Advance Praise for

BRIGHT LIGHTS, BIG EMPTY

"Ron is a gifted teacher and healer who has helped thousands of people transform their lives, myself included. Let his story and soul medicine guide you to your more authentic and fully embodied self."

—Kris Carr, *New York Times* bestselling author, speaker, and cancer thriver

"Ron takes you on his journey, setting out as a pathfinder and wayshower for your own *re*-remembrance. This is a story of 'green lights,' magic, synchronicity, and intuitive hits to finally bring you into full alignment and deep connection with yourself and beyond."

—Yanik Silver, creator of *The Cosmic Journal*, author of *Evolved Enterprise*

"In *Bright Lights, Big Empty*, you will meet the man who has helped me get out of my own way and work through anxieties that prevented me from having deeper relationships with my friends, my family, and myself. I now have a deeper sense of calm, a more open mind, and a richer compassion for my fellow humans."

—Jimmy DiResta, designer, author, YouTube sensation, and cohost of the *Making It* podcast

"Ron is one of those individuals who makes you feel better about your-self when you are in his presence. Calming and supportive, Ron truly cares. I am better by knowing him. You will be too."

—Garrett Gunderson, entrepreneur, educator, and *New York Times* bestselling author

"Ron's work and approach to healing opened my eyes, my mind, and my heart to an entirely new way of feeling and seeing myself, in addition to what's possible going forward. His method and understanding of the human journey is not like any traditional therapy—it's unique, and it's powerful!"

—Bill Miles, Co-Founder of Best Self Media

"Ron was the first man to show me the transformative power of loving myself. I'm eternally grateful for the impact his tender presence has had on my life, and am so thrilled for the world to experience that love through this book.

—Raj Jana, Founder of JavaPresse Coffee
Company, host of the podcast *Stay Grounded*

BRIGHT LIGHTS, BIG EMPTY

A JOURNEY OF PROFOUND AWAKENING

RON BAKER

LIONCREST
PUBLISHING

BRIGHT LIGHTS, BIG EMPTY
A Journey of Profound Awakening

ISBN   978-1-5445-2708-6   *Hardcover*
        978-1-5445-2706-2   *Paperback*
        978-1-5445-2707-9   *Ebook*

The journey of you!

For Robert...
without whom none of this
would be possible.

CONTENTS

III. ADULT

IV. SOUL

INTRODUCTION

Even as a child, I just *knew* there were deeper truths about Life and why things happen as they do than people around me were able to offer. While so many things about the world seemed unfair and confusing, I always had a nagging feeling that so much more was possible. What I could never have guessed, however, was how exciting, challenging, and inspiring the path to those more complete answers would become, or that the reason my initial hunches never wavered was that they were coming from the deepest part of myself: my own Soul.

I will begin my story in 1990 because that's the summer when everything changed for me. Making my debut on a major New York City stage became the gateway to doing more than sixty leading roles on important stages around the world. Though I'm grateful for all of it—singing with celebrities, dining with royalty, sharing the stage with two Supreme Court justices—these beautiful opportunities are not what ultimately led to extraordinary levels of personal fulfillment.

Those achievements, exciting as they were, did not have the power to outweigh my constant inner battle with emptiness and Self-doubt.

Fortunately, other doors opened for me as well that summer—this time as two pivotal connections. One became my dearest friend and business partner, and the other was a profound teacher whose wisdom blew my mind. Not only did he provide priceless clues for resolving my fear and doubt; he also showed me how to align with my Soul purpose.

My hope is that the journey I now share with you—which reveals the specific steps that allowed me to immerse myself in this new sense of Self-value—will help you understand how to make similar enhancements by learning to become the nurturing authority in your own life. In the early years of your life, your Soul set up important challenges for you. Once you learn how to turn them into gifts and guideposts, you will discover how essential those past challenges will become.

Before I experienced the adventures I will share with you, I would have never believed how differently I would eventually see my own painful and confusing challenges, but the truth is that I actually appreciate and value them now.

I also want to mention how much it meant to me to discover some of the practical realities of being on an extended Soul journey. Just relieving the pressure I had always felt to figure everything out in one lifetime was priceless. By learning how to integrate the profound layers of education about the Self, I was able to shift from a desperate attempt to prove myself to a much more immediate commitment to Self-love and Self-value. That made all the difference.

Once my day-to-day experiences became predictably richer, I felt inspired to share all that I was learning with the people around me. Once they, too, began to experience reliable enhancements in their lives, word spread rather quickly. As more and more people began showing up to explore the unique, nurturing approach that I was gradually forming, it became clear that nothing could be more meaningful than creating deeply authentic connections and being able to impact others' lives. Those motivations led me to establish a School of Self-Mastery in New York City.

In the twenty-five years since I made that pivotal decision, I've had the privilege of walking beside thousands of courageous individuals who have initiated a broad spectrum of personal transformations. Some have shifted from jobs that were not so fulfilling into careers that are more aligned with their particular gifts and interests; others have focused on investing in relationships that consistently grow into meaningful intimacy and trust; while others have worked more fully on healing physical ailments, from simple issues to advanced stages of cancer. In each case, positive changes in people's lives were made possible when they learned how to become their own nurturing authority.

Based on what I have witnessed, I now live in a state of deep trust that we can all build more intimate, fulfilling relationships. We can all inspire more passion for our lives, focusing on the things that are truly important to us as individuals. We can also sustain more consistent health than what our traditional systems have taught us, and even go for decades without getting sick. Those are just some of the things that my own experiences have taught me.

Still eager to reach as many people as I can with this unique education about what it means to claim our Whole Self, I decided to write this book. The process of sharing my story so intimately has been a profound one. The thought of sharing my life—including many of my core challenges—with people I've never met brought up distinct fear.

While I was concerned about how some people might react to such vulnerable parts of my life, my motivation to affirm how safe we can all be to admit our challenges, fears, and doubts in order to take back our personal power was much stronger. Besides, the last twenty-five years had already taught me that the most meaningful way to inspire others is to simply walk the walk, offering a clear example of willingness, courage, and compassion.

I'm so glad to bring you a clear message about what is possible in this world of accelerated shifts, affirmed by my work with thousands of individuals through the School of Self-Mastery. The exciting truth is that we all hold much more potential than most of us were ever taught to access. I now live with meaningful capacities and depths of intimacy in every aspect of my life, and I watch that taking place around me on a daily basis. I've even had the opportunity to experience the reality of miracles, which I look forward to sharing as my story unfolds.

The last thing I will say in these opening remarks is that I'm fully aware that the challenges and gifts in your life will differ from mine. However, the principles of healing transformation that I will pass on to you are universal. In other words, they will work for you, just as they have worked for so many others who have explored this awesome approach with me.

Know that no matter where you find yourself in your journey, jumping into healthier, nurturing choices is always an option. I'm glad you're here and that you're willing to explore possibilities with me. When you have a deeper understanding and alignment with your own journey to Self, so much more will be possible. The choices you will begin to make will be a clear investment in what is most important to you, rather than doing what I initially did—magically hoping some outer achievement, job, or relationship would be the main source of fulfillment. You hold the power to make the biggest difference in your own life, and that is exciting.

So let's begin.

THE
CALL

1

THE
CURTAIN
RISES

STANDING BEHIND THE IMPOSING RED VELVET CUR-
tain that dressed New York City's Lincoln Center stage, I could
hear the excited buzz of three thousand people finding their
seats. Heightening the moment were the muted sounds of a sixty-piece
orchestra warming up in the pit and the more immediate pounding of
my nervous heart. In just a few short minutes, the lights would dim, and
I would walk out to the other side of that curtain in complete silence—
the first actor to appear in the 1990 revival of Stephen Sondheim's *A
Little Night Music*.

Since this would be my New York debut, staying grounded was
a challenge. At some point in my dance between excitement and

nervousness, I was interrupted by a tap on my right shoulder. The last thing I expected to find when I turned was Mr. Sondheim himself, standing beside me.

"Ron, I've been meaning to tell you. I'd like to change some of the lyrics in this first number. Would you mind making a few shifts?"

Oh, my God.

Don't get me wrong. I would have done backflips if this musical theater genius had asked, but I also knew that Sondheim's lyrics, known for being quick and witty, could sometimes be a mouthful. Of course I agreed, which meant that my nerves went into overdrive. Once Mr. Sondheim turned and disappeared into the darkness, I started feverishly repeating the new words in my head. What I did not remember in that moment was that I'd been preparing for this opportunity for years.

Without warning, I became aware that the muted whispers of the audience had ceased, which meant that the lights in the theater had likely been dimmed. Confirming my suspicions, the stage manager gave her cue that it was time to make my move. Ready or not, two stagehands pulled the curtain aside, and within seconds, I was hit by a bright spotlight from the back of the theater. This meant the giant space in front of me that boasted four impressive levels of balconies now became an endless cavern of darkness.

Just as I had rehearsed, I found my way to the grand piano that waited for me like a reliable friend. After the strike of a single key, I launched into the opening passage, which brought me rather quickly to the excitement of a sustained high G. Fortunately, four other cast members soon joined me for the opening number. We were off, and there was no looking back.

The following morning, the New York press hailed *A Little Night Music* a resounding success. In fact, the inspired guidance of director Scott

Ellis, choreographer Susan Stroman, and conductor Paul Gemignani turned our show into the hottest ticket in town. I will never forget the rush of excitement that moved through my body when a wall of deafening cheers hit the stage at the completion of the first act and then at the finale of the show when that huge red velvet curtain returned to its familiar resting place. Without a doubt, this debut was a real milestone in my life, complete with the unique memory of having successfully delivered last-minute lyrics from one of Broadway's most important icons.

"Wow, you are certainly living the dream!" friends and acquaintances claimed when they heard the New York City Opera had hired me to perform a handful of roles over the next six months.

While I was aware that being part of that historic company was an incredible opportunity, what most of my supporters couldn't see—because I had become so well practiced at hiding vulnerabilities—was that on the inside, I still felt like the insecure boy from North Carolina whose father had never engaged in a single conversation growing up.

While I enjoyed each expression of congratulations, I was also filled with Self-doubt. I simply had no idea how to value myself as a person. Now that I had reached my goal of performing at Lincoln Center, it was clear to me how deluded I had been to think that proving myself on major world stages would somehow erase my insecurities. Instead, the main thing this milestone affirmed was that I had a real gift for magical thinking. Fortunately, the string of performances I was scheduled to do that fateful summer of 1990 was not my only opportunity. Much to my surprise, an entirely different event ended up changing the trajectory of my life.

Backing up a bit, this second opportunity took place prior to *Night Music*'s opening night in the big city, when the cast and crew were traveling to do performances in the charming town of Saratoga Springs, New York. "Out-of-town tryouts" were a long-held tradition in the theater community. They were established to give creative teams an opportunity to make shifts and enhancements to their shows prior to facing the make-or-break reviews of New York City newspapers.

When we boarded the bus for our ride to Saratoga, I took my place in an aisle seat near the front. Not long into the three-hour journey, I heard an interesting conversation taking place behind me. Curious about who was doing most of the talking, I turned my head just enough to see a slight, unassuming man in his early forties. The story he was recounting, which centered around a near-death experience on his last City Opera tour in Thailand, was so compelling that it sent a surge of energy up my spine.

The man's experience began in a ground-floor hotel room, with him lying on a single bed. While staring up at a light bulb hanging at the end of a simple black cord, he suddenly discovered he couldn't move his body. Almost immediately, the light bulb started to shine much brighter. The next thing he knew, he was somehow hovering above his own physical body, which was visible on the bed below.

I was on the edge of my seat as he talked about moving through a tunnel of light that eventually brought him to a vast, empty space. Once there, he experienced a surprising depth of pleasure, connection, and peace—sensations that were quite new to him. Just recalling it was so moving to him, I heard his voice crack with emotion as he continued.

"After spending a few brief moments enjoying those new sensations, I suddenly heard a voice inside my head announcing, *You must go back. You have not yet learned how to love.*" With no time to respond, he was suddenly back on the hotel bed, focused on the gradual sensations of his physical body becoming mobile again.

Hearing the man so honestly share the details of his spiritual experience caused distinct memories from my own past to rise to the surface. Though what occurred to me was not so direct or dramatic, it still reminded me of how connected I had felt to something spiritual ever since I was a young child. For instance, when an especially upsetting or confusing event took place, I, too, would be filled with a strange sense of peace—as if I were being offered some unspoken assurance that there were deeper answers waiting to be discovered. I couldn't explain it logically, but that was how it had always felt.

In addition, the surge of energy that had shot up my spine while listening to the man's story was a sensation that had occurred many times over the years. This typically happened in moments when I heard something that seemed particularly important and true. By the time I was a teenager, I started referring to those energetic releases as my "internal green lights." For me, they were like a mysterious nudge, encouraging me to pay close attention to whatever was happening or being shared.

Over the years, I figured out that whenever I ignored one of those green lights, I'd end up regretting it. With that in mind, I was determined not to miss out on making a connection with this interesting new person who was now sitting behind me.

As soon as he finished his story, I turned around and said, as calmly as I could manage, "I don't know who you are, but I know that I'm supposed to talk with you."

From our first meal together, that night in Saratoga Springs, Robert Baker and I became immediate friends. The moment we sat down, we began to swap stories about our lives, starting with some of the synchronicities that had led us both to choose careers in the performing arts. The more we shared, the more excited we became about the parallels we discovered, starting with the fact that we shared the same last name, Baker.

Though we were born twelve years apart and grew up on opposite sides of North America, we had both started out in tiny towns and were brought into the world by parents who were quite young. My family lived in Pinetops, North Carolina, while Robert's family had settled into a logging camp near Vancouver, British Columbia. I remember how comforting it was when Robert told me that his parents had almost no idea how to provide help or guidance when he was growing up. This was something about my own life that I'd long felt frustrated by.

Hearing Robert share his experiences so openly was like a breath of fresh air. The experience was so unusual that I realized I'd never felt safe enough to share myself like he had. It was comforting to find someone I could relate to, someone who had also figured out so many things on his own as a young person. Even though this was our first real conversation, these similarities between us created an immediate ease that made me feel less alone.

The impact was so clear that I eventually shared some of the more personal and unusual spiritual phenomena that had taken place in my own life. One of those events took place almost ten years earlier, when I was performing at the Brevard Music Center Summer Festival in the Blue Ridge Mountains of North Carolina.

The main highlight for me in the festival involved being cast as Billy Bigelow, the brooding male lead in the musical *Carousel*. The icing on the cake was that my mom and younger sister, JB, would come to help me celebrate the opportunity. An extra bonus was that my mother had spent a summer or two performing at this very place when she was young. From the moment they arrived, I relished introducing them to my summer home. At some point during that first afternoon together, I reached over to give JB a sideways hug. Much to my surprise, she winced and pulled away.

It turns out that she'd been diagnosed with a kidney infection a couple of days earlier and was still experiencing some pain.

"Wow. That is so strange," I responded. "That same part of my back has been bothering me today, and even though I haven't seen a doctor, I've been guessing that I might be having an issue with my kidney."

We both thought this was an interesting coincidence but tossed it off and moved on with our weekend together. Things got a bit more intriguing when my family left to return home, and the pain I'd been feeling simply disappeared.

Over the course of the next year, I noticed that whenever JB developed any physical discomfort, I would feel the exact symptoms she was manifesting. At first, I imagined it was the strong sense of protection I felt for her, as she was my baby sister. However, I started to experience physical symptoms that other members of my family were going through as well. At that point, I knew there had to be more to the story.

It was during my fateful dinner in Saratoga that I learned there is a name for this phenomenon.

Robert listened to my story and then simply informed me, "Some people have a heightened sensitivity to what is taking place energetically in other people's bodies. When that empathetic sense is particularly heightened, it is known as clairsentience."

"Wow." Yet another way that Robert was able to comfort me. Of course I had to ask, "How do you know about things like that?"

"I have some wonderful teachers in New York City who've been educating me about many things over the last couple of years," he replied.

Up to that point in my life, I'd worried that someone would think I was crazy if I shared these phenomena. Now I felt encouraged and accepted, so much so that I decided to take it one step further, telling Robert about the most surprising clairsentient experience I'd gone through.

On what seemed like a typical day in grad school, while listening to one of my professor's lectures at the Cincinnati Conservatory of Music, I was jolted by an intense surge of pain in my stomach. The sensation was so strong that I ended up doubling over and falling out of my chair and onto the floor. At that same moment, a fleeting image of my mother flashed through my mind.

Wanting to find out what was going on, I left class and went to call my mom. When I wasn't able to reach her at home or at work, I contacted a family friend. It turned out that my mother had an undetected stomach ulcer that had ruptured around the same time I felt the surge of pain. What made the experience so hard to believe was that she was six hundred miles away.

Robert nodded knowingly, moved but unfazed by what I was telling him.

I told him that my mom had lost almost seven units of blood before an ambulance was able to get her to a hospital, which had left her in a truly vulnerable state. Fortunately, she was in stable condition by the time I spoke with her that evening, but the whole experience had taken my gift to a completely new level, leaving me a bit confused.

If there is nothing I can do, what is the point of having this gift? I wondered. I told Robert I was curious. Was there a way for me to use this unusual capacity to feel? Could I use it to help the people who were in trouble?

Robert told me that he had also been wondering, since his near-death experience, how he might use everything that had begun to shift in his life to help and inspire others. He said that his experience had opened and shifted him so much that he no longer felt as satisfied with his life as he had previously felt. As one example, he had worked as the head of the makeup department at the New York City Opera for almost twenty years, a position that had provided him with a wonderful way to express his creativity. Now he was questioning whether there was something different he was supposed to be doing.

One of the first differences he noticed when he returned from Thailand was a strong desire to meditate. He decided to follow his intuitive hunch and joined two meditation groups. There, he found the teachers who were now so important to him. Prior to making those moves, he hadn't approached his life from a very spiritual perspective, which I found interesting. By the time our evening came to a close, we both sensed that we had begun what would surely become a rare and beautiful friendship.

Once our performances in Saratoga were over and we returned to the city, Robert and I started spending more time together. The fact that we both needed to be at the opera house on most days for the next six months gave us plenty of opportunities. Going out for Mexican food was one of our favorite things to do, which typically included me enjoying iced tea, chips, and guacamole, while Robert sipped blue margaritas.

I was pleased that it didn't take long for Robert to invite me to join him at his meditation groups. The first was led by June Graham and Jim Spencer, two wonderful people whose home in the West Village quickly became a safe haven for my beginning explorations of the inner Self. A few weeks later, I accompanied Robert to my one and only visit to the second meditation group. This one was led by a gentlewoman named Alma Daniels. Alma lived in a beautiful apartment that overlooked Central Park.

Once everyone had arrived for the evening, we all took our places. We formed a circle on various cushions and chairs that had already been set up. Alma began by asking us to close our eyes, and then she had us take some deep breaths, encouraging us to let go of the day's stresses. Not long after I began settling into a more relaxed state, I was startled to hear Robert's voice. Because interrupting someone seemed so out of character for him, I opened my eyes to find out what was happening.

As it turned out, when Robert had closed his eyes to begin deep breathing, he experienced an intense energy moving through his body. Rather quickly, he grew concerned that he wouldn't be able to stay conscious, and he was correct. The next thing he remembered was opening his eyes again, only to find the whole group staring at him. He later told me that he had felt embarrassed, assuming he must have fallen asleep and had likely begun snoring or some such thing.

What the rest of us witnessed and experienced in those moments was quite different. As soon as I opened my eyes, I noticed that the words I was hearing didn't match the way Robert typically spoke at all. *Dearly beloved, children of light, we are called Gabriel, and we are most joyous to be in your divine presence.*

The group was then blessed with a beautiful message. Gabriel, who identified himself as an Archangel, told us that this was the first time Robert was discovering his capacity for channeling. I wondered if this was as new to the others as it was for me. Even so, I was fully intrigued and grateful when Gabriel suggested that what was taking place was much like listening to a broadcast coming through a radio. He then reminded us that the radio had initially been a real stretch for people to consider, even if it was now accepted as quite normal.

Gabriel drew this parallel to focus on the radio as proof that energy and information could move through the air and be picked up and transmitted through radio receivers. Channeling was possible through a similar process, and Robert was the receiver. I imagined that Robert had acquired this ability when he went through his near-death experience.

Gabriel encouraged us to focus on his message rather than getting too caught up in the mechanics of channeling. This seemed wise to me, so that's exactly what I did. As a matter of fact, I remember being disappointed that after only a few more introductory remarks, Gabriel brought his message to a close.

It was only when Robert opened his eyes that we discovered he had been completely unaware of what happened. When we told him, he initially thought we were playing a prank on him. Of course, we assured him this was not the case. Alma then chimed in, informing Robert that Gabriel had included some personal reassurance for him—that even though his Soul had chosen this unusual capacity to connect with higher guidance prior to being born into this lifetime, he always had a choice whether to continue allowing it or not.

Alma then encouraged Robert to choose a moment over the coming days when he could sit quietly and invite Archangel Gabriel to connect again. Of course, I loved that idea and secretly hoped Robert would allow me to be with him for that next attempt. Robert did his best to take it all in, and then, with such a mind-boggling opportunity to consider, he took a few days to evaluate how such an invitation might impact his life.

Fortunately, Robert was like me in yet another way. He loved to learn and to experience new things. He also wondered if this might be the path through which he could help others more fully. And so we set a day that we could meet to call upon Gabriel.

As that time approached, I did my best to balance my own excitement with a sensitivity to what Robert must be going through. Even as a witness, I could hardly wrap my head around the opportunity. When it was finally time, I reflected on how much my life had opened and expanded in the few short months since I'd made my New York City debut. And now it seemed that so much more was in store.

2

SURPRISING TWISTS

THE ONE THING ROBERT REQUESTED AS WE PREPARED for his next attempt to channel was that we record the session. He thought it was important for him to hear whatever might come through. He hoped that hearing Gabriel's voice speaking through him would not only make it feel more real but would also allow him to trust and feel included in the unfolding.

I agreed and showed up to Robert's apartment with a cassette recorder in hand. It was only a few seconds after we sat down that Robert closed his eyes and I noticed something happening with his body. I assumed this must be Gabriel's energy creating a connection. The first time Robert channeled, my eyes had been closed, and I had missed this part of the process. What I now witnessed was almost a solid minute of twitching body movements. Then, much to my relief, Gabriel began to speak once again.

I found it interesting that his opening words were exactly the same as the first time: *Dearly beloved, child of light, we are called Gabriel, and we are most joyous to be in your divine presence.* He then continued, *One of the most important reasons we have come in at this time is to make certain things clear—starting with the fact that you are a world filled with sacred individuals on unique Soul journeys. You each hold a tremendous depth of potential in your bodies, much of which you have not yet learned to access.*

Most people don't take the time in their busy lives to consider the reality of being on a Soul journey or how much time you all actually need to explore and grow from one stage of personal and collective potential to the next. In order to afford you the time that you all need, your Soul journeys evolve over the course of many, many lifetimes.

For most of my life, I had tried to make sense of why we all have such different experiences, so this was exciting to hear—and at the same time, experiencing the phenomenon of an Archangel talking to me directly was almost too much to take in. However, I did my best to stay present.

Most of you have been unaware that your lives are set up with distinct structures and stages, all of which create a sense of Divine Order. For instance, each of your lifetimes is set up in the early years with specific gifts and individual challenges—all of which provide important elements for the unfolding of your individual Soul plans. Those initial setups are what form the foundation of your Soul curriculum for a particular lifetime.

We know that it will likely be a stretch for you to consider that each of your challenges is set in place to serve and guide you. This is true for your simplest challenges as well as your most complex. The main purpose of challenges is to provide an opportunity for you to explore, discover, and claim a particular layer of your personal potential. The process that you move through as you face each challenge allows you to build skills and to develop specific qualities. Each challenge that you resolve teaches you, starting with revealing which of your choices work well and which ones do not. In each case, you all learn through a process of trial and error. Having time with each step of that process allows you to gradually build confidence in your emerging individuality.

Each gift and challenge is set up to encourage you in the specific directions that you, as an individual, most need to develop. In other words, each lifetime is set up with clear and purposeful opportunities for you to take some perfect next steps on your journeys toward wholeness and empowerment. This also involves encouraging you with specific interests quite often. Someone whose life will be well-served in science will have those natural interests. Someone else will be more fully drawn to sports or the arts. By having specific interests and gifts that you want to pursue, you are more willing to face the challenges that are necessary for you as well. These are just some of the ways you are all encouraged into personal development.

If you pay attention, you will see what a wide array of challenges individuals are negotiating around you. No matter what challenges are set up in any of your lives, we want you to feel comforted in the knowledge that each of your challenges is intended to serve you, encouraging and supporting you on the most meaningful journey possible. What we refer to is the all-important process of learning how to love and value yourselves—your most authentic, sacred Self.

Hearing about Soul journeys in such a direct, practical way was both exciting and a little confusing. Particularly new for me was the idea that my individual challenges had been specifically set up to serve me, and that they were somehow perfect for what I most needed to explore. Up to this point, I had considered many of my challenges to be a royal pain in the ass; I had certainly spent a lot of time trying to avoid and even deny them. The truth is that I had spent most of my life trying to hide the fact that I even had challenges.

Now that Gabriel presented a more encouraging way to look at them, I felt glimmers of relief, and I hoped that what he claimed would eventually prove true. For the moment, just receiving hints of inspiration concerning challenges was a great contrast to the relentless frustration and confusion I had known prior. I particularly loved the idea that our lives might actually be designed with care—in some kind of Divine Order.

This was such a departure from what I had felt growing up. Left to work out most challenges on my own, I had so often tried to figure out why different individuals were born into such different circumstances, and why each person faced such different obstacles. Some people's difficulties felt so severe, while others' seemed relatively mild. I had also been taught that this was our only lifetime, and within that context, I could never work out how having such different setups could possibly be fair.

Just hearing these new perspectives and realizing we have lifetime after lifetime to learn and grow provided me with great relief—especially as a driven achiever. I had often wondered how I would possibly work out all my confusions or achieve all that was necessary to prove my worth in such limited time. I had also wondered if everyone else was feeling that same pressure. Perhaps most compelling was that these were some of the deeper answers I had been seeking since I was a child—answers that allowed our lives to make more sense.

I had always asked big questions, like "Why do you suppose one person lives for only a short time, while other people live for a hundred years? Why are some people born into families with money and others are not? Why is one person naturally intelligent, while others seem to struggle so much?"

Hearing Gabriel's words stimulated my hunger for more knowledge. Always thinking ahead, I began to hope there would be more opportunities to hear about Divine Order. I also found it interesting that Gabriel paused at various points during his message, as if he were allowing me the time to take in each idea before throwing out the next perspective. In some of those moments, images began to form in my mind.

As I considered having time to move from one stage of learning to the next, the experience of being in school came to mind. After all, in a single school, many people were in a broad spectrum of grades, exploring different sets of lessons, challenges, and individual needs. In school, each person was encouraged to focus on the specific things they most needed to learn—whether they happened to like the curriculum or not.

Even in those first moments of considering Life through this new lens, these perspectives about Soul journeys just felt right to me. Comfortable. Sensible. And once Gabriel finished his introduction to having multiple lifetimes, he encouraged me to ask questions. I could hardly believe it. I had been a child who asked questions relentlessly. And this was one of the first times someone actually encouraged me in this way.

Dear one, wanting to ask questions is a sign that you are curious about Life. This is healthy. So pay close attention to your questions. They often emerge from a deep desire to understand something that Life is trying to reveal to you. What we are saying is that your questions often come out of truths that are already held inside you, pointing you toward something that is attempting to emerge and become known. We would even suggest it is crucial for people to question. Questioning allows all of you the opportunity to explore and evaluate what feels true for you—as well as finding out what does not—at every stage of your development.

When Gabriel completed what he wanted to say, he ended the meeting with, *As we now take our most joyous leave, we encourage you to remember to love one another.*

Once Robert was grounded again, I couldn't wait for him to hear the recording. He felt a similar excitement, so we sat down right away to review what he had channeled. As I began to hear the message again, I watched Robert closely. After a few moments of getting used to what was likely very strange for him, he started to look calmer and eventually even seemed touched. Because I hoped there would be many more channeled gatherings, I was thrilled with his response.

Once the message was complete and I went home, the subject of Soul journeys remained on my mind. Robert later confessed it had been on his mind as well. In the days that followed, Robert and I spent a lot of time discussing various possibilities. While many things about our lives seemed clearer within this new context, we still had tons of questions to ask. I was pleased when Robert suggested we set a date for our next meeting.

After opening with the now familiar greeting, Gabriel surprised me by acknowledging that I seemed genuinely interested in starting this meeting by asking more questions. I not only appreciated that he could sense this without me needing to say anything, but I also enjoyed getting to play a proactive role in the direction of the conversation.

I began by sharing how I had started to put the big subject of Soul journeys into practical contexts. "What I think you are saying, Gabriel, is that our individual Soul journeys are very much like moving from grade to grade in school. I imagine we first experience lifetimes that are focused on our more primitive lessons, much like we do in first grade.

Each of us is then naturally supported to move through each level at our own pace," I said.

"I imagine that means we have as many first-grade lifetimes as we need, to work through the foundational challenges that are perfect for that level," I continued. "Then, when we are able to navigate and trust those areas and skills, we naturally begin to focus on the potentials of the next level. Sticking with that same metaphor, I will call those our second-grade lifetimes—which present us with new sets of challenges and opportunities. Is that right?"

Dear one, over time, you will likely trust that one of your particular gifts includes a capacity to understand complex ideas, and then to relate those ideas through practical, grounded contexts. This particular gift will help others who become interested in this greater education about Life and the Divine Order that guides you all. For now, we will respond to the specific subject you have brought back to us.

Gabriel then concluded our meeting with the following: *You have understood the foundation of Soul journeys quite well. Over time, we will add much more to what you have just shared, such as helping you understand that there are seven primary Soul levels, all of which coincide with the seven primary energy centers in your bodies. For now, we honor that you have not yet learned about such things. We only hint that there are deeper layers of information about every subject that you can look forward to as you continue investing in this education about the Whole Self.*

Robert and I soon established a regular weekly meeting time with Gabriel to receive more clues and hints about our lives. And although Gabriel broadened our conversations into other topics, most of the focus was the Whole Self, as he would call it, for the first couple of years that we spent together. Robert and I also continued meeting up each week to explore and spin ideas about whatever Gabriel had presented.

Gabriel affirmed in one of our meetings that he was purposefully giving us time to ruminate on each new idea before introducing too many layers about a particular subject. He suggested that having time to explore, experience, and discover new possibilities on our own was a vital part of learning to trust ourselves. Spending time with each subject also allowed us to become intimate with each layer of this novel education.

Gabriel was also quite clear that our true development of Self included much more than simply understanding concepts. *Mental understanding is an important starting place. However, it is important for you to consider that you learn most fully and create the deepest transformations in your lives based on what you actually experience. After all, what you experience is what you end up trusting most fully, starting from the time you are young children. What you experience impacts you deep within your bodies. We would even suggest that you can't fully trust what is only a concept in your heads—particularly if your experiences don't align and agree with that particular concept. When concept and experience don't match, the concept will simply not feel true.*

I loved this explanation. It reminded me of how frustrating it would be when, as a child, I was told to behave in a certain way, or to do one thing and then witness my parents or other adults do the exact opposite. This made it hard to know who or what to trust. The message seemed to be "I want you to trust what I say, not what I do," and that *sucked*.

Fortunately, each lesson Gabriel presented made great sense to me. I can hardly express how powerful the experience was for me, the ability to trust the new ideas Gabriel had imparted. Until this time in my life, so many things I'd been told about the way Life operated hadn't felt like complete or reliable truths. Over time, I began to appreciate having a gift that I called my bullshit meter. Whenever something didn't resonate as truth, I would feel a sort of contraction in my body—a clear contrast to my green lights.

Much to my delight, in those first years of exploration with Gabriel, I started getting used to a consistent stream of green lights, and my inner affirmations became an important part of building trust in this new education. At the same time, I still felt compelled to add my own form of testing into the equation—particularly in the moments when Gabriel's ideas required a real stretch of the imagination.

One example: when I noticed that Robert seemed even more energetically sensitive than I was, which was a first for me, I would sometimes come up behind him and send a small jolt of energy from my hands. I just had to see if he could truly feel what was happening. Fortunately, he passed every test. Robert's body would always jump when I did such things. And much to my relief, Gabriel also passed each test. He even revealed in one of our sessions that he knew I'd been testing him and suggested that I turn this into discernment rather than fearful skepticism.

You see, dear one, your motivations are a truly important part of your choices. For instance, your tests can be motivated by trying to protect yourself from being hurt or deceived—both of which you experienced as a child.

He explained that we all create "comfort zones" to define the specific areas where we learn that we must defend ourselves. Therefore, he encouraged me to continue testing, but to do so with the intention of building affirmations of trust more than fears.

We have made sure you have healthier ways of negotiating your fears, having introduced some specific tools for Self-nurturing in this new education that we are providing. We want you to feel safe with the process of stretching your familiar comfort zones. When you have a nurturing approach that becomes reliable, it is easier to let go of your protection rackets, discovering for yourself when they are no longer necessary.

It felt nice being able to trust how clearly all the pieces were fitting together.

Another experience that allowed me to build trust in these new directions and conversations came from a small group of people who were interested in hearing weekly messages from Gabriel. At first, most of them were in our circle of friends from the opera house. Having the chance to see others find peace and encouragement was comforting. It also allowed for some much needed conversations and connections regarding things that truly mattered to us.

Even so, in the first few years, I felt self-conscious about sharing with other people that I had begun having personal conversations with an Archangel. While I was secretly thrilled for each moment of learning, I was too concerned about what others might think. I was afraid to share that something so extraordinary—and hard to believe—was taking place. I had spent so many years trying to control others' opinions of me. I just wasn't ready. I needed time to grow into each new experience, to build more trust in these approaches.

To aid in the process, Gabriel would often encourage us. *We don't want you to ever take anything we say for granted, blindly accepting any of these new concepts as personal truths, just because an Archangel is sharing them with you. Unless a particular concept resonates in some way—which will often take place as an idea feeling like something you already knew somehow—don't force that idea. Simply keep the concept in mind. You might then find that it makes more sense at some later date. Our main goal is to help you open to awaken the truths that are already held inside you. That is what will inspire you to truly open to the greater possibilities we are highlighting.*

What will often happen when something doesn't fully resonate is that you will need a more complete context or some time to start paying attention to how it feels in your day-to-day life before you are able to understand the potential benefits. Much like when you are in fifth grade, you are able to evaluate a certain idea about Life in a more complete way than you were able to evaluate when you were in earlier grades.

Until something begins to make sense to you, just consider each new idea as a seed of possibility. And feel free to toss any ideas that don't feel comfortable. We don't need you to validate us or to try and please us. That is the best way for you to become more aware of the Whole Self—one natural step at a time.

In addition to teaching us how to feel safe facing our challenges, Gabriel also encouraged us to identify and appreciate our individual gifts, which included authentic interests, capacities, talents, and qualities of Self. One of the first ways Gabriel approached this subject involved affirming that Robert and I had both discovered some natural interests when we were young children, such as our love of learning. Both of us had always wanted to understand as much about Life as possible.

Your natural desires to learn and to understand were seeded in your initial Soul setups. Your Souls knew that these gifts would be of great help at various points in this lifetime, particularly supporting your willingness and likelihood to invest in this deeper education when the time came.

Each person has gifts seeded inside them. Some of those gifts only become accessible when a person accesses some new depth of their inner Self. In your case, a gift that you discovered when you were about ten years old involved a gut feeling that you were being prepared for some purpose. You had no idea what that purpose might be at the time; but nevertheless, the feeling was distinct. We now suggest that your Soul was giving you glimpses of the opportunity to be educated about the Whole Self and about the Divine Order through which Life operates.

Gabriel's awareness of those early gut feelings was profound to me. I hadn't even told Robert about some of those premonitions—having a sense that I was not only being prepared for something but that I was also being protected. Because those were not sentiments I had heard anyone else expressing around me as a kid, and because I was afraid they would make me sound arrogant as I got older, I had kept both of those things to myself. It felt wonderful to be encouraged to trust my inner awareness, which Gabriel affirmed as one of my gifts.

There are many reasons we have come to offer this more complete education with the two of you, as well as with the Soul grid of people—or Soul family, as you like to call it—who have begun to gather each week. One of the most important opportunities is to assure you that your world is now moving into a period of accelerated change and awakening that is unlike anything you have known in the history of your planet. Over time, we will help you understand how many of the outer shifts you will see taking place around you are also attempting to take place in your bodies.

Over the coming decades, you will discover many unprecedented shifts, awakenings, and changes taking place in the world around you. It will be more fully evident in the coming decades than anything you have known in the last several thousand years—which brings us back to the importance of helping you understand the practical realities of being on Soul journeys.

Over the coming years, you will discover a growing need for more complete solutions in your world. So many things are out of balance, and using the same old approaches will not allow you to create the solutions that you need. As things begin to accelerate, revealing those imbalances, you will all need to know how to negotiate your fears. Rather than habitually going into contraction or trying to hold on to what has been familiar, your world will need this much more complete education about what is taking place. What we are teaching you now about nurturing and valuing your Whole Self will become crucial for people to understand.

We also want to point out that the two of you have chosen, at least on a Soul level, to spend time receiving this education when these unprecedented shifts have only begun to become evident in the world, so that you will be ready to share and inspire others when more of them are ready for a fuller understanding of all that is taking place. The journey from "survival consciousness," which is what most of you have known at this point in your journeys, into the consciousness of empowered adults, and then into the tremendous potentials of the Soul will be a formidable depth of change to navigate.

We encourage the two of you to focus on each experience and symptom as you awaken each level of Self so that you will feel prepared to help others understand more of the journey they can expect as they are faced with similar levels of awakening. Only as you learn to nurture your way through fear and challenge will you become truly effective as an inspiration that so much more is possible.

It was overwhelming to consider that I could help others through the stages I was beginning to navigate. And yet, it felt right. Even though I was hesitant to talk about Gabriel with many people, I had never lost my desire to help others. His words gave me even more motivation to continue forward with this beautiful new education. With so much to learn, I felt grateful to be cast in more seasons of shows at Lincoln Center over the next few years. Those opportunities gave me lots of in-person time with Robert and Gabriel to continue exploring.

3

NEW
POSSIBILITIES

EVEN THOUGH MY LIFE CONTINUED AS USUAL FOR three solid years—going to work, preparing for performances, continuing to train and grow as an artist, and making sure to spend some much appreciated time with friends—nothing was more important to me than continuing to invest in this new understanding about the Whole Self.

Most of the time Robert and I spent with Gabriel was focused on teaching us how to show up as empowered adults, rather than remaining stuck in core challenges like wounded children do. Only once that journey was well underway did Gabriel focus on revealing all the ways in which the three primary aspects of the Whole Self—child, adult, and Soul—work together. Just as Gabriel had shown us that the Soul sets up a curriculum for each lifetime when we are children, he helped us see that we are meant to spend our adult years facing and resolving those challenges.

The more pieces of the puzzle he handed us, the clearer it became that most people were moving through their lives without an education about Soul journeys, the Whole Self, or an awareness of fulfilling their core purpose. To make this point truly clear, Gabriel explained that we all share some foundational qualities that are crucial to claiming the three main levels of Self.

For instance, in an optimal scenario, childhood is the time when we are meant to build a foundation of innocence, wonder, and trust. When those three core qualities are not established, we end up with gaps and blocks in the developing Self. Without being taught that we are sacred individuals, reinforced by consistent nurturing from our caregivers, we typically end up accumulating experiences of fear, shame, and judgment instead.

We are meant to spend our adult years figuring out how to resolve this. What typically happens instead is that most of us become entrenched in the myths of the wounded child. We then spend our adult years playing out the agendas of the wounded child that are still inside us. This is certainly what I had been doing prior to that pivotal summer when I arrived in New York.

Gabriel acknowledged that Robert and I had begun to claim three of the core qualities of the adult Self in our time together: empowerment, clarity, and passion. To continue growing, we needed to deepen our understanding of the role that nurturing is intended to play in our growth.

Whatever each of you experienced in your early years became your first impressions about Self and the world around you. When you are nurtured, you naturally develop a trust that you matter and that you deserve support.

When you aren't, you end up creating limited beliefs about yourselves. You develop a limited view about what you think you deserve—all based on personalizing whatever your early experiences seem to have affirmed. That is how powerfully your experiences color what you trust, and when nurturing is missing, you create layers of Self-doubt.

That is exactly how I had always felt.

Most people have unknowingly remained in the more primitive stages of their potential, simply because very few leaders and caregivers have known how to model the greater depths of nurturing encouragement to connect to the inner Self. Of course, we say this with no judgment. Every stage of your development is sacred and important. At the same time, we continue to encourage you with how much you have to look forward to as you learn to show up and nurture yourselves.

Hearing those words was a great comfort to me. I had spent the last few years learning to identify some of the missing levels of nurturing, and I had already begun to nurture myself the best I could.

Only when you feel safe through nurturing—whether in childhood or as adults—do you allow yourselves to open and grow. This is why creating the practice of nurturing is crucial for you if you want to gain access to the deeper parts of your Whole Self. Without nurturing, you can only create a more peripheral connection with the inner Self and with one another.

The good news is that it is never too late to introduce nurturing into your lives. You already know this is true from direct experience. More and more, this is becoming your new, reliable state of being. It is so important that you continue to build on that foundation and identify throughout your lifetime where you still hold perceptions of fear, shame, and judgment.

The more I heard about these early setups, the more compassion I began to feel for the wounded child within me, as well as for the wounds that others were carrying. The more I learned, the more I felt sure that no one I knew had received the depths of nurturing education needed to build a truly solid depth of Self-value in their early years. That was certainly true for me.

I knew I hadn't been happy or at peace for much of my early life, and only now was I learning how to identify why that had been so. Even with this information, it felt daunting to consider identifying each of my fears and the specific things about myself that I had learned to associate with shame. Reaching this vulnerable point of the healing process made me appreciate that I had already built so much trust in Gabriel over these first few years together.

Once I began to evaluate what Gabriel encouraged, I realized that none of us reach adulthood without building up the energy of fear, shame, and Self-doubt. For me, one of the most telling experiences of this came from having a chance to perform in a star-studded gala at Carnegie Hall.

Though it was thrilling to be included in a performance with so many celebrities from film and Broadway, getting to see how some of them were negotiating their own versions of fear and insecurity was a rare opportunity. It also helped to solidify my growing awareness that great achievements did not automatically provide a trusted sense of Self.

In one of my first private sessions after the Carnegie Hall event, Gabriel affirmed, *We are so pleased for you to find out firsthand some of the things we've been telling you. No matter what levels of glamour or achievement any of you reaches, you all need to become nurturing authorities in your own lives, encouraging one another in the process. No matter how many other people think you are wonderful, it is ultimately what you feel about yourselves that determines more of your day-to-day experiences. Once again, the more you begin to nurture yourselves, the freer you will become.*

One step at a time. Just having conversations about fear and shame got me used to their reality in my life. I was safer to bring those things into the light of day than I had long imagined.

Before you become overwhelmed by the task that stands before you, we remind you that you already understand many things about the process of facing challenges. When you were in first grade, the primary way you developed was through facing challenges. Even if no one talked about the importance of facing challenges directly, you still had to face the challenges of learning to read and write, to share with other children, and to be away from home for the first time in that way. Facing those challenges is what allowed you to discover and develop some of the first important layers of your personal potential.

What you can now begin to evaluate is that what you learn at one level prepares you for what comes next. Little by little, you gradually claim more levels of the authentic Self. This is also what allows you to have more to offer into the lives of those around you.

Once Robert and I began to understand the importance of identifying where we were still held in fear and shame, we started helping each other identify the core challenges set up in our early lives. For both of us, many of those challenges seemed to revolve around feeling alone, without the support of conscious, nurturing adults. The more we showed up to support each other, the more we affirmed that we could create new and healthier experiences of trust. In short, we were teaching each other that mutual support was possible.

One of the memories Robert shared one evening was how his parents had expected him to babysit his younger brothers when he was only five years old, sitting alone in a truck in a dark parking lot while his parents were drinking inside a pub. It was touching that he allowed himself to admit how much fear this had created for him. By showing up to support him in that moment, I was able to demonstrate to him that he was no longer alone. It provided the exact new experience that would allow him to trust the opposite of what he had feared for so many years.

The more we began to identify challenges—some we had already faced and some that still loomed before us—the more we saw that the process of facing fears had allowed us to develop certain qualities that we now appreciated and counted on in our lives. For instance, because we had to figure out so many things on our own as children, Robert and I had both developed more confidence in our ability to find creative solutions than some of our peers. Seeing that a much needed gift resulted from a challenge was quite encouraging for us.

The more we acknowledged the challenges that we had already faced, the more we began to feel proud of ourselves. We could both see how much courage it had taken to show up on our own, to invest in our specific talents, and to move far away from home to pursue our dreams. Each challenge we identified gave us chances to search for the gifts we had developed. Over time, this became a great game we enjoyed. How strange and surprising this nurturing approach was turning out to be.

One of the things we both appreciated about the careers we had worked so hard for was that, in the process, we had gained an important world education. Both of us had met and interacted with people from many different cultures, religions, and approaches to Life long before there was the internet to provide easy access to such things.

My experiences in other countries confirmed something I had always imagined was true: that people from all around the world are more alike than we are different. We all share the same emotional needs and desires. We all want to feel safe and to trust that we matter. We all want to create meaningful lives, and we all want to feel safe in the revelation that what is meaningful to one may differ from what is meaningful to another.

Seeing so many variations in the setups of people's lives helped me develop further compassion for a broad spectrum of wounds and challenges. I also became more aware of how we all need to learn how to create nurturing solutions to our unresolved pain and fear. Now that I had met so many people from around the world, this became a much more personal revelation.

Gabriel continued encouraging us by explaining that we could only replace our old choices with new, more nurturing approaches *gradually*, as we grew accustomed to identifying the specific choices that we wanted to replace. In other words, he was assuring us that a healthy process of transformation can only take place by percentages—shifting from the habitual approaches that we had learned as wounded children into the more empowered ones of adults.

Another wounded tendency that I had to admit at this stage was that the habitual overachiever in me now wanted to reach new levels in record time—anything that might end up with me being seen as impressive or pleasing to the authority figures in my life, which now included Gabriel. It was all so humbling to realize and to admit. Some days, it seemed that no matter where I looked, there were constant examples of wounded distortions to transform. And now, hearing that it would be wise for me to slow down and accept change as a gradual, multilayered process presented me with one of my biggest challenges.

Being kind to myself was something I had to continually remind myself to do, especially when I made mistakes. Only gradually was I able to interrupt my Self-judgment and the high expectations that I held for myself—just as Gabriel suggested would be the case. One of the most effective ways to get out of those traps involved redirecting my focus toward specific experiences I preferred to create for myself, or to simply remember that I was showing up and willing to learn.

Little by little, it was clear how much I preferred the more nurturing adult choices over the wounded ones that had kept me in fear. I liked having clear solutions to work toward. One step at a time, I was learning that Life provides us all with a constant opportunity to learn, grow, and evolve. We truly do have more power to impact the quality of our own journeys than I would have guessed.

CHILD

4

SNAKES
AND STITCHES

ONCE ROBERT AND I BECAME MORE PRACTICED AT identifying challenges and turning them into gifts, Gabriel informed us we were now ready to look much more fully at the setup of our early lives—one of the most important parts of healing and claiming the authentic Self.

To get to the core or root of the challenges that your Soul has set up, we now suggest you go back and do a more complete Life review. As you look back at each stage you have already moved through, you will be able to see more clearly how your core challenges were set up as important lessons and focuses that are there to guide you. You will also be able to identify and appreciate how early you began to awaken your most natural gifts, interests, and qualities. This more thorough investigation will teach you to recognize the Divine Order of your life.

Whenever you find limitations and wounded experiences, we also encourage you to consider the many ways you wish your caregivers had known how to nurture you in those early years. The more specific you are, the more fully you will be able to identify healthy options that you can now begin to practice on yourself—nurturing the child that is still held inside you. This approach will teach you to show up as the nurturing authority in your own life, which is something everyone needs to do in their lives.

By offering various forms of nurturing and encouragement, you will show the inner child that it is possible to finally feel safe, seen, and heard. When you feel safe, you will free more of the authentic Self that is waiting inside you to emerge. This approach will allow you to build more innocence, wonder, and trust, which are the core gifts of childhood that became stunted.

In short, as you move through this life review, it is important to see yourself through the eyes of compassion. Take time to visualize and experience some of the new options that are now possible. By offering new alternatives, you will encourage old layers of fear, shame, and judgment to release more easily.

Robert and I both committed to doing this deeper life review. We also appreciated that we had already spent years learning to nurture various wounded feelings before we jumped in at this deeper level. Gabriel reminded us to take our time with each event we uncovered, assuring us yet again that it was introducing new, nurturing experiences that would allow us to make the most progress. It didn't take long to realize this was great advice.

The moment I closed my eyes to begin this in-depth review, something surprising emerged from deep inside me.

"I'm *so* sorry!"

As soon as I heard the words, I felt a sharp pang of regret that was quite unfamiliar. I had no idea what memory was coming up for me.

However, instead of worrying about it, I simply showed up for this part of me that was in distress with the tenderness and compassion Gabriel had encouraged. To ease myself in as the nurturing adult, I asked the unidentified part of myself, "Why are you sorry?" Almost instantly, more words came hurtling up to the surface.

"I hurt my mommy!"

I was dumbfounded. What could this possibly mean? I did a quick scan of my childhood, trying to remember a single moment when I might have hurt my mother. Nothing came. So I continued to dialogue with the child that clearly needed to be heard. "When did you hurt your mommy?"

"When I was born!" came the answer without hesitation, followed by a flood of sobbing. Though this took me by surprise, I landed in the moment and allowed the feelings to come up. I did my best to honor them and to allow their release. At some point in the process, it occurred to me that I had no idea I'd been carrying such a huge pool of charged feelings about my birth somewhere deep inside me.

I was moved by the fact that this vulnerable part of me had not only been waiting so long to come up but also trusted me enough to allow such deep sadness to emerge. It helped to remember that allowing those feelings to surface was in no way threatening to my adult reality. Honoring that nothing negative was happening to me in that moment gave me a sense of safety that allowed me to fully surrender to the release of those old feelings.

That was the first moment I felt such clarity about showing up as the nurturing authority in my own life. It was all quite natural, spending time listening, and then rocking the wounded infant that had been me. The whole experience humbled me. I was amazed that I could release such a well of old feelings in such a safe and meaningful way. But it was more than that. It was satisfying. Not just safe. The longer I nurtured the child, the calmer my whole body began to feel. Instead of the shame and regret that my child had held, I replaced that space inside myself with an experience of compassionate nurturing and acknowledgment. I noticed that my child also allowed himself to settle down and become calm.

After sitting with these discoveries for a few days, the vulnerability began to transform into a deeper sense of solidity and trust. I took that as a great sign, and I was ready to look at the next pieces of my past. I was also convinced that it isn't an intellectual understanding of something that helps us move through some buried upset. It was the willingness to feel the feelings with nurturing that created the magic. Who would have guessed that honoring sadness, vulnerability, remorse, and worry would have such an impact? When I tuned in to what I was feeling as the adult, I felt less afraid of the next time I would inevitably face similar wounded feelings.

True to what Gabriel had suggested, it was allowing a new experience of nurturing that had made all the difference. It was also clear that every past experience I relived might involve surprising feelings that needed to be released. Therefore, I decided it would be wise to be as thorough as possible in my review. So I went back as far as I could to find out.

In October of 1960, my family lived in Pinetops, North Carolina. The only thing I could remember about that small town was that it had just two stoplights, a hardware store, and an A&P grocery. Since it was too small to support a big hospital, when my mother began to have contractions that announced my pending arrival, my parents had to drive twenty miles to the nearest and bigger town called Rocky Mount.

When my mother's labor had gone on for hours and she was still not showing any real progression, the staff encouraged my father to go home and get some sleep—a choice that unknowingly heightened the drama of my birth. My dad left without signing any documents, which included the forms that would give doctors permission to perform any surgeries that might be needed.

At some point in the early morning, things accelerated. Only then did they discover a real problem. Apparently, my umbilical cord was tightly wound around my head and neck. This meant that my mother's contractions were putting us both in deep trauma. Soon after that discovery, the hospital called my father and told him to get back as quickly as possible. Once he arrived and was in the process of signing the surgical release papers, my mother and I were rushed into the operating room for an emergency C-section.

As I looked back at what had come up in the processing of these events, I was astounded that even as a newborn, I had perceived the pain my mother was going through—and I had blamed myself for it. As an adult, I knew the blocked birth process and surgery had caused her tremendous pain. However, as a child, I personalized that she had only gone through that pain to bring me into the world. This brought me back to what Gabriel had told us, that in our first years of life, we personalize everything in the limbic brain. But this was the first time I had discovered such an undeniably clear example.

As I continued to move forward from my birth experience, I found that I remembered hardly anything at all. Fortunately, Gabriel had also informed us that a lack of logical memories from our earliest years comes from the fact that the logical part of our brain is not "turned on" at that point. Prior to ages four, five, and six, most people only have general impressions about the events that took place.

As I began to scan, I was only able to recall moments that involved strong emotions. The first of those took place when I was three, a memory that began with some commotion in my grandparents' bedroom. When I went in to find out what was going on, I discovered my mother and grandmother nervously hunkered by the front windows. Apparently, after encountering a snake on the front porch, they had run inside. They were now waiting for a signal from my grandfather that everything was safe.

Several things became apparent to me, looking back at this early memory. I had already heard that in our earliest years, we are taught how to feel about specific situations; these feelings are mostly based on how our caregivers respond to what is happening. This was my first experience with snakes, and I recognized that my first impression was how threatening snakes must be if they frighten adults.

Clearly, as a three-year-old, I picked up on my mother and grandmother's fear, and I wanted to feel the safety of connection. As I tried to reach my mother's side, my timing was unfortunate. Just when I was passing by my grandmother, she turned with her Chesterfield cigarette held at the same height as my face. The lit end of her cigarette went directly into my open eye.

I remember feeling shocked and terrified by the pain. After that, I could only recall vague glimpses of lights flashing on and off as I was rushed to the hospital. My next impression was being on a cold, silver table and hearing one of the doctors say that my eye had turned an awful yellow-green color. Looking back, I focused more fully on being grateful that my eye hadn't sustained any permanent damage, before remembering that my family eventually referenced that night as "one of Ronnie's close calls."

It just so happens that my only other specific memory from those early years also involved a snake. On some random day when I was four,

I was excited to spend time outside, riding my tricycle. Wearing nothing but shorts and a pair of socks, I ventured outside by myself. Focused on the fun I was about to have, I didn't even notice the thick, coiled snake sleeping on one of the brick steps I had to cross to get to my trike. So of course, I ended up stepping directly on the snake.

Perhaps if I hadn't had such a fearful association from the first memory, I might have been curious or even indifferent. What occurred instead was a surge of the fear and perhaps even the pain I associated with the first incident. Apparently, the adrenaline that surged through my terrified little body was so great that it enabled this four-year-old to climb all the way up to the roof of our family car, which was where my parents found me, screaming at the top of my lungs.

Fortunately, those two events didn't dampen my natural love of adventure nor my tendency to get into unfortunate mishaps. By the time I started elementary school, I was given free rein to explore the neighborhood and the surrounding woods, which meant I had plenty of opportunities for both excitement and trouble. As I scanned forward in my review, it was again a mishap that came to mind. This time, I was seven.

On that day, I was out scouting the neighborhood on my bike. Fascinated with the pavement that passed so quickly beneath me, I soon discovered that looking straight down wasn't such a wise choice. All of a sudden, my view of pavement was replaced by grass. When I looked up to find out how I had gotten off track, my face slammed into a wooden mailbox—one that happened to belong to Mrs. Andrews, the local kindergarten teacher.

The fact that our logical memory is more developed by the age of seven was validated by the fact that I could remember more specific details about this event. The structure I had hit was made from three pieces of wood: a tall vertical four-by-four post, a horizontal two-by-four that reached out toward the street, and a third angled two-by-four that supported the wooden mailbox perched on the end. I even remembered someone saying that the force of the collision had disengaged eight nails and three screws. Once I hit the mailbox, nothing but the vertical post was left standing. Included among the wreckage was me, lying on the ground completely passed out.

Since no one was around when it all went down, when I eventually regained consciousness, I had to get myself up and then back to my house. As I scanned my experience of that day, I remembered crying and feeling dizzy—distinctly aware that I was drenched in blood. I also remembered encountering two people along the way. The first was a schoolmate out riding his bike.

All he said before riding off was, "Oh, my God. I hope you don't die!"

The other person who happened by was one of the teenage babysitters who sometimes stayed with my two sisters and me when our parents went out. I remembered how surprising it was that she didn't come over to comfort me. Instead, she turned and ran the other way, which I eventually realized was so she could get help. I remember her shouting for my mother, "Help! Help! Ronnie has split his head wide open!"

Perhaps most amazing was that the most poignant memory of the event was my mother nurturing me in the upstairs bathroom of our house. Receiving that nurturing was more important than having a huge gash in my forehead, which I briefly glimpsed a couple of times in the large bathroom mirror. I also remember how comforted I felt on the drive to the hospital, nestled next to her on the front seat.

How powerful to discover that even in the face of real trauma, my focus was most drawn to the nurturing. Once that was clear, I suddenly remembered one final mishap.

This time, I was eight, moving really fast up the metal steps of a high dive, propelled by the excitement of having another adventure. How I loved the feeling of complete freedom that came each time I soared off that diving board. However, just as I reached the final step of my hurried climb, my hand slipped from the wet metal rail, and I fell backward, plunging all the way down to the unforgiving cement below.

Though the experience solidified a distinct fear of heights that lasted well into my adulthood, this memory brought up something even more immediate for me. A number of adults came rushing over to help me as I lay there on the cement, but none of those included my parents. They weren't even at the pool. Though that part of the experience hadn't stood out to me when I was young, it was distinctly obvious to me as an adult.

How could my parents allow a young kid to be at the pool without their supervision? Once that question was clear in my head, I began to scan through the next years of being at the pool with my two sisters, Beverly and JB. The vast majority of the time, we were there by ourselves, even though JB was much younger than both Beverly and me. The lack of supervision was so common that we thought nothing of it. However, when I scanned back over those early summers, I could easily recall other parents sitting in chairs next to the pool. They were there to watch and protect their children.

As I continued my review, it felt good to remember how much we loved being at the pool, even if I could now see that it had been our replacement babysitter. We all loved those little frozen pizzas that we ate each day for lunch. However, once the subject of being on our own entered my consciousness, I knew it was important and that I needed to investigate it further.

I started by scanning each of the first houses we had lived in during those early years. The fact that I could remember tons of specific details about the rooms and furniture, down to the quilting of the green bed-spread in my room, was telling. And yet, I hardly had any memories of my parents being around. This was disturbing to me as an adult. While logic told me that our parents must have been at home quite often, it was still telling that I didn't remember interacting with them. In one specific house, I could recall us all being at the dinner table, though the food we ate stood out more than any conversations or connections that had taken place.

As a child, this was simply our "normal." However, as an adult, this really bothered me. At first, I wanted to find a way to justify their absence. I even found myself wanting to deny what I had discovered. But no matter how much I scoured our many houses in my memory, I mostly remembered being alone.

This pivotal discovery inspired a great deal of compassion from me. When I remembered that besides being alone so often, we had also moved twelve times in my first fifteen years, my feelings of loneliness only grew. The adult part of me realized that never staying in one place for very long hadn't given me much of a chance to establish memorable connections or lasting friendships.

Because Gabriel had encouraged me to pay close attention to the kinds of nurturing I wished I had received, I noted that no one had ever sat my siblings and me down to talk about the changes that took place each time we moved. Our parents never acknowledged how profoundly their choices would affect us, or that we'd have to let go of everything that was familiar. Nor did they help us or teach us to focus on some-thing we might look forward to in each new location. No one talked to us about anything, really. Again, the contrast of what was simply nor-mal to me as a child and what I could now recognize as harmful as an adult was stark.

Of course, I also learned that it is never too late to go back to the child inside me to offer the clarity and nurturing that had been missing. Each time I recalled something hurtful from my past, I took the time to create new memories, with me as the nurturing authority I had always longed for. As a result, I was able to help the child build trust in new possibilities, which felt more and more comforting over time.

Prior to this life review, I had only known the choice to keep marching forward through each event, without any awareness that processing feelings was even an option. I realized this didn't mean I hadn't been feeling insecure, confused, or sad the whole time; it just meant that no one acknowledged those feelings, and so I had learned to belittle them. What became familiar was packing up, putting my feelings aside, and moving on to a rather constant stream of "new normals." No one discussed anything or reassured us. As kids, we were just left to deal with figuring everything out on our own.

At this point in my review, I realized that a pattern was developing. As I looked back, I would make what seemed like an important discovery, and then I would begin to scan for evidence and confirmation that my realizations were correct. For instance, in the case of being on my own, I remembered that I was expected to find my own way to and from school each day, starting back in the first grade. Just like every other situation, I couldn't recall any discussion about options or whether I felt safe with the things my parents asked of me. I can only guess that they considered it safe for a six-year-old child to make that journey each day.

I also remembered coming home from school on many days to a dark, empty house. If I needed anything in those few hours after school, prior to our parents coming home from work, I simply figured it out. If I was hungry, I ventured into the kitchen to see what I could find. This typically involved going for the Honey Buns that were always in the freezer. I remember loving them, and though they were hard and cold, I worked my way through as many as I could eat. I don't think my parents ever noticed how quickly I went through boxes of those frozen treats.

Doing this much of my life review took many months. Once I made a discovery, I would stop and take time to feel, always making sure to reassure my inner child. At this point in the process, I realized how many of my discoveries were tilting toward the negative. So I decided it was time to shift my focus, purposefully looking for moments that I had enjoyed. Even though many of those positive memories also involved doing things on my own, after all the wounded feelings I had processed, it was fun to find positive feelings and pleasurable experiences.

As a child, I was always curious. I was constantly seeking ways to keep my active imagination engaged. I loved doing all things creative. I remember watching *Mister Rogers*, *Captain Kangaroo*, and cartoons like *Shazam!* and *Johnny Quest*. I also remember one day when I discovered two sets of green-and-white books etched in gold on a shelf in the den. The ones on the upper shelf were called *World Book Encyclopedias*, and just below them was a second set of thinner books called *Childcraft*. Specifically designed for children, those books gave me my first hints that I had an insatiable desire to learn—a gift that I grew to appreciate more than I can say as I got older.

Reading *Childcraft* was one of my favorite things to do. The highlight of the bunch was volume 9, *Make and Do*. The excitement that I felt delving into that book was easy to remember. While reading, I discovered so many projects that were intriguing to my young mind. Only in looking back did it occur to me that my mom must have been aware of this, as being able to fulfill those projects meant I needed some very specific items—items that I would never have found in random drawers. Realizing this gave me some glimmers of peace.

Even though this seemed like a small thing, I couldn't quite reconcile the feelings of loneliness with the ones of adoration for my mother. She was precious to me, and so recalling that last string of memories had made me really sad. I didn't want to feel negative things about my mom. And even though I had trouble finding her in my life review, I still had an overall impression of feeling loved that I looked forward to exploring in the future.

What had been easier to remember was being with my older sister, Beverly, in a handful of situations. One of the most fun things she and I did was acting out skits for our babysitter from *Rowan & Martin's Laugh-In*—one of our favorite TV shows. One of the most memorable skits involved two old people sitting on opposite ends of a bench. The whole sketch boiled down to the man gradually finding excuses to scoot over to flirt with the old woman, culminating with the woman hitting him with her giant purse. Once she knocked him to the ground, she ran away.

To pull this one off, we needed gray hair. What we came up with was going into our parents' bathroom and dumping a bunch of the powder from my mother's makeup table onto our heads. When my sister eventually knocked me off my seat, using a purse we had found in our mother's closet, powder flew everywhere. I really loved the moments I spent playing with Beverly, particularly when we could make each other laugh, reenacting skits or doing handstand contests.

What I couldn't remember was cleaning up the mess that we had made from our skit. Nor could I remember anyone even mentioning it afterward. Again, there never seemed to be any feedback or guidance about our choices. Big things and small things simply happened in our lives without note.

Another one of my pleasant memories involved spending time pondering and exploring big subjects in my mind. Starting as early as four or five, I remember lying in bed contemplating Life and how it all worked. My best attempts in those early years involved working my way back through history. "Before I was born, there was my mom and dad. Before they were born, there were my grandparents. Before them, there were lots of other people, and way before that, the planet was created. At some really distant point, there was just God." I then imagined God out in space—also alone.

After I spent a while wondering what God might have done with his time, I continued. But each time I got to the point "Before God was born..." I moved into a state of discomfort. Whenever I couldn't find a clear answer, I got so uncomfortable that I jumped out of bed and searched for something new to distract me. Most of the time, that didn't take much effort.

A number of years later, when I asked my mother to share some of her early impressions of me as a young child, she said one of the most obvious things she remembered was that I was relentlessly curious. She said I asked questions about everything. "Why?" and "How?" were constants from me. Hearing that my mother had distinct impressions of me from that time felt really nice, though it was oddly disconcerting that I could hardly remember any of those times with her.

One interaction we had shared did stand out for me. Unfortunately, this was also a charged memory. I was five and I could remember how very much I wanted to have a real conversation. In this case, I was preparing to take a bath. Even though I couldn't recall what my mom was saying, I do remember her reaction when I jumped in to offer one of my ideas. She exclaimed, "Young man, are you contradicting me?"

This took me by surprise, and I distinctly remember feeling confused, shut down, and hurt. Although that specific moment might not have seemed significant to my mom at all, I could see, looking back, that her reaction sent a clear message to me that it wasn't safe to disagree or challenge adults, and that left me feeling quite frustrated and sad.

I absolutely hated when something ended the possibility of exploring and connecting—two of my favorite things. It just didn't make sense to me. One of the other versions of this abrupt end to conversations was simply "Because I said so." Even though I was too little to challenge an adult who said this to me, I would secretly continue exploring possibilities in my own head.

Over time, I concluded that adults didn't have answers to many of my important questions, at least in ways that were satisfying to me. I remember disagreeing quite often with things they told me. Sometimes this involved hearing comments that seemed hurtful. Growing up in the South, I sometimes heard people make racist comments—though I was relieved that it was never my mother. I do remember feeling angry when people made comments that put other people down. Even from a very young age.

After all, when I was in kindergarten, my best friend was a Black girl who lived at the end of Ivanhoe Drive. I loved her a lot. When adults made derogatory comments that included the people I cared about, I couldn't stand it.

I also didn't understand many of the claims that were made about big subjects, like heaven and hell. When those discussions came up with my mother, I found ways to imply that I disagreed without the risk of contradicting her directly. For instance, I would innocently ask, "Are you telling me that some of my friends from school are not going to heaven, simply because of where they go to church? Or because they don't go to church at all?"

Looking back, I felt proud of my inner child for this workaround, and I made sure to tell him so. At the same time, I had to remind myself that I was supposed to be looking for positive memories. Shifting gears, it was time to focus on one of my favorite early moments with my mom.

One day when I was five, she called me out to the garage. This time it turned out that our family dog, Cleo, was starting to give birth to five puppies, and I got to watch the whole thing! Amazed and excited, I could hardly believe those little babies were coming out of Cleo.

Of course, I asked lots of questions, and I spent tons of time in the garage watching and holding those little dachshund puppies. It was all so exciting, and I didn't want to miss a thing. One afternoon, not too long after the puppies arrived, I called my mom out to the garage to ask what the puppies were doing with their faces nestled so close to Cleo's body. She told me they were drinking milk, and then she went back inside the house.

When she returned a short while later, she found me on the cement floor alongside the puppies, trying to figure out how to drink some of Cleo's milk. Cleo was a trooper, giving a curious little boy a loving place to explore.

5

THE LAKE

WHAT BECAME CLEAR AS I BEGAN LOOKING FOR positive memories from my early years was that there was one place that was my favorite. Without question, my grandparents' house in Lake Waccamaw, North Carolina was most special to me—probably because it was the one true constant in my early life, and it was also the one house where I was always surrounded by people.

I will never forget taking the final turn off the two-lane highway each time my mom took us to this most magical place—lovingly referred to by all of us as "the lake." Looking back, I was pleased to find that almost every detail of being at the lake was still beautifully etched in my mind, including the fun I had with my mom and sisters in the car on the way down.

Lake Waccamaw is a quaint community situated along one main road that winds its way around the lake. As soon as I began to focus on the time I spent there, my heart warmed. I would even say that something about the place seemed sacred. Its mystique was only enhanced the day I found out that the lake had originally belonged to the Waccamaw Indians, after being formed by a meteorite falling out of the sky. That was just about the most fascinating thing I had ever heard.

Each time we began our drive down the final stretch of road, I started looking for the beautiful blue of the lake in the distance. I then looked forward to seeing the alligator farm on our left, just after the turn onto the main road. I loved the towering trees covered in dangling Spanish moss and hearing the lap of small waves hitting the rocky edges of the lake. Those were all constants in my life, and they were dear to me.

I also loved that our grandparents' house had a name. The Good Shepherd Home was a rehabilitation center for male alcoholics—though that didn't really mean anything specific to me in those early days. It was only later that I found out my grandfather had been an alcoholic for a number of years before I was born. Once he turned his life around, he became a Methodist minister and eventually the director of The Good Shepherd Home.

The main house was situated on the largest piece of property I had ever seen—even though I realized as an adult that it was no more than a handful of acres. I loved remembering the details of every building, starting with the main white house. The long, screened-in porch that lined the front had a wooden bench swing that our whole family loved. The right side of the first floor was where the private family apartment was situated, complete with a living room, kitchen, and three bedrooms—all of which had bathrooms attached.

Outside "the apartment" was a huge gathering room for guests, an office, and an equally large dining room that held three long tables where everyone gathered for meals. My favorite time of the day was dinner, because it was when we got to spend time with "the men," which was how everyone referred to the guests seeking treatment at The Good Shepherd Home. For me, it was definitely the more the merrier.

On the wall behind the main family table was a huge mural of Jesus holding a lamb, drawn in chalk by a guest. I remember being mesmerized by the mural and the calm feelings it evoked. It felt particularly special because I had watched the man create what I considered a masterpiece. I also appreciated that the dining room provided easy access to the large kitchen, which was filled with silver tables, sinks, and large stacks of all-white dishes.

The kitchen was also where I would often find Alan, the warm, jovial man who was one of the other constants of the house. For as long as I could remember, he was the cook who prepared meals for the group. I loved it, of course, when he would give me special attention. I often created excuses to be in the kitchen so I could spend time watching him, and sometimes chatting too. A moment that stands out involved him secretly offering me some raw biscuit dough to take away and play with, very much like the Play-Doh I had back at our house. Thinking of Alan, I recalled that he had given me my first, and only, cup of coffee, which I absolutely hated.

The centerpiece of those beautiful memories was the lake, located just across the street from the house. To get there, we had to cross the main paved street, move past the long wooden benches that lined the upper edge of the cliff, and then walk down about twenty-five steps to reach the private pier reserved for people staying at The Good Shepherd Home.

There were other places dotted along the huge property that my sister, Beverly, and I enjoyed. We spent hours exploring. We liked to wait each day for the much anticipated mosquito truck to drive past the house. Looking back, I'm not sure how we were allowed to run behind a truck that sprayed thick clouds of toxic gas intended to kill mosquitos.

However, without knowing that it was deadly poison we were inhaling, we looked forward to the adventure of disappearing into the mysterious fog. It was pure magic. As per usual, the adults somehow allowed everything without comment.

Out of all the places I enjoyed at the lake, I did have one clear favorite—the chapel that was located on the second floor of the house. That was the place where everyone gathered for weekly meetings. It was also the first place in my memory that I associated with music.

The most special memories I have of that chapel typically took place at my favorite time of year: Christmas. It was when all my favorite things happened at once. The holidays were filled with music, particularly on the rare occasions when we were treated with visits from my uncle Jason, who was one of my favorite people in the world. Perhaps the reason he was so special to me was that he was the first person who took a real interest in me.

This very tall and gentle man was the eldest of my mother's two brothers. All I knew about my uncle was that he lived so far away that he had to fly in a plane to come and see us. Though I had never seen a plane, just hearing about it created a grand adventure in my mind. My uncle's life was a glamorous fantasy to me, filled with endless adventures.

He and my mom both grew up involved in music. Uncle Jason was quite gifted on the piano, and my mother had a stunning voice, just like my grandfather. My mom and my uncle had both been offered opportunities to pursue careers in New York City when they graduated high school—something that was almost unheard of for people from rural North Carolina in the fifties. While my uncle ended up following that path, it seemed that my mother must have felt it was too much of a stretch to consider. I often wondered what her life might have been like. Once, I heard that she had been invited to study with Estelle Liebling—the most famous voice teacher of the time. I loved knowing that this gifted woman had personally written to invite my mother. After all, Liebling had also taught the world-famous opera singer, Beverly Sills.

While my mom chose to get married and start a family immediately after high school, my uncle Jason went to New York and eventually to Los Angeles, where he built a career as a musician and an actor. In our eyes, he was a celebrity. After all, we were the only kids in our neighborhood who had an uncle they could watch on television. Jason was featured on any number of commercials, which was cool and exciting. However, nothing compared to the time he appeared on *The Brady Bunch*, one of our all-time favorite shows.

The few years when Jason would come to North Carolina for Christmas, I would sit and watch him practicing classical pieces on the piano whenever I could. I remember being so impressed. I almost couldn't believe what I was hearing. Sometimes he would also play for the services that my grandfather led. My grandmother played her part in those gatherings as well, accompanying others in singing hymns from an electric organ.

While my grandfather gave sermons intended to inspire the men in treatment, what stood out for me was that this was nearly the only time I heard him say anything. I loved it when we reached the part of the meeting when he invited the men to stand up and share some of the meaningful experiences they'd been having. They often affirmed that The Good Shepherd Home was just as special for them as it was for me.

As I looked back on all the years I spent in Lake Waccamaw, I was struck by how many pivotal first experiences and impressions took place while I was in that amazing chapel. Of course, I had no idea when I was young how many of those moments would have long-term impacts on the man I would become.

Some of the clear highlights were the times I got to hear my mother and grandfather singing duets, particularly when they were accompanied by my uncle Jason. How well I could remember the resonant baritone of my grandfather—who seemed surprisingly accessible when he was singing—and the warmth in my mother's eyes as they sang, "It Took a Miracle."

It took a miracle to put the world in place.
It took a miracle to hang the stars in space.
But when He saved my soul, cleansed and made me whole,
It took a miracle of love and grace.

Each of the memories I reclaimed from those early years were distinct and strong and still evoked powerful feelings for me. Being true to what Gabriel had suggested, I made sure to have conversations with my inner child after I discovered these more positive pockets of memory, reliving each experience with him. Since no one had acknowledged how important or beautiful these experiences had been at the time, I thought this would be a wonderful way to nurture the part of me that had experienced moments of innocence and wonder.

Recalling these memories of being at the lake provided a real boost for me at this point in my review. The timing was perfect because I knew that there was one thing I could no longer avoid. In order to continue moving forward, I needed to face my most obvious challenge: my father.

6

THE PIVOTAL CHALLENGES OF EIGHT

HAVING A FATHER WHO LIVED IN THE SAME HOUSE with us but who never engaged me in a single conversation in my childhood years had quite an impact on me. You might think I'm exaggerating, but I'm not. No matter how thoroughly I scanned, I couldn't remember my father ever initiating a real exchange between the two of us. Only the bark of occasional orders. The main feelings I experienced when tuning in to this part of my life were longing and confusion, followed by a sense of loneliness and rejection.

Although I had spent years practicing Gabriel's teachings by the time I got to this point in my review, I was still hesitant to relive some of the more upsetting experiences I associated with my father. As I eased my way in, the first place I could remember my father being around was at our house in Burgaw, North Carolina. When I was five, I could picture him out in the backyard, working in his garden.

Because I desperately wanted to connect with my dad, I made sure to find my way outside whenever he was there. The meticulous process he went through in the garden came back to me easily, a process that started with him carefully forming long rows of raised dirt with a hoe. He then poked little holes in the top of each mound for seeds. I loved watching for the plants that first appeared as tiny shoots and gradually became a lush wonderland over the course of the summer. Witnessing my father's dance with nature made the garden he created the second most magical place of my childhood.

Towering beanpoles covered with vines, all suspended along the strings that my dad had hung with care, provided a place of great adventure. As the summer progressed, a mix of vibrant greens, reds, and yellows made the space seem alive and even more remarkable. Looking back, I realized that the most positive thing I learned from my father was a love of gardening and connection with nature.

The darker side of these memories was that all the time I spent in the garden with him took place in complete silence. Even though my dad was right there in front of me, there was a constant distance that I didn't know how to resolve. When I first started showing up, I hoped he would include me or teach me or even just start a casual conversation. But inexplicably, he never said anything, so neither did I.

Naturally, I wanted to ask him a million questions about everything he was doing, but somehow, he never sent out the energy of permission. Still, I watched in wonder. And even though I couldn't explain it at the time, looking back as an adult, in my father's love of plants, I could see clear hints that he had a deeply hidden potential to care.

Over the years, I heard from others that my father had grown up on a large tobacco farm, which was apparently quite common for families in rural North Carolina at the time. He was the youngest of nine children, and his father died when he was just a boy. Though he never said a word about those experiences, I imagined losing his father must have been devastating.

The only other times that I remember being next to my father were the few times he would drive the family somewhere. What made those moments exciting was that if our dad was in the car with us, it usually meant we were going on a long trip. For those journeys, most of which took place before JB was born, my parents always sat in the front, while Beverly and I sat in the back—very much like the Cleaver family in *Leave It to Beaver*.

It seemed strange that I could recall more memories of family time in a car than I could of being together in our home. And yet, even in the car, I can only remember my dad speaking when he was demanding that my sister and I be quiet. Other than that, he remained a silent mystery.

On those longer trips, Beverly and I usually got bored, and we would bicker. Our mom then drew an imaginary line between us that we were not allowed to cross. True to form, this drove me crazy, and I would typically figure out how I might get a silly, loud reaction from Beverly. Our dad would get upset, demanding, "You kids be quiet!" That was our mother's cue to tell us to look out our respective windows. To have those rare moments of being together as a family and not be allowed to say a word was excruciating for me. I so wanted to connect that I looked for any excuse to break the silence. That usually meant doing something to make Beverly laugh.

It was not lost on me that it was only when Dad was in the car that we had to be quiet. On our weekend trips with Mom, we always had fun.

We played games, sang, and laughed. Mom used road games to keep us entertained, like hunting for letters of the alphabet on license plates or on signs and billboards. The songs we sang were silly, but they were dear to me. It wasn't until I was an adult that I realized the lyrics of one of Mom's favorite tunes, "Mairzy doats and dozy doats but liddle lamzy divey," was actually a string of English words. "Mares eat oats and does eat oats, but little lambs eat ivy."

A few times when Beverly and I pushed a boundary that my parents had set, my father warned us in a stern, loud voice that he would take off his belt when we got home if we didn't listen. It only took a couple of times for him to follow through on that threat—taking us into a bedroom, bending us over the end of a bed, then hitting us quite firmly with his belt—for us to know that he meant what he said. All of that just for talking.

Moments like that left me more afraid of my father than anything else.

Still, I liked going on the long drives together because sometimes, they meant we were on a family vacation. Of course, our parents never told us where we were going. However, my father loved to go camping with tents and sleeping bags. The two places that were special to us were Nags Head Beach and one really cool journey to the Blue Ridge Mountains. On that particular trip, we were treated to an old-fashioned train ride at the Tweetsie Railroad, which included being held up for a mock shoot-out robbery between cowboys and Indians, just like the ones I'd watched on TV. This was even more exciting because I got to sit next to my dad on the train.

We also visited a Cherokee Indian reservation while we were in the mountains. As an adult, I realized that opportunity awakened in me a special connection to Native Americans. When I was young, I remember wanting as many souvenirs as possible to take home as mementos from the reservation. I was so happy that Dad allowed me to get a drum, a tomahawk, and a small headdress filled with colorful feathers.

When my scan for positive impressions with my dad was done, I knew I could no longer avoid the other events that took place when I reached the pivotal age of eight. In 1969, we were living in our second house in Raleigh, North Carolina, and for the first time, we had a large yard. Somehow, at the age of eight, that full acre of land became my responsibility. It all began one Saturday morning when I heard my dad calling my name from the back patio. Once I was there, I watched him put gas in the mower and then pull the cord to start the motor—all without saying anything. He then turned to me and said, "Go," before heading back inside the house.

I reached up to the handle that was located at a height just below my neck and started to push the mower around the yard. Each Saturday from that point forward, I was expected to go outside and spend what seemed like hours pushing and pushing and pushing. Naturally, there was one Saturday that stood out. It was the day the lawnmower jammed up and wouldn't start again. It seemed my dad had forgotten to tell me about something important called "oil," which apparently needed to be checked as well.

Based on my father's angry reaction, I imagined this was something I was supposed to have figured out for myself. What he discovered was that the engine had overheated to the point that it was completely ruined. Even then, my father said nothing to me directly, nor did he take any responsibility for not teaching me more effectively. I just remember him seething in silence, leaving me with the impression that having to buy a new mower was my fault.

Most of the other difficult moments that took place at that age boiled down to him letting me know that something I had done was wrong. Looking back, it was clear that if I'd had any guidance, each one of those challenging moments could have been avoided. Even so, I never spent any time thinking about most of those moments once they were done.

Unfortunately, there was one event that I could never forget—nor avoid any longer in my review. I would even say that this event became the centerpiece of Self-doubt that I still carried as an adult.

The predicament started with my dad barking for me to "go and put on a clean T-shirt." When I returned, he mumbled, "Your hair is too long." He then went inside the house, only to return with a pair of scissors. Once he came back, he began to randomly chop off clumps of my hair. My confusion and discomfort only deepened when he told me to get in the car. It would be the first time he and I drove anywhere, just the two of us.

I had no idea where we were going, but during our twenty minutes in the car, I kept looking at this warrior athlete out of the corner of my eye, deeply wishing that he would reach out and connect. I kept trying to think of something we might talk about. I so wanted to please him, and it was confusing to me that he never gave me any clues or invitations.

When we finally pulled into a parking lot, I saw several other boys in T-shirts, walking with their dads toward a large brick building. When we reached the front door, I looked inside and saw two large, brightly lit basketball courts. Apparently, my dad had decided it was time for me to play a team sport.

The moment was confusing for many reasons, even as an adult. I had always been fearless as a child, willing to soar off high dives and do complicated tricks on the neighbor's trampoline. I was comfortable doing athletic things. I had also heard from my mother that my father had played semipro baseball for a few years and that he had been the coach for a high school basketball team before I was born. But not once had he ever invited me to go outside and play catch.

Each of those things made this moment at that gym impossible to process. My dad had to have been aware that we had never even talked about sports. And yet, he had somehow thought it made sense to bring me to the city league basketball tryouts, even though I had never even held a basketball in my hands.

Naturally, the tryouts boiled down to all of us being asked to demonstrate certain skills. I had never even heard the terms they were using. To shoot what they called a layup, one had to bounce the ball with one hand, direct that ball forward while simultaneously watching the approaching goal, and while still in motion, grab the ball and leap into the air, throwing it off the backboard and into the hoop. I was a complete and utter disaster. And I was not only going through this in front of my dad but all of the other dads as well.

The whole experience was humiliating. I felt scared, confused, and deeply embarrassed—though no one seemed to notice or care about what I might be feeling.

After all the evaluations were done, it was time for the coaches to pick teams—a process that began with choosing the most practiced, gifted boys and ended with dividing up the two or three of us who were at the other end of the spectrum. The whole time this went on, I tried to find some sense in what was happening. I had always been an avid adventurer, and I had never been afraid of trying new things. *How did I end up here? What was my dad thinking?* I wanted to disappear.

Making matters even worse, after the whole devastating process was over, my dad drove us all the way home...in complete silence. He said absolutely nothing about what had just taken place. No reassurance. No words of comfort or encouragement. Nothing but an endless twenty minutes of awkward, scary silence. Though I didn't have any words for what I was experiencing, looking back, I could easily remember how raw and exposed I felt. And there was nowhere to escape.

Over the next few days, I kept hoping my dad would show up to teach me what I so obviously needed to learn. The very least he could do was buy me a basketball so that I could try and figure out some of it on my own. Each day passed like any other. Basketball was never mentioned—until it was time to return to the gym for what was to become my weekly visit to hell.

The very next Saturday turned out to be our first game. It began with running through the same drills we had done at tryouts. And now there was a bigger audience. Because this was now my second time holding a basketball, I was just as hopeless as I had been on the first day. Not even the coach, who was supposed to be our guide, offered any help. I had no option but to simply endure.

Once the drills were over, I quickly found a place on the end of the bench, as far away from the coach as possible. Still preferring to disappear, I sat there for the duration of the game, secretly panicked the whole time that the coach might put me in the game. All the while, I was painfully aware of my silent father sitting behind me in the stands, watching his clueless son just sit there.

Week after week, this same scene was repeated, each time ending with my dad driving me home in awful silence. Each week, I shrank a little more, knowing that the whole experience would all take place again in seven days' time. Looking back, I could remember how trapped I felt, knowing how much I needed help and being too afraid and ashamed to ask. And the fact that my dad never showed up for me was completely baffling.

Like a scene out of a bad movie, our team kept winning. And yes, we actually ended up competing in the city championship game. That's also when the inevitable finally happened. In what was clearly the most important game, our team was so far ahead that there was no possibility we could lose. That was when the coach called my name. To be honest, I don't remember much about the moments that followed. There was just a general sense of terror. I had no idea what I would do if anyone threw me the ball.

Fortunately, the other boys were so focused on winning that no one even considered making that choice. They simply kept scoring points, while I ran back and forth, up and down the court like a frightened animal. At some point, the final buzzer sounded, at which point I remember a loud celebration happening all around me. Moments later, I was handed a trophy: my lifelong reminder of shame, which is still hidden away in a trunk—hidden much like the feelings I had buried deep inside. And then that entire string of torturous events was capped off by one final drive home with my dad, with absolutely nothing to celebrate.

Looking back, it was clear to me why I never considered playing a team sport again. Perhaps even more devastating was having to acknowledge that this was the last time my dad ever asked. Little did I know that this experience would impact me for decades to come.

This core event began a new cycle for me. I became fully aware of a growing insecurity, and I felt unworthy whenever I was around my dad. I felt like I had lost any chance of him being proud of me. I imagined that his silence was an affirmation that I had no worth. Without any way to understand what had happened, even as an adult, I was left with the impression that my dad had never actually cared about me. It seemed he had only cared about basketball.

My only relief and escape during that eighth year of my life came from becoming friends with a girl named Lisa Brown, whose family lived just down the street from us. Lisa introduced me to horses. From our very first trip to what became known as "the barn," I was swept away with passion for those remarkable animals. Once I was able to get on the back of her beautiful chestnut gelding, Piper, I was hooked.

Each time we were dropped off at the barn, we were left to explore on our own. Lisa and I spent hours getting lost in our adventures, building forts out of hay bales, and then riding off together, both on Piper's back, to get lunch at the country store. Just when I thought things couldn't get any better, Lisa told me she was getting a second horse—one that was more suited for her to ride in competitions. This meant I would have a chance to ride Piper on my own. The more I rode, the more I started begging my mom for a horse. She just kept saying that we couldn't afford one. This was something I had never heard, nor did I really understand what it meant.

Even so, I remained obsessed with horses. The best way I had of indulging my fantasies was to join a Book of the Month club for horse lovers. Each time a new book arrived, I would disappear into my room and dive into a different world, imagining myself as the main character in each tale.

This went on for months before my mom surprised me with news that my dad had given the go-ahead for me to take some actual riding lessons. This qualified as one of the most thrilling things I'd ever experienced. I couldn't even sleep the night before my first lesson. When I finally got home from school on that special day, I ran into the house to get ready. I pulled on some jeans and scampered into Mom's yellow car for our trip to the barn.

As we backed out of the steep driveway, I was completely lost in what promised to be one of the most exciting days of my life. That's when everything went terribly wrong. Soon after my mom set the car into motion, I felt a strange up-and-down movement, like when a tire rolls over a curb or some other large object in the road. As we continued to back down slowly, I looked out the window, curious to see what we had run over. Words cannot convey what I felt when I realized it was Cleo, our precious dachshund.

Shock and disbelief flooded over me. We had run over Cleo. *No! Take it back. I am sorry that I asked for lessons. If only I hadn't asked, she'd still be alive* was what I thought when I eventually realized I was sitting on some stupid horse.

What happened after I saw Cleo was a blur. My mom somehow got me to the riding lesson, which only added to my confusion. Even as an adult, I couldn't make sense of the choices that were made.

I felt even more frustrated when I realized that no one ever talked about what had happened. I had so many feelings that needed to be addressed, and I needed to be nurtured. Never was that so clear. It was unbelievable to me that almost everything from my eighth year was filled with deep sadness and incredible confusion.

Though I didn't know how to put all the pieces together at this point in my healing process, I did figure out that in the midst of this event, a troubling belief emerged. I decided it wasn't safe for me to ask for something for myself and that if I did, there'd be a price to pay—a price like Cleo's life. It was all too much to process.

I knew this was a biggie for me to work through and nurture. And I knew a one-time meditation wouldn't heal the deep pool of feelings I felt. For this one, I needed Gabriel's help. It was hard to find words that felt adequate to comfort my inner child. So I settled for just letting him cry. We cried together. It was safe to cry. If only my parents had let me see *them* cry, it might have made all the difference in the world.

Gabriel had suggested that many of our core challenges are set in place by the time we are eight. Maybe that was why so many things were jammed into that one momentous year. Whatever the case may be, I spent a great deal of time in mourning as I eased my way into the process of nurturing these core events.

Several months passed before I felt remotely prepared to continue my review. Fortunately, once I finally decided I was ready, the next core challenges I found to unpack were from later, when I was ten.

One Saturday in my tenth year, two cousins we'd never met from my father's side of the family—Mickey and Cindy—showed up at our house. It turned out they'd be living with us.

The way I found out about that change felt like another personal blow. I was told that Mickey, who was sixteen and in need of his own space, would be taking my room. Without any discussion or explanation, I found myself sleeping on a recliner sofa in the living room, expected to simply accept this as my new normal. Because I felt painfully awkward asking for anything after the incident with Cleo, I squashed any objections that I felt and quietly accepted the new arrangement.

Years later, I found out that the reason my cousins had come to live with us was that my father's sister—their mother—had a serious drinking issue. Things had apparently gotten so bad that it was no longer safe for them to live with her.

The only memory that stood out from my time sleeping on the recliner was one night when my parents went out for dinner on their own. Sometime later that night, I was abruptly awakened by the sound of my father in a fit of rage. What I discovered once I got my bearings was my dad barreling his way through the house, screaming and ranting as he stormed by my chair again and again. My sisters and my cousins were somewhat protected behind the closed doors of their bedrooms, while I had a full view of him grabbing every ceramic ashtray he could find. One by one, he took them to the open back door of the house and smashed them on the back patio.

That rampage went on for what seemed like a long time, with me terrified and pretending to be asleep, secretly praying that my dad wouldn't notice me. When it was finally over, the house became eerily silent again. Par for the course, no one ever acknowledged what had happened or made sure we felt safe. Strangely and predictably, silence was the only thing adults ever offered.

It wasn't until years later that I found out the event had been triggered by my mother discovering that my father had been having an affair. He had tried to turn the blame on her by focusing on his disgust of her smoking. Perhaps the pressure of trying to care for Mickey, Cindy, and his own children had gotten to him. Or perhaps this was just my father's pattern—building up and then exploding. I didn't know. But that evening set a new series of changes into motion for all of us.

The next thing we knew, my cousins disappeared just as mysteriously as they had arrived. I then began to hear hints that we would be moving again.

This time, we left Raleigh for Jacksonville, North Carolina. Our first house on Kathryn Avenue was just half a block away from the elementary school that JB and I would attend. As baffling as things were at home, I found that I loved being in this new school. This was the first place I'd attended where there was a system that allowed us kids to learn at our own pace. We would each finish one lesson and then return to a box full of laminated lesson cards to grab the next. For the first time, I could learn as quickly as I wanted, and I loved having that new sense of freedom.

In addition, the teacher in charge of gym class offered some wonderful guidance, which was a definite first for me, especially from a man. He introduced me to individual sports, and it was in that setting that I reclaimed my athletic potential. Much to my surprise, I even stood out as a leader in some of the events, particularly in broad jump and gymnastics—the perfect sport for me to develop strength, coordination, and more command over my body.

The shift of starting elementary school in Jacksonville provided a natural move in my review, from a barrage of core challenges to the introduction of more meaningful experiences. Gymnastics, as one example, became a love that I continued to pursue all the way through college. The only thing that dampened my initial joy in that sport was that my father never paid any attention to my successes. He continued to show a lack of interest, even after it was clear that I was a standout. This only left me more confused about our relationship and about my value as a person.

Little did I know that those first years in Jacksonville would create more of a shift in my life than I imagined. As it turned out, our days living in the same house as our father were numbered. Naturally, the problems in my parents' marriage were not magically solved by moving to a new city. And as bad as things were, they hadn't changed that much in my eyes. Even so, I never considered that our family might split up. After all, I still wanted to find a way to connect with the most important male figure in my life.

Once my parents divorced, I lost all hope in that possibility.

7

MUSIC TO
MY EARS

N EEDING ANOTHER RESPITE BEFORE I BEGAN TO look at the years surrounding my parents' divorce, I knew I should spend some time balancing the scales with more positive influences. After all, the whole point of this review was to learn how to set myself up well, starting with offering all the nurturing that I could to my wounded inner child and looking for any gifts that I could find.

Keeping in mind that Gabriel had identified our core gifts as natural interests, qualities, talents, and capacities, it didn't take long to choose two for this deeper search for the things that mattered most to me: music and spirituality.

How wonderful it felt to recognize that I initially discovered my love of music and spirituality in the small chapel of The Good Shepherd Home. What I first noticed about music in those early memories was that it brought out the best in the people I loved. My mother and my grandfather both seemed much happier and more alive when they were singing. Knowing that I had some musical gifts was really exciting for me.

A particularly meaningful story that my mom shared with me was about when my uncle Jason found me at the piano in the chapel, plunking out a tune I had recently heard. I was only six years old. Apparently, this was meaningful to him as he was eager for the next generation of our family to continue expressing themselves through music. After he saw me, he bought a piano for Beverly and me to learn on. When we received the beautiful spinet with "Chickering" displayed in gold letters, little did any of us know what a cornerstone that piano would become in my life.

As I began to relive those first years of playing piano, I appreciated that my mother was equally responsible for making that part of my journey possible. Even though our family didn't have a lot of money for extracurricular activities, she always made sure we were able to participate in the activities that interested us. For me, that definitely included piano lessons. *Priceless.*

Right from the beginning, expressing myself through music was like a new world opening for me. Because of my enthusiasm, no one ever had to force me to practice, and I ended up making great progress. According to the people in my family who had a clear idea about what was typical for a child my age, it was surprising how quickly I was playing advanced compositions.

Feeling a sense of achievement in music created an important first for me. Through music, I received some definite acknowledgment, which was one of the few things that made me feel less alone. One moment that solidified that new reality involved my grandmother, who had never been a particularly warm presence for me. However, I will always be grateful that she noted the progress I was making. One afternoon, she surprised me with an invitation to join her on the piano for evening services. I couldn't believe it. This was exactly what I had seen my uncle do any number of times. And even though I needed to move through a steep learning curve to build those particular skills, for the first time, I felt I had something of real value to offer.

Fortunately, there was also some awesome support for the arts in North Carolina schools during the seventies. This gave me other opportunities to explore. After a less-than-thrilling introduction to a flute-like instrument called the recorder in fifth grade, I was given the opportunity to choose my own instrument for sixth grade. I initially chose the viola.

I still remember the deep-purple velvet that lined the inside of the viola case that the school provided for that year. I also remember the beautiful, shiny wood and the smell of resin that I applied each day to the bow. Unfortunately, my time playing viola was short. That was the same year my parents had their major blowup, which led to our quick move to Jacksonville. And unfortunately, that school system had no offerings for strings.

By this point, I was quick on my feet at figuring out solutions for myself. It occurred to me that Beverly, who was two years ahead of me in school, had picked the trumpet for her sixth-grade instrument. My parents had purchased one for her, but she had given it up after only one year. So I was now able to consider the trumpet as an option.

Out of sheer habit, I didn't consider asking my parents or telling anyone my plan. I simply took the initiative of going to the band director a few weeks after we arrived. "I'm curious if there is any way I could join the band. I already have a trumpet," I assured him—leaving out the important detail that I hadn't yet made a single sound on the trumpet in question.

Thankfully, I was a quick study. At the same time, because I was months behind the other kids, I didn't stand out in any way. As I looked back, I could see how that small detail ended up serving me in the long run. As we approached the end of sixth grade, the band director asked some of us if we would consider switching instruments in order to meet the greater needs of the middle school band.

Having chosen the trumpet out of necessity more than real desire, I was thrilled to make a new choice. By that point, I had heard a much broader array of instruments, and I chose the one whose sound appealed most to me. Once I got my hands on a French horn, my whole experience of being in band transformed.

Out of genuine enthusiasm, I excelled for the next six years. This meant that I ended up with opportunities on both the piano and the French horn, each of which allowed me to develop different parts of myself. Playing the piano was something I did completely on my own. Being in a band allowed me to share a musical experience with a whole group of people, which of course, I loved.

I was initially introduced to spirituality because my grandfather was a Methodist minister. In addition to services in the upstairs chapel, we would often go to church in a neighboring town, where my grandfather was once again preaching from the pulpit. True to form, I often wanted to ask questions about the things that were taking place, but that didn't go over well in church.

I had discovered a desire to chat and discuss things when I was only three or four years old, and I didn't like being shushed. One Sunday morning, I had apparently had enough of being stifled. I decided to announce at the top of my lungs, "Well, my granddaddy's talking!"—which got quite a laugh from the congregation.

Looking back, I had to admit that it wasn't hearing my grandfather's sermons that inspired my love of spirituality. I was way too young to understand anything that he said. What first got my attention were the moving moments in the chapel when the men in residence would share what was meaningful to them. It was people speaking from their hearts that first awakened an initial sense of sacredness for me.

But it wasn't until the summer after third grade that I had my first truly personal experiences with spirituality. That's the summer I was old enough to attend Ambassador Camp, an interdenominational camp located just down the street from The Good Shepherd Home. The Ambassador Camp was the perfect place to introduce the principles of love and value in ways that were appropriate for kids.

For me, what made the biggest difference was that all the adults I met at Ambassador Camp were so loving, accessible, interested, and engaged. I felt nurtured by every activity they offered. Adding to the intimacy was the fact that everyone on staff was referred to in a familial way. The leaders, for instance, were Uncle Bobby and Aunt Sara.

I felt particularly close to Aunt Sara, who was one of the most loving people I had ever encountered. Another favorite for Beverly and me was Aunt Jacque. Blessed with a beautiful voice and spirit, she was the one who led us all in singing.

Uncle Jackie and Uncle David were the two male counselors who lived with us in the boys' cabin. They were both great examples of loving, accessible men—strong, gentle, and generous. Those qualities made a huge impression on me.

The impact was so clear that in my review, I couldn't find a single memory from camp that wasn't positive and loving. Even mealtime was filled with surprises and outbursts of song. As one example, when someone was caught with their elbows on a dining room table, one of the counselors would start a chant to tease that person in a loving way. Gradually, the whole room would join in.

It was especially fun when a camper would catch one of the staff doing it and we'd get to chant, "Uncle Jackie, strong and able, this is not a horse's stable. Get your elbows off that table!" Afterward, everyone would laugh and clap. Innocence at its best.

The campsite was simple, consisting of four wood cabins that were spread out over a large piece of property located just across from the lake that I loved so much. Each week, there were about forty kids in attendance. As an adult, I appreciated that the staff focused on providing grounded experiences of each loving principle that we were intended to learn—rather than giving us a long list of rules and expectations. What better way to teach? Even the ways they introduced stories from the Bible, which mostly focused on the loving example of a man named Jesus, were creative and nurturing.

Many of the stories the camp leaders shared made a real impact on me. The fact that their lessons only reinforced the experiences we were already having at the camp made them seem more accessible and real. This was another time when Gabriel's suggestion about learning most fully from what we *experience* became clear for me.

One of the memories that stood out as I scanned those summers at camp involved Aunt Sara showing us how we all learn from the choices we make. She suggested that when any of us acts out our frustrations or anger on others, we create a blemish in our hearts. To make her point, she dabbed a white piece of heart-shaped cloth with a bottle containing a dark mystery fluid. When she showed us the heart-shaped cloth again, it was marked with an ugly brown blemish. Every time she suggested another unhealthy choice that we might make, like shoving someone or being disrespectful, she would dab the heart and create new marks.

When there were a bunch of stains on the cloth, she spoke in a caring, gentle way about Jesus and how he practiced love, nurturing, and forgiveness toward the people around him. He taught people to learn from their choices and not to judge others for making mistakes.

She then pointed out that when any of us chose to take responsibility for our choices, forgiving ourselves and asking for forgiveness from others, we could make our hearts pure again. While she was making this important point, she took the blemished cloth and placed it in a second bowl that contained a different solution. When she finished talking about forgiveness, she removed the cloth, and we could see that the heart had been washed clean, made completely white again.

With tenderness and grace, Aunt Sara made the power of forgiveness seem like a real possibility. I remember gasping when I saw the demonstration. By physicalizing the story, Aunt Sara was the first person in my life to demonstrate that we are all capable of creating positive experiences for ourselves. Even then, it made great sense to me. I remember how inspired I was by the story and this woman, and how much I wanted to do whatever I could to keep my heart pure.

Another thing I appreciated about those teaching sessions was that we were encouraged to ask questions. Sometimes we even had a chance to share how a particular story had touched us in some way. This was just like what I had seen the men doing in The Good Shepherd Home chapel, only now, kids got to participate. Yet another remarkable way to teach loving principles to young people, acknowledging that what we had to share truly mattered. I remember thinking how Aunt Sara must be very much like Jesus. Not only did her compassion have an impact, but it made it so easy to believe that this man was just as real and accessible.

The staff also introduced us to our lessons through a process of memorizing Bible verses. This was even more meaningful because Uncle Jackie and Uncle David would spend time helping us with those verses in the evenings before bed. Having never had any direct male guidance or connection, this was such a poignant opportunity for me. I imagined, looking back, that this must be how some children felt when someone read them bedtime stories. I found comfort in being able to ask these two men about their own experiences within those conversations. With great patience, our gentle teachers moved from one bunk to the next, making sure everyone felt seen and heard.

Because Gabriel had encouraged me to look for the ways that I needed to be nurtured as I moved through my review, my time at Ambassador Camp offered vital clues. Each moment of feeling seen, heard, acknowledged, and encouraged was so powerful to my young Self. So much so that my week at camp became my new favorite time of the year—even better than Christmas.

The only negative thing I could possibly think to say about camp is that my time there always ended much too quickly. Looking back, I could see that my experiences at Ambassador Camp literally changed my life, planting seeds of possibility that have stayed with me ever since.

How blessed I feel that my spiritual awakening came from real human experiences rather than from speeches delivered from pulpits in formal churches. Looking back, it was clear that my first real sanctuary had been made up of wooden cabins, a giant playground, and the magic of a lake. This part of my review was so meaningful that I wanted to stop the clock and remain in these deeply content feelings.

So for a while, I did just that, making sure to enjoy the celebration with my inner child.

Once that sense of sacred experience was firmly in place, I felt ready and willing to begin reviewing the confusing contradictions of adolescence.

8

WHAT MAKES
A MAN GREAT?

HO AM I REALLY? DO I MATTER? WHAT DETER-mines my value? What parts of me are safe to share? Perhaps every adolescent is like I was, trying to put together different influences and perspectives to ultimately answer these big questions. Given my painful relationship with my father, it makes sense that my core questions included *What determines a great man or gives him real value?* and *How do I fit in or measure up as a man in the world?*

It wasn't just my father who didn't provide consistent and meaningful clues about being a man of value. Other than the few hints I gleaned in my few weeks with Uncle David and Uncle Jackie at Ambassador Camp, most of the other men in my young life left me with more questions than answers. Therefore, I moved into my first years of adolescence with these questions and needs at the forefront of my mind.

I also began to wonder if it was the absence of meaningful guidance that made my questions so immediate. Without clear answers, I spent a great deal of time, starting in my most formative years, trying to figure out what would make other people proud of me or at least impressed enough to engage. Most often, this boiled down to watching other boys who got consistent attention.

The main male figure whom I quietly looked to for clues was my grandfather. At six foot four, he was a giant, and the most immediate example of a leader in my world. As a minister and the director of a home for alcoholics, he was clearly doing meaningful things with his life. At the same time, what I couldn't figure out was why he rarely seemed happy or joyful. I also wondered why he almost never had anything to say to me. While I was never able to answer those questions as an adolescent, I still loved my grandfather—even if it was from an all-too-familiar distance. In his case, I was able to be grateful for some of the qualities that he had always demonstrated, from his willingness to become a leader to caring for all the men at The Good Shepherd Home.

The only other male who occasionally dropped into our lives was my mother's younger brother, Lamon. Just like my other uncle, Jason, Lamon had also left rural North Carolina to do some important things in the world. The most obvious to me had been his service as a Green Beret in the Korean War. By the time I was thirteen, this made him my first example of a hero. Secretly, I wanted to ask him all about his wartime experiences, but true to what I had always known, he never brought it up, and I didn't feel confident enough to initiate a conversation.

I do remember feeling proud that he must have endured really difficult things, which only became more obvious to me after seeing a number of propaganda films released in the sixties and seventies about the Vietnam War. Each time I watched one of the horrors depicted in those movies, such as the booby traps that ended with soldiers impaled on spikes or suffering some other horrible death, I assumed it had been just as bad in the Korean War, and I would secretly feel afraid and sad for my uncle. I couldn't imagine anyone having to face such devastating traumas.

The few times Lamon visited over the years, I predictably wanted to connect. Since I didn't know how to make that happen, I spent some time imagining what his life was like, based on the few facts I had heard or the few mementos I'd seen—like the eight-by-ten pictures of him sitting and laughing with famous people, such as Goldie Hawn. How cool that I had a second uncle who had achieved such impressive things in the world. In his case, after serving in the Army, he had become a national production manager at Warner Brothers, located in a city that kept seeming more glamorous to me: Los Angeles.

Sadly, the only direct experiences I ever had with Lamon made me feel embarrassed or ashamed. I remember one summer day when we were at the lake. I was four or five, and Beverly and I were standing on the pier with some of the adults in the family. When one of their conversations revealed that Beverly and I had never learned how to swim, Lamon decided this was not acceptable. Without any warning, he picked me up and hurled me off the pier, way out into the water. Naturally, there was no adult out there to catch me or show me how to stay afloat. I vividly remember my terror. There had been no warning, no nurturing guidance, and no choice—just like so many of the other sad, frightening, or confusing things that had occurred in my young life.

Quite honestly, I don't remember what happened next, though I imagine someone must have come in after me. Looking back, what was quite clear is that events such as this one added to my confusion about what was expected of me as a boy, and that only became heightened as I moved into adolescence. I was distinctly aware that I grew up with some real warriors, but almost all of those memories involved me feeling inadequate and out of control. It was painfully obvious that this was a key factor in my growing fear of looking like a failure or being a disappointment—particularly in the eyes of strong men.

So I entered puberty with tons of Self-doubt, often wondering what the men in my life really felt, what they feared, and what was important to them. I desperately wanted to know what they thought of me and how I would ever fit into the pack. I had no clue what I might do to improve or change my place, and true to form, I didn't feel comfortable going to any of them for help.

My review of those adolescent years brought me back to the confusion of my parents' impending divorce. I remembered noticing that none of the adults in my life were demonstrating that they had any trust in each other. None of them talked about much of anything, much less opened up about their fears or feelings.

Since I was starting to better understand challenges through my work with Gabriel, I could easily imagine that they, too, carried their early insecurities, and they seemed better left hidden. Perhaps that is why they appeared to blindly march forward in their lives, with no sense of resolution or hope for making things better. It all seemed so sad.

Since my parents didn't seek any professional help, things continued to deteriorate in their relationship. This eventually led to my father returning home one evening, only to find his things packed and out on the front porch. Naturally, for years, I didn't find out what actually happened. I only knew that big changes always came without warning, and one day, my dad was simply gone. No explanation and no comfort.

Soon after that pivotal change, I realized that I was now the "man of the house," though I was totally clueless what that might mean. Just another new normal.

With my dad no longer around, I felt even more desperate for male connection, guidance, and reassurance. As a matter of fact, I started spending so much time focused on searching for male connection that I hardly noticed when my desire for validation and comfort turned into the very confusing experience of attraction as well. *Wait a minute. That can't be right!* I remember thinking. *What is happening to me?*

I grew up in the Deep South, where no one ever suggested that someone could have feelings of attraction for people of the same gender. At first, I hoped that the feelings would go away. *Please!* Much to my deep dismay, they only grew stronger, which left me more confused and alone than ever. I remember thinking that I was literally the only person in the world who felt this way, which of course meant I was doomed. As far as I knew, growing up in the South in the seventies, my new feelings didn't even have a name.

I now feared that all the people who mattered to me would always remain on the other side of an invisible wall that I could never cross. That was when sorrow and anxiety truly became my constant companions. Being different meant that I had no possibility of fitting in, and that was almost too much for me to handle as a teenager. It also seemed quite clear that my newest discovery meant I would likely never experience a meaningful relationship in my life. Once that reality began to sink in, I wanted to disappear.

Adding to my growing list of confusions was that I had always felt such a natural connection to spiritual things in my young life. Now that I had turned out to have such unusual feelings, that connection felt shaky. I spent a lot of time trying to figure out why God would have given me attractions that so clearly set me apart. *Was it possible for God to make such a mistake?* I wondered. I had always felt protected and guided by some unseen force, but this newly awakened part of me made that sacred force seem inaccessible. With no one to ask for help or guidance, the only thing I could think to do was bury what I had discovered and get on with imitating others whom I admired.

I spent a lot of time praying about my conflicts and confusion. "God, please help me understand what is happening to me. I want to be loved—more than anything. Please make these feelings go away. Please!" More than praying, I would often scream those words in my head. I put all my passion into this core wish. Without an awareness of the truth about Soul setups—an awareness that would have calmed my panic—I felt so unheard, and I imagined that the familiar rejection I had experienced with my father must now be happening with God as well.

What I found helpful to consider when looking back at all of this was that my fear of rejection had nothing to do with a religious conflict. My connection to God had never come through religion, and these confusions had nothing to do with religion either. It was all about the personal and immediate spiritual connection I had always felt. As a young teenager, I had no way of knowing that the reason my connection with God felt so inaccessible was that I had shut myself off within the fear and shame of being different. The adult truth was that I was the one hiding. I was the one who couldn't imagine that this new discovery, which I believed set me apart from everyone, could possibly be lovable.

What was deeply clear to me as an adult was that this part of my life would need tons of time and nurturing attention in order to find any real resolution. When I got to this point in my review, I realized I had never brought up this topic with Gabriel. That is perhaps how scared and ashamed I still felt. At the same time, it was becoming clear to me how innocent I was in those early years of childhood and adolescence, and that no matter what this new confusion presented to me as a young teen, I still cared deeply about people, and I still wanted to keep my heart pure.

What I hated seeing in my review was that I began to compensate for anything that might make me seem different by cutting things out of my life that were truly precious to me. I just couldn't bear facing rejection. First, I quit taking piano lessons. That choice only made me more unhappy, of course. As my despair grew, I began to skip school, and I hid in my room. In truth, those years of middle school were riddled with constant doubts about my value. At the same time, my family was breaking apart. And I wasn't the only one seeking to escape. My mother began her own version of escape, which mostly involved drinking.

As usual, no one seemed to notice when I became disconnected and depressed. No one even noticed how much I was skipping school. There were nights when I sat on the living room couch with my mother passed out drunk next to me. Beverly had figured out that getting out of the house was her best escape. That meant that on many occasions, it was just me, the thirteen-year-old man of the house, scared, alone, and distinctly aware that my seven-year-old sister was sleeping in the next room with only me to protect her.

Pleasing others, proving myself, and trying to avoid any kind of rejection or invalidation became my three biggest motivations. I began to feel myself split in two, unable to be fully authentic for the first time in my young life. In some ways, that was what I hated most. Authenticity had always been priceless to me, and I feared it was something I would have to let go of for the rest of my life.

One of the only things that helped me cope was shifting my focus to achievements and having a place to fit in because of my talents. I also continued doing gymnastics, and after only a short break, I resumed piano lessons. The piano teacher that my mother found when we had moved to Jacksonville was remarkable—except for the fact that she lived thirty minutes away. This meant we had to travel to her house down a narrow, windy, two-lane byway called Gum Branch Road. Each Monday, JB and I would get in the car for that drive to see Gladys Sylvester.

While at my lesson, I knew my mother went to the Toot-N-Tell-It Drive-In to drink beer while my little sister got something to eat. Of course, that only meant she would then drive us back along that same windy road in some stage of inebriation. Looking back, I felt grateful that we remained safe each time we made the trek.

When my review started to get too heavy and dark again, I began scanning for happier memories. The first thing that came to mind was that toward the end of seventh grade, I heard an exciting announcement. As fortune would have it, the high school had decided to offer an unprecedented opportunity for their upcoming musical. Rather than limiting the spring production to students who were attending the high school, they had decided to use a bunch of younger boys to complete the cast of *Oliver!*

This opportunity was a real lifesaver for me. Prior to auditioning for that production, however, I had never sung or acted. Fortunately, they ended up selecting me as one of the boys anyway. The timing was perfect. I *needed* a new adventure and a distraction. Not only was I going to have the chance to spend time with high schoolers in a theater, but I was also about to meet the people who became my first "accessible heroes."

One of the perks of being with older kids who were interested in the arts was finding out about other exciting events taking place in town. One that drew my attention was a performance called "Celebrate Life" by a group called Joy Choir. This nondenominational group of local young people was led by Steve Barnes, who happened to be the minister of music at Jacksonville's First Baptist Church. Little did I know when I arrived for the performance that both the Joy Choir and the church were about to become really important to me.

Once I was able to find a seat quite close to the front, in a sanctuary that was already packed, I settled in and waited for the performance to begin. I was thrilled when the lights eventually dimmed, and over the course of two hours, I was moved to tears a few times. My feelings were inspired by the combination of beautiful music, a meaningful message that centered around the life of Jesus, and the fact that some of my friends from *Oliver!* were performing the leading roles. This made everything feel so personal and accessible. By the end of the evening, I was completely blown away.

At various points during the performance, I kept thinking how much I wished I could be part of the group. Although I knew I was too young—according to the official rules—that was exactly what ended up happening. Looking back, I realized that night was the first example of what would soon become a welcome new pattern in my life: improbable doors opening at just the right time, giving me unforgettable opportunities and encouragement as well.

After so many years of intense challenges, this night ended up being a real turning point for me. The first key moment was when someone introduced me to Steve and Susan, the two directors of Joy Choir, after the performance. I remember gushing about how much I had enjoyed the production. Steve then asked me if I sang. I confessed that I did sing a little but made sure to clarify that I was more accomplished on the piano. Steve then asked if I also played the organ. Just as I had fudged about playing the trumpet, I said that I did play. I just didn't volunteer that I had only received a handful of lessons in recent months.

Steve then shared that the church had just started looking for an organist. He wondered if I might like to come and play for a service the very next weekend. I said yes right away, unaware of how unusual it must have been for an adult in his position to offer an opportunity like this to someone so young.

When I showed up for choir practice the following Wednesday night, I can only imagine how surprised and skeptical the twenty adults were when a thirteen-year-old kid walked in to play for them.

Because the rehearsal involved me playing the piano rather than the organ, and I had gotten used to sight-reading from my years of playing for services at The Good Shepherd Home, everything went really well. Looking back, I realized how I had been prepared for this opportunity by having worked through earlier challenges and investing in my specific gifts. In some ways, this was the first time in my review that I could sense the possibility of Divine Order guiding my life—particularly when it came to challenges serving me.

Once rehearsal was over, I got the green light to play for the service on Sunday. I made sure to prepare two simple pieces that I could manage as solos on the organ. When Sunday arrived, I got through those pieces well enough. When it was time for the minister to deliver his sermon, and I left my spot at the organ to take my place on the front pew, I didn't realize that things would soon go awry.

Knowing I had twenty minutes of relief during the sermon, I waited for my next cue, which involved the minister shifting to a closing prayer. While he was praying, I was supposed to quietly return to the organ and be in place, ready to start the final hymn by the time he said, "Amen."

When the minister started that prayer and everyone had closed their eyes, I tiptoed to the organ. It was when I placed one foot and then the other onto the lower keyboard of the organ—a necessary step for climbing up to the bench seat—that the room was shocked from a contemplative silence into a horrible cacophony. You see, after I had finished the previous hymn, I had forgotten to release the buttons that deactivated the lower keyboard. So when I stepped onto the pedals, my foot caused an earsplitting blast of dissonance from which I had no way to recover.

After everyone figured out what was happening, they ended up showing great compassion for this young kid who was now sitting red-faced and frozen. Naturally, I was expecting my dismissal after the service. However, since Steve had already seen what I could do on the piano, he exceeded all my expectations by offering me a second invitation. I could hardly believe it when he asked if I would be interested in continuing to accompany services—but I would use the grand piano located on the other side of the room.

From that infamous Sunday forward, I became the official accompanist for services at First Baptist, all the way through my final year of high school. During that time, the acceptance and encouragement the congregation offered me was more healing and meaningful than I can say. This, too, became a clear sign of support, hinting that others could find value in this young, confused adolescent.

Much to my delight, other doors began to open. Only a few months after I began playing the piano at church, I arrived early for a choir rehearsal. With time to kill, I headed straight for the grand piano in the sanctuary. Except for the time I spent with Mrs. Sylvester in piano lessons, I didn't have opportunities to play a grand piano. On this particular evening, I had the whole church to myself. The longer I played, the more fun I had, and the more confident I began to feel. I eventually surprised myself. Knowing I was completely alone, I started to sing, loudly and unabashedly, just as I would do when I was alone at home.

What I didn't know was that on that night, Steve had also arrived early. One floor below me in the rehearsal room, he heard someone playing the piano. Knowing that it must be me, he headed up the stairs to discuss something that would be needed for the upcoming rehearsal. As it so happened, he arrived just in time to hear me launch into my song. I can only guess that he sensed how tender or private the moment was for me because he ducked behind one of the back pews until I was done.

As soon as I finished, the sound of enthusiastic clapping shocked me back to reality, complete with an embarrassing awareness that I had not been alone as I sang. As he made his way down the aisle toward me, he was grinning full-on. He then proceeded to not only invite me to join Joy Choir as their new accompanist but to also sing a solo in their next concert. Both offers were shocking to me. However, that is exactly what took place in the coming months. Steve ended up once again creating another important turn in my life—me singing my first public solo.

Little did I know that the opportunity would lead me to finally understand what I had witnessed with my mother and grandfather years earlier. Even though singing in public was one of the scariest things I had ever done, it was also one of the most exciting. The rousing ovation that I received at the end gave me a glimpse of the power that music—and singing—has to inspire and move people.

Adolescence was turning out to be a more confusing negotiation of challenges and gifts than I would have ever guessed. How I got through it was by focusing on the fact that I finally had some meaningful connections.

9

CONTRADICTIONS
AND MIXED
MESSAGES

S I CONTINUED REVIEWING THE LATER YEARS OF my adolescence, I was grateful that the new compassion I brought to my inner child also allowed me to see my mother through new eyes. Instead of only seeing how deeply lost I felt at home, I learned to shift some of my focus to the fact that my mom had also faced profound challenges and wounded feelings that she had never learned to nurture or resolve. This inspired a real sense of gratitude in me. Despite all she had on her plate, she continued to show up and stayed with us through some intensely difficult times. No matter what, she worked hard to provide all the foundational things we needed.

My review also showed me that by spending time with Steve and his wife Jackie, whom I adored, I had a chance to replenish the nurturing

I'd been missing at home. They practically adopted me into their family. Perhaps sensing my needs, they treated me like a third son. Over time, the people at church also became like extended family. Even so, I was constantly aware that I could never share certain aspects of my life with any of them. There was no way I would risk messing up the new comfort I had found with them.

The fortune of unprecedented opportunities continued in my life. One prime example took place during the summer before eighth grade, when our middle school announced an advanced academic program. This program was created for students whose testing qualified them as "gifted and talented"—a precursor to today's Advanced Placement (AP) courses. In this case, the school decided to begin the program with just one class.

A wonderful woman named Betsy Travis led the G/T English class, and the small group of us who were chosen to participate landed an opportunity that felt like a small miracle. Even as an adult, I still viewed it in a similar way. That is because Betsy Travis was unquestionably the most innovative teacher I'd had in all my twenty years of formal schooling, including the eight years I spent acquiring three college degrees.

Living in a small town, we had no obvious connections to or awareness of the bigger world, and yet Mrs. Travis somehow brought the world and its history to life in our classroom. Just as astounding was the level of talent present in our small group of students.

Mrs. Travis empowered each one of us by giving us as many leadership roles as she could. One of her greatest geniuses was offering us countless chances to become fully immersed in a broad array of topics. Reflecting on the masterpieces that resulted from practical assignments like creating our own bulletin boards (a pedestrian term that doesn't remotely signal the artistry and expansive thinking displayed in these projects), I could see that Mrs. Travis inspired our imaginations and talents.

Of course, I was even more impressed as an adult, knowing that the two students who drew many of those bulletin boards were master artists-in-training. One of them even ended up working as a product designer at the Metropolitan Museum of Art in New York City in his adult years. How we all found ourselves in one small classroom in Jacksonville, North Carolina is anyone's guess.

One of Mrs. Travis's assignments had us moving through the entire history of the English language. From the Old English of *Beowulf* to the Middle English of Chaucer's *The Canterbury Tales* to the masters of the modern era, she made history and literature real and accessible. She even made an exciting project out of memorizing and then reciting the prologue to *The Canterbury Tales* in its original form. The stunning impression this made on my young mind was affirmed by the fact that I could still recall those words as I continued my review.

When we examined the Wars of the Roses, learning about every king and queen who had ruled England, Mrs. Travis made each player seem so human and relatable. We also explored how language has the power to inspire feelings. We learned more about the structure of language in eighth grade than most adults ever do—beginning to understand and work with litotes, hyperbole, and synecdoche.

What was equally amazing was that I was somehow able to handle the demands of Mrs. Travis's class, even as I was skipping school to escape the challenges of divorce, my mother's struggle with alcohol, and my own suppressed sexuality. The only real sign that those deep emotions were having an impact on me came from a bout of shingles—a resurgence of the chickenpox virus that is typically triggered by unusual amounts of stress and far more common in middle-aged people than in fourteen-year-olds.

During eighth and ninth grade, I continued appearing in productions at the high school, and by the time I turned fifteen, I performed in my first professional production. This transpired because Steve and Susan, the leaders of Joy Choir, decided to mount a dinner theater production of *Godspell* at a wonderful restaurant called The Country Squire. They asked me to play the role of John the Baptist with none other than my champion, Steve Barnes, portraying Jesus. Topping it all off, being cast in that production gave me lots more time with my older friends.

My best friend during those few years was a great guy named Phil, who was already a freshman in college when we did *Godspell*. It was a dream come true for me to be accepted and included by someone who, for all intents and purposes, became the older brother I had always wished for. It was also during that summer that I first tried dating. Kandy, a beautiful girl from the cast, was four years older than me. My adult Self guessed that if she hadn't just broken up with her twenty-five-year-old fiancé right before we began rehearsals, she wouldn't have been interested in spending so much time with me.

Sadly, the fun we all had that summer was the end of an era. After *Godspell* closed, Steve—in his mid-thirties by then—decided it was time to fulfill one of his lifelong dreams of becoming a doctor. Even though I knew it would be a great personal loss when he, Jackie, and their two sons moved away, I felt proud of him for making such a courageous choice.

Perhaps the greatest gift the Barnes family gave me in our time together was showing me that surprising levels of personal support were indeed possible. My own experience showed me that it was true, and I was grateful that two other adults from the church took me under their wings after Steve and Jackie moved away. Nance and Pete Anderton, gym teachers and coaches at local schools in the area, were used to investing tremendous amounts of love and energy into their students. It didn't take long for their home to become a new centerpiece of love, joy, and fun in my life.

It turns out that I wasn't the only one who felt Steve and Jackie's absence. Nance recognized that the departure of Joy Choir created a real gap for the kids in our community, leaving many without a nurturing place to gather. Responding with enthusiasm and sensitivity, Nance and Pete were the perfect candidates to take on the challenge, which they did by forming a new youth group at First Baptist. Pete even supported the endeavor by creating a gorgeous space on the third floor of the church that was soon filled with more than fifty kids.

On a more personal level, Pete ended up teaching me important and practical things, like how to change the oil in a car. After much coaxing, he even convinced me that it might be fun to return to a team sport for one season. Based on his encouragement, I spent a whole summer learning to be one of the catchers for the church softball team. Nance, on the other hand, taught me how to trust being playful and to enjoy myself more fully than I ever had. The two of us got into frequent mischief over the years. One day, for instance, Nance was melting chocolate on the stove for one of the goodies she baked. As I walked past her, she took the opportunity to dab a bit of chocolate on the end of my nose.

"You better not do that again," I mock-threatened, relishing my assumed role as a troublemaking little brother. "Revenge can be hell." When she took the dare and streaked more chocolate across my cheek, I grabbed a tub of butter from the counter and tackled her. I literally buttered an entire leg before the escapade ended with both of us in hysterics on the floor.

Through these experiences with Nance and Pete, I continued building trust that nurturing support and connection were indeed possible for me. Naturally, this didn't mean an end to the challenges I had to navigate. When I was in tenth grade, a teacher who had always recognized my talents and raw potential as a leader invited me over for dinner;

he said he had something important to discuss with me. I showed up, intrigued, and I sat in the living room while he finished preparing a meal in the kitchen. I passed the time by thumbing through a book about celebrities that I found on his coffee table.

Just as I was beginning to read the chapter on Carol Burnett, he came back into the room. When I casually mentioned how much I loved Carol Burnett, he said, "It's really interesting that you mention that particular celebrity. The book describes a time when she needed financial support. As the story goes, someone in her community recognized her need and decided to give her one thousand dollars, with two distinct stipulations: one, that she wouldn't tell anyone where the money had come from, and two, that she would do something similar for someone else in the future when she could afford it," he said. "The reason this is so interesting," he continued, "is that I invited you over this evening to acknowledge a similar need in your life. I know that your mom has to support you and your sisters, and you have a lot of activities that demand travel. To help you all out, I have searched and found a Volkswagen Beetle for about the same amount of money that Ms. Burnett received. I want to offer that car as a gift to you, but only if you agree to the same two conditions."

I was stunned and moved. I couldn't quite believe what was happening and didn't have words that felt adequate as a response. While we ate the dinner he had prepared, we also talked about some of the upcoming opportunities for me while I was in high school. When we'd finished eating, I thanked him again and he responded by leaning over to give me a hug. As he hugged me, I felt him lean more heavily into me. He slowly pushed me back onto the couch, and while I wasn't sure what was happening, I definitely felt awkward.

What was particularly confusing was that this teacher had always been so supportive, just as he had been that very evening. In this moment, however, he continued to push forward until he was lying on top of me. While I lay there in stunned silence, he began to move his body. Fortunately, we both had all our clothes on. And although he never attempted this move again, on that one occasion, he had ignored any sense of healthy boundaries. Unsure what to do, I remained silent and waited for the moment to be over, at which point I said I had to go.

Because I still had no examples of adults talking openly about their difficulties or challenges, I didn't consider it an option to share with anyone what had happened. Therefore, this became one more secret that I buried somewhere inside myself. Looking back, I realized I had no way of evaluating the harm he had done. I was just relieved it never happened again. Perhaps confusing on some level, that teacher did follow through with the gift of the car, and even though it created a positive impact all the way through my first year of college, I just did my best to ignore the rest.

During my second year in high school, I started to develop a great friendship with someone who was, yet again, older than me. This time it was a young marine named Thom who had recently been stationed in town. I was older now, so it was becoming more difficult for me to avoid the perplexing desire to be physically affectionate with someone, though it was quite clear that Thom was crazy about girls.

Even so, I decided to use my friendship with him as an opportunity to share more personal things about myself with someone I trusted. The most obvious time I was able to do this took place when he was away on a tour. For that short period, I used the benefit of distance to tell him in a series of letters how much I valued having him in my life. Of course, I was careful not to jeopardize the friendship, and fortunately, Thom received my loving words in the innocence with which I had shared them.

I knew that my love for my friend was deep and genuine, and that choosing to express those authentic, heartfelt feelings was an invaluable step that required real courage for me. As an adult, it was quite clear that those bold gestures gave me the first hints of what it might be like to be in a more complete relationship—even though I couldn't imagine at that point that I would ever fulfill such a reality.

As a result, I spent long hours hiding out in my bedroom in a kind of depressed longing. One thing that helped me deal with the weight of those feelings was the fact that my mother had decided to get help to stop drinking. Her courageous choice ended up creating what would become a lifelong transformation for our whole family. By getting sober and welcoming the support from a group of friends in Alcoholics Anonymous, our mother showed us all that it is indeed possible for someone to turn their life around—a gift that had a priceless impact on all three of us.

Looking back, it was clear that our mom had grown up with almost no nurturing support and that she, too, had no safe place to work through the confusing experiences of her childhood. I could also imagine why, at a crazy young age, she had chosen to get married to a man who gave her lots of attention. And the fact that neither she nor my dad knew anything about healthy connection or communication meant that for many years of her adult life, she lived with a partner who didn't know how to value her or to be faithful. Even so, she eventually showed all three of us kids that it was possible to face deep challenges.

Continuing with the momentum that her initial shift created, once Mom got herself on her feet, she began to use her passion for recovery to help other people. She sponsored many in AA who were struggling. Eventually, she returned to school for a master's degree in social work, and later became the head of two treatment centers. Each of those important developments encouraged my sisters and me to find ways to help others in our lives too.

Watching my mom make these inspiring choices encouraged me to wholeheartedly pursue the things that mattered to me. This meant exploring as many different opportunities as I could manage in my remaining years of high school. At the same time, I didn't know how to trust that people liked me or included me for reasons other than my talents and achievements.

On the positive side, investing in my gifts allowed me to continue preparing for more opportunities that showed up in the next stages of my life. This included excelling in academics as well. After two years with Mrs. Travis in middle school, I found that high school was a piece of cake. This meant I was able to get top grades with minimal effort. Once my mother noticed, she attempted to give me a great compliment. "Ronnie," she said with a big smile, "you are so smart that I bet getting anything less than an A would be like failing for you!"

Hearing those words, my heart sank, and my anxiety spiked. My mother had no idea that her comment exacerbated the pressure I already felt to prove myself. To me, her words meant "If you get anything less than an A, you will be a failure in my eyes." Looking back, my distorted thinking was obvious, but at the time, her words sparked a new possibility for being rejected and alone. In fact, I remember a distinct moment in eleventh grade when I was walking along the school corridor from one class to another. I literally stopped in my tracks and made a conscious decision. "I can no longer afford to make mistakes. It is simply not acceptable for me."

Trying to live up to that wounded decision became a core focus for me. Fortunately, the added pressure didn't diminish the innocent enthusiasm I had always appreciated about myself. My desire for adventure, my willingness to help, my love of learning, and perhaps most important of all, my heartfelt desire for deep, authentic connections all remained intact and true.

Performing continued to offer the greatest opportunities to deepen each of those qualities. I loved how moved people seemed to be each time I sang. After having such a positive experience with dinner theater, I jumped at the chance to be in my next professional production. This time, it was *The Fantasticks*, also directed by Susan Howard from Joy Choir. Another highlight of my junior year was the school's production of *Camelot*, in which I portrayed the role of Lancelot.

Imagine me playing a man trapped in his own expectation of perfection until his overwhelming desire for someone he could not have destroyed his life. Looking back, I thought Life itself must have a great sense of humor, and it certainly corroborated the adage that "Art imitates Life."

By this point in my review, many of my choices were becoming easy to predict. Whenever I was faced with a conflict I couldn't resolve, I would shift my focus to achieving something new. In addition to the opportunities to distract myself with theater, I now had other avenues, such as the goals I set playing the French horn. Even if each goal I reached became padding for my unspoken need to impress, it was exciting to go to band camp and be awarded first chair and then audition for All-State with the same results.

Just as it got easier for me to count on those accolades, my Soul apparently thought it was time for yet another frustrating interruption. This challenge came in the form of a birthday gift from an adult who was quite special to me. Excited to receive her package in the mail, I soon found that she had written a lengthy personal message in the front of a book. She first acknowledged how much she valued me, highlighting how talented she thought I was. She then followed up with a sentence that took the wind out of my sails. "As gifted as you are, and as often as you are the obvious choice for many things, I encourage you to occasionally step aside and give others a chance to shine."

Shame, guilt, and confusion washed over me. *Oh, my God! Am I blocking others from being able to shine? I wouldn't do that! I love people way too much to cause them pain or Self-doubt.*

The conundrum this created was that I was just learning to count on my achievements as the primary way to be attractive or interesting. I was doing my best to ensure that others would include me. Achievement was also a primary distraction from the deprivation of not being able to date someone special, which was a constant source of angst for me. Now I was being told that by choosing to achieve, I simultaneously caused others to experience their own versions of the same wounded feelings.

Looking back, I could see that my friend never in fact said I was hurting anyone. Nevertheless, her note created a new form of confusion for me to work out—one that would get more complicated as I moved forward. Yet another new normal.

10

FINDING
MY FEET

B Y THE TIME I REACHED MY JUNIOR YEAR IN HIGH school, I was playing major works by Liszt, Chopin, and Rachmaninoff on the piano. At one of my afternoon lessons, Mrs. Sylvester surprised me with an unexpected compliment. She informed me that she considered me her "once-in-a-lifetime" student. She said the reason she had decided to tell me such a thing was that she wanted to return some of the joy I had brought her in our years together—which she did by gifting me with free lessons for the rest of my time in high school. I was so moved by her loving gesture that I couldn't find words.

This was only one of the enhancing shifts that took place in my junior year. After my mother became sober and more present in our lives, Nance invited her to become one of the counselors for the youth group. That decision created many meaningful moments with my mom. Beverly ended up developing some beautiful friendships and excelled even more fully with her impressive athletic gifts during that time. As a matter of fact, she became the only girl at our high school to letter in four sports.

Though JB was younger, she also found distinct places to plug in and shine. As a small child, she had thrived in swimming competitions, well ahead of other kids her age. She now spent time shifting back and forth, spending one season on the basketball team and the next season cheering for that same team from the sidelines. Equally drawn to individual sports, competing in roller skating became her favorite way to explore.

The summer before my senior year, I was ready to spread my wings a bit, exploring beyond North Carolina, just like I imagined my uncles had done. How fitting that my first plane trip took me all the way to Utah, where I was scheduled to spend a couple of weeks with my uncle Jason. Some years earlier, he had taken a job as the director of the musical theater program at Brigham Young University.

While I was visiting, I got to witness more of his creative gifts in person. We had purposefully chosen dates that aligned with the summer stock season of musicals. This meant I would have chances to spend time with the talented college kids who had been cast. Experiencing a more developed level of talent up close created a real high for me. I was so moved by the opportunity that I made an important decision before I left Utah: I would return after high school graduation to attend college at BYU with these wonderful new friends.

Of course, the only way I knew to take big steps in my life was by following my own gut. In truth, it never even occurred to me that I might ask anyone for permission or guidance, or that I might explore more than one option. Once any moving option was clear to me, I moved forward with gusto. The only other school I secretly wanted to apply to was Harvard. I didn't actually consider going there. I just wanted to prove that I could get in—mostly inspired by wanting a new way to impress my dad. I knew we'd never be able to afford Harvard, a reality upheld by the fact that when the time came, I didn't even have the money to pay the application fee.

To compensate for living on my mother's salary, I always worked part-time jobs from the time I was hired to play for church at thirteen years old. I wanted to do whatever I could to take financial pressure away from my mother. By working a few different jobs, I was able to pay for most of the things that I personally needed, such as clothes, gas, meals, and extras throughout high school. In hindsight, I felt proud of myself for showing up in these ways, eager to stand on my own feet whenever possible.

Similarly, I appreciated that my mother never put any guilt or pressure on us financially. When doing my review, I was stunned to truly comprehend the fact that our mom had been supporting our family of four on a meager salary of only fourteen thousand dollars a year. With hardly any reliable child support, she even managed to go back to school for her master's degree.

I was proud and moved by all that she had done in my final years living at home. It made me all the more determined to work hard in my own life. I must also admit that working hard was part of an attempt to assuage the guilt I now felt about continuing to achieve, burdened by a new sense of how my achievements might impact others. I did everything I could to feel worthy of the opportunities that continued to come my way.

Even so, there were moments in my senior year when my distress about achieving versus depriving others got the better of me. On one particular Saturday in the fall, I drove myself to a nearby city, eager to participate in a piano concerto competition. It was exciting that first prize would include getting to play as the soloist with a full professional orchestra. As soon as I completed that audition, I jumped back in the car for a three-hour drive to audition for All-State Band on French horn.

A couple of days later, when I received word that I had been awarded first chair on horn, I was thrilled. However, when I got a call that same evening confirming that I had also been offered first prize in the piano competition, I went to bed and cried myself to sleep. I worried that I couldn't possibly have worked hard enough to deserve both honors and wondered who else might have deserved it more.

A similar phenomenon occurred the day I was scheduled to perform with the orchestra. It just so happened that on that day, I needed to be in the capital city of Raleigh to receive another award. This time, I had been named Outstanding Youth of North Carolina. How strange it was to feel truly honored and guilty all at the same time.

Since I was now used to moving through Life with any number of unsettling feelings, I simply marched forward. By the time I graduated, I had served as the class president, drum major, head marshal, lead in a musical, and even valedictorian. I was also chosen to represent our high school at Boy's State, a chance for upcoming leaders from all the major high schools in North Carolina to create a mock government. Topping it all off, a congressman asked if I wanted to be nominated for an appointment to West Point.

As my time to leave for college approached, I considered any number of ways I might give back to the community of people who had played such huge roles in my young life. I decided that giving a final concert would allow me the best chance to acknowledge them. As I began to put the performance together, I also came up with the idea of asking my mother to sing with me in our first public duet—an experience that I had imagined since I was a child.

At some point during those few weeks of preparation, I received an unexpected phone call from my uncle in Utah, who wanted to share some news. He had just been offered a last-minute position at Illinois Wesleyan University, where he was to act as director of the graduate acting program. While I was aware that this was a beautiful opportunity for him, it meant that he would no longer be at BYU when I was scheduled to arrive—in just one month. I congratulated him, hiding the fact that for me, this was extremely upsetting news.

Having an extended amount of time with him was the main reason I had chosen BYU. It originally seemed that so many synchronicities had supported the decision. I had even accumulated just enough money, mostly through awards and scholarships, to head west with my first year fully covered.

Without my uncle there, I didn't feel very motivated to continue with that choice. It now seemed rather empty. Since I had decided to only explore one option for college, it meant I hadn't applied to any other schools. Working in my favor was the fact that I'd spent my whole childhood coming up with creative solutions. I was rarely willing to be bound by logical limitations and obstacles. So I decided in a rather matter-of-fact way to phone another school that one of my close friends was planning to attend.

When I considered that my long-term plan was to work my way toward medical school, using my talents to acquire certain scholarships, Baylor University made great sense.

Though I had never heard the word "gumption" while I was in high school, I had certainly developed plenty of it by the time I was eighteen. Looking back at my choice to phone a major college out of the blue, just one month before school was to begin, I imagined the administrators at Baylor must have thought I was crazy to ask for such a consideration. It must have seemed equally strange to hear the request directly from the high school student, instead of a guidance counselor or some other adult in a position of influence.

Perhaps it was my innocent enthusiasm and determination that moved them. Whatever the reason, this was yet another case when an unusual door opened. After asking a few questions about my stats and qualifications, they ended up saying yes to me right there on that phone call. Now I had to figure out how I would pay for this new opportunity. After some initial evaluation, I realized I would need one thousand dollars more at Baylor than what I had put together for BYU. No matter. I decided to take the leap of faith. Besides, I didn't have time to worry. I needed to focus all my attention on the farewell concert.

When the evening of the big event finally arrived, I welcomed the chance to pay tribute to a number of individuals and to the church family as a whole. The truth is that I couldn't have asked for a more wonderful, nurturing group of folks in those pivotal years. In addition to the regulars from First Baptist, what a joy it was to have so many other key players from my life sitting together in what had become a truly sacred space for me.

Getting to sing with my mother was priceless. After taking a moment to acknowledge her and the inspiring changes she had made in her life, I spent time honoring many of the other people who had been important in my life. With those words shared and received, I had just one final surprise to offer. When I told everyone about the events of the last few weeks and how I had recently decided I would be heading to Baylor University, the room erupted into cheers and applause. Though I hadn't made this decision based on religion, I was glad that my choice made them so happy.

Once the applause died down, I believed we were done. What happened instead was a surprise they had all prepared for me. Reverend Sides came forward to thank me for having been such an integral part of the church for so many years. He revealed that while I had been away on a recent summer trip, the congregation had responded to his suggestion that they all prepare a farewell gift for me.

Surprised and teary-eyed, I opened the envelope they handed to me and found that it contained a check in the amount of one thousand dollars. I was fully aware, both as a teen and as an adult, what a powerful, touching affirmation this gesture turned out to be. Relieved and grateful, the final pieces for me to attend Baylor with complete financial support for that first year fell right into place.

After the concert, when everyone gathered for refreshments in the dining hall, one of the guests presented me with yet another surprise. Tommy Herndon was a robust man who had grown up in Jacksonville twenty years earlier. He was now a professional opera singer living in Germany. He just happened to be in town visiting family when someone told him about my concert. His gracious consent to attend gave me the chance to meet a living, breathing person who was enjoying an international career in the arts.

Imagine my surprise when he asked if I'd be willing to meet with him a few days later. When he said he'd been intrigued by what he had heard and wanted to find out the true scope of my vocal potential, I jumped at the opportunity. After spending almost an hour singing for him, he said, "I believe you could also have a successful career if you chose to train as a singer."

While I was thrilled at receiving such beautiful encouragement, I had just declared to Baylor that I would be entering school with a double major—piano performance and biology premed. So far, my plan to use my talent scholarships to pay for the foundation of my path toward becoming a doctor was working out. I knew I wanted to do something with my life that focused on helping others. Unsure how to respond to Mr. Herndon, I simply thanked him for his kind words.

What a meaningful launch that farewell concert turned out to be for bringing my final year in Jacksonville, North Carolina to a close. I remember feeling both happy and blessed that so many synchronicities seemed to be supporting my next steps. As I prepared to move from a rather small pond to a distinctly bigger one, I continued to receive what felt like a combination of mixed messages. While a part of me that was desperate to continue achieving shouted *"Please* see me!" another part of me continued to compete with a well-practiced plea of "Please *don't* see me."

Having negotiated both sides of that coin for all my years of adolescence, I worried this would be a burden I would always carry. Fortunately, I was utterly motivated toward the one thing that mattered most to me—something I reiterated to others in the final words of my valedictorian speech. After acknowledging the many adventures my fellow seniors and I had completed, I closed with one final encouragement. "No matter what any of us chooses to do with our lives, I hope we will all have powerful opportunities to love and be loved. That is my greatest wish for us all."

11

NEW TERRITORY

I N AUGUST OF 1979, I GOT INTO MY LIGHT BLUE VOLKS-
wagen Beetle, equipped with a cool flip-page map created by AAA,
and began my first real move out into the world. Driving to a college halfway across the country felt strange, and yet doing it alone did
not. At this point in my journey, I was quite comfortable exploring
things on my own.

The many miles of unfamiliar territory that I passed through on
my way to Texas were constant reminders that I was venturing into
the unknown in a way I never had. When I finally pulled into the
campus of Baylor University, I was ready to land and start this new
phase of my life. Because I'd applied so late, it wasn't possible for me
to live in one of the freshman dorms, so I was prepared to move in
with three older students from the music school who had fortunately
been looking for a fourth roommate—a convenient arrangement for
all of us.

Believe it or not, one of the few things that made me nervous about this new living situation was knowing that I would need to take a turn each week cooking dinners for four. How remarkable that I had an angel back in North Carolina who'd volunteered to help with this issue. When Ann Carroll, my advanced biology teacher in high school, heard me express concern about this daunting task, she decided to help in a big way. Perhaps this came out of her class having been my favorite in high school. The class had a reputation for being difficult, but because I loved finding out how everything works, I enthusiastically drank in all the beautiful detail she offered about the human body. As a matter of fact, I learned so much from Mrs. Carroll that I was able to place out of my first-year college biology courses.

Who knew that the long dissertations I had handed in for each test would eventually inspire such huge support from her in that first year of college? Even if my roommates never knew it, she became a real lifesaver for us all.

I will be forever touched by the care packages that Mrs. Carroll sent each week. When I opened the first one, I discovered that she had taken the time to purchase each ingredient I would need to prepare the recipes she included. In addition, that week and every week following, she sent the money I would need to purchase any meat that she couldn't ship. Though I certainly thanked her at the time, I can only hope she understands today how much her consistent reminders assured me that I was not alone.

Having acquired twelve hours of course credit before the first semester of classes began, I was able to put most of my focus on getting settled in the music school. What I didn't know prior to arriving was that getting a degree in music required that I not only focus on one specific major but that I also invest in a secondary music focus as well. When

I found out that soloists from New York City's Metropolitan Opera would join the Oratorio Choir, which was a rare occurrence, I chose that choir as my secondary focus.

Since this was the first time I had ever been in a choir, I had no idea how much it was not a vocal fit for me. My voice was bigger and darker than most others my age. Up until this point, I'd only performed solos and leading roles in various shows. Having to stifle much of my sound to fit into a choir was not fun for me at all. After a few weeks of negotiating that frustration, I was relieved that the conductor—who happened to be the dean of the music school—announced that there would be an additional performance of Verdi's "Requiem" that would feature student soloists.

He then surprised us by asking for any volunteers who might be willing to audition right then and there. Without thinking twice, I raised my hand. I figured this would give me a chance to finally express my whole voice. For this first round of auditions, he needed one volunteer from four vocal categories, from the highest register of soprano to the lowest, which I hoped to fill as the baritone. As I made my way to the front of the room with the other volunteers, I once again felt grateful to have had so many chances to practice sight-reading.

After we took our places, the choir began to sing the opening phrases from the "Requiem." After the soprano, mezzo, and tenor moved through their solo lines, it was finally my turn to sing. As it turned out, I was concentrating so hard that I didn't even notice when the dean stopped conducting. Only when the choir went silent did I look up to see Dr. Sternberg staring blankly at me.

Without making a big fuss, he simply asked if I would come to his office after rehearsal. At the end of the hour, I found myself sitting with the man in charge of the whole school. When I told him I was a freshman and a piano major to boot, he merely shook his head. He then made an offer that took my breath away. He promised to provide me with a four-year full scholarship if I'd be willing to shift my focus and become a voice major. Though I felt a bit dumbfounded, I also felt tremendous relief and gratitude. It seemed that my secret plan for paying for an education in premed would be realized after all.

The dean closed our short meeting by telling me about a baritone voice teacher in the opposite wing of the school whom he believed would be perfect for me. That's what led me to John McFadden, the man who became the next pivotal influence in my life. After only a couple of months of voice lessons, Mr. McFadden told me he thought I was ready to enter the big vocal competition that took place each year.

The National Association of Teachers of Singing (NATS) hosted the biggest competition offered to undergrads, which brought together singers from four different states. I had no idea what to expect, but if Mr. McFadden felt I was ready, I was willing to follow his lead. As it turned out, I actually won second prize as a freshman.

Once that first life-changing semester was over, I moved from the apartment to a freshman dorm, where I roomed with a great new friend named Crockett. From the beginning, I loved that Crockett was so authentic and open. Gifted in a number of directions, he not only had a beautiful tenor voice, but he had also been a star swimmer specializing in butterfly in high school. We hit it off right away. Once we were joined by the rare-voiced soprano, Natica, our trio of best friends was complete.

Living with Crockett was my first opportunity to get to know someone whose early challenges were so radically different from mine.

Rather than having to figure everything out on his own, Crockett came from a family who was overly protective and did practically everything for him. Though that sounded great to me at first, I soon realized he was now faced with needing to figure out tons of things about Life that I had already worked my way through. I was happy to help Crockett with some practical things, like showing him how to mail a letter or explaining how his girlfriend having cramps each month wasn't something dangerous he should worry about.

Gratefully, he was also there to support me in many ways. The most immediate example took place soon after I was accepted as a pledge in the Sigma Chi fraternity. While I was excited by the opportunity of getting to know people from many different schools, backgrounds, interests, and majors, being accepted into the fraternity also brought some negative attention.

A guy in my dorm who hadn't been accepted during Rush Week felt resentful and decided to make me a target. One night when I returned to my dorm room particularly late, Crockett was already asleep, so I slipped in quietly. Not wanting to wake him, I undressed in the dark and collapsed into my bed. Within seconds of hitting the pillow, I felt something wet and cold on the sheet at the back of my neck. I sat up and felt the sheet, expecting to find that someone had spilled a liquid there by mistake. When I found nothing but a dry sheet, I laid down again. Just as before, my neck felt immediately wet and cold. At that point, I had no choice but to turn on the lights.

When I pulled back the sheets to explore, I found nothing. It was only when I lifted my pillow that a long black snake shot out across the bed, trying to hide under my now crumpled sheets. I screamed out in panic, practically clawing at the door to get away. Beyond all logic, I once again became the little kid who had scrambled to the top of the car when I was four. Later, just the thought of a snake curling up under my neck in the dark still gave me the skeevies.

I hadn't received enough information from Gabriel at the time of my review to fully understand how we continue to manifest repeated patterns as we get older, but I remembered that it had something to do with attracting the very things that we need, which reflect and reveal any unresolved feelings that are still being held in the subconscious. The main reason we continue to attract those things going forward in our lives is so that we have the chance to face similar situations from the wiser perspectives and capacities of an adult. This encourages us to face the wounded feelings and to reeducate the wounded perceptions of a child.

Though I wasn't prepared to do any of that when I was in college, just looking back at the reality of attracting similar experiences was serving me in this life review in a big way. Who would have guessed? Out of all the ways that guy could have chosen to act out, he had picked a snake.

When I yelled out, I shocked Crockett out of his sleep, and he quickly came to the rescue. Once I was able to communicate what was happening—*There's a snake in my bed!*—Crockett went over and calmly captured it with his bare hands, as if the whole thing was no big deal. He then took the snake outside.

Even though I couldn't see the true gift this experience with Crocket had offered at the time, I was grateful to have time to explore the event with Gabriel when I reached this point in my review. What Crockett had shown me was that other perspectives and truths existed about each thing we experienced when we were young. We most often made decisions about what those events "meant"—based on the limited perspectives of a child—including snakes. The deeper adult truth is that most snakes are not terrifying or even harmful. Because Crockett didn't have any childhood traumas that involved snakes, he was planting new seeds of possibility for me, all with a beautiful sense of calm and safety. This memory allowed me to reflect on how meaningful my experiences with Crockett had been in our four years together.

Crockett, Natica, and I were fully immersed in each other's lives. One of my favorite opportunities came out of accompanying both of them for voice lessons and recitals. This created a beautiful intimacy that is tough to convey, not only making music together, but sharing milestone moments as well.

Much like high school, I took advantage of a huge spectrum of opportunities while I was at Baylor. I also continued to feel the familiar pressures for achieving and pleasing during those years. Receiving a 4.0 GPA at the end of my first semester reassured me that I could handle this new level of academics, which alleviated some of the pressure I'd continued to feel about getting As. That GPA led to an invitation into the freshman National Honor Society, which in turn gave me the chance to connect with other new friends, who ended up inspiring me in more directions.

After yearning for deeper connections for so long, I soaked in every chance I had to get to know the new people around me. Because I remained naturally curious, I didn't hesitate to ask them lots of questions about their lives. I wanted to know all about their interests and challenges. When any of them expressed an opinion or perspective that was clearly different than my own, I'd ask them to explain how they'd come to their particular conclusions. I made sure they knew I wasn't questioning whether their conclusions were right or wrong. I just liked understanding what motivated people or made them tick.

What I found, more often than not, was that most people didn't have clear answers as to why they felt the way they did, nor did they understand how they had arrived at many of their beliefs. Most of the time, it seemed they merely adopted the perspectives that had been modeled by their parents. Even so, what made me the happiest about those conversations was that my friends were more than willing to explore and share with me, and I loved considering tons of new possibilities.

Being in college gave me an abundance of chances to learn about singing and about connecting with a broad spectrum of people. I also couldn't believe that in such a short time, I had the chance to speak with Metropolitan Opera stars, sing with orchestras, and see grand productions at the Dallas Opera, which Mr. McFadden made sure Crockett, Natica, and I were able to do.

Experiencing the reality of professional opera up close made quite an impression on us. One evening really stood out. It was the evening we were able to sit extremely close the stage. From a distance, it was easy to get swept away by the grandness of the sounds, lights, and sets. From up close, I was able to see that the actors were real people—as strange as that might sound. That specific experience created a revelation that performing on professional stages just like these might be a real possibility for me.

The main problem I eventually had to face was that I never took the time to ask myself whether pursuing opera suited my personality or gratified me. I had simply followed the open doors that led me to my first opera. Prior to the offer of a full scholarship, I'd never even said the word "opera" or expressed a desire for such a career. I had simply said yes to the specific opportunities that presented themselves. I never took the time to explore other options or to consider if it was what I wanted.

Once I immersed myself in the realities of being a double major— and now a triple major—I decided to let go of piano as a focus. Naturally, I was concerned about letting down Mrs. Sylvester, who had invested so much into me. The last thing I wanted to do was hurt her feelings.

Little did I know at the time that this was only my first big example of "letting go" while I was at Baylor. When performance opportunities continued to take most of my time during my second year, I felt I was somehow being led in a clear, new direction, and it was time to let go of my original plan for medical school as well. True to form, I never consulted any adults about the decision.

Once I settled into having just one major, I could much more fully appreciate the opportunities to sing leading roles. I was now invested in a real career path. I also enjoyed learning rare language skills from Mr. McFadden. One of the things I valued most about our time together was him teaching me how to create an intimate connection with words, using them to not only enhance the music but also to create an emotional impact.

During those pivotal years of college, I also continued to develop my tendency for taking initiative. Wanting more opportunities to express my talents, I set up concerts in various churches in North Carolina for the summers when I would be back home. Those venues also gave me chances to share some of the things I had been learning about Life.

The summer before my senior year of college, I felt compelled to use one of those concerts to offer another tribute—this time to my grandfather. Though I couldn't explain it logically, I felt compelled from that intuitive place inside me. Following my green light, I programmed one of his favorite hymns, "How Great Thou Art," as a setup for honoring him. Sadly, it turned out that his arthritis had progressed to a point that he was unable to attend that concert in person.

Refusing to be deterred, I decided I would take a recording of the concert directly to him. Even though we'd still never had much personal conversation, sitting next to his bed while I played this segment of the concert touched us both. Tears formed in his eyes as he listened to my words about his impact on my life, which were heightened by the music that followed. The next day, when it was just him and me hanging out in the living room, I had another impulse. Since my grandparents' old upright piano was just across the room, I asked my grandfather if he would consider singing "How Great Thou Art" for me while I played. It had been so many years since I'd heard him sing in that little chapel. He agreed.

His vulnerable condition made the whole experience childlike and beautiful, particularly because this time, he was singing just for me. What neither of us knew was that these were to be our final moments together. About a month after I returned to school, I woke up quite suddenly from a deep sleep, and somehow, I just knew my grandfather had died. A couple of days later, I flew home again—this time for the first funeral I had ever attended.

When my grandmother asked if I would sing "How Great Thou Art" for the service, I hesitated. I didn't want to disappoint her, but I had no idea if I would be able to sing without breaking down. Fortunately, the night before the service, I found out there was a tradition that involves people coming to say their last goodbyes. Still needing to make a decision, I waited until everyone had left the church before I went in to say my own goodbyes.

As soon as I entered, I felt a heightened quiet in the space. I was also aware that this was the first time I'd ever seen an actual casket. With great reverence, I went to the most familiar place I could find—the piano bench. For some reason, I began to talk to my grandfather out loud. I told him that although I wished we could've shared more in our lives, I appreciated that music had always given us a way to communicate. I then told him I would sing for him—just for him—one final time.

As I half-sang and half-cried, something incredible happened. I had the distinct feeling that my grandfather was standing right there next to me. I could literally feel his presence, which was a sensation I'd never experienced before. It was palpable and deeply comforting, and just as I hoped, having that final moment to release the well of feelings that I'd been holding on to created a sense of peace about singing the next day. When the time came for me to share at the actual service, I simply focused on sending love to my grandmother, hoping the experience would help her just a little with the huge loss she was facing.

Only weeks after my return to school, I was faced with the reality of death yet again. This time it was much more shocking. Mr. McFadden, who was only thirty-five years old, suddenly passed away. Crockett, Natica, and I guessed that his unexpected death must have come from him having just lost a tremendous amount of weight. Perhaps his body didn't have the strength to handle the virus that the doctors told us he had contracted. They let us know through the adults who were allowed access to the information that within twenty-four hours of being admitted to the hospital, a rapid growth of some sort had occurred near his heart and had somehow destroyed his aortic valve. No matter what the logical explanation might have been, we began to land in the reality that this dear man was now gone from our lives.

The three of us were devastated. In the fall of our senior year, we had lost a friend, a mentor, and a trusted advisor. Unsure what to do or where to focus, we felt like we were trying to navigate a boat without a rudder. The only thing we figured we could do to honor his memory involved putting all our energy into preparing for the annual NATS competition that was about to take place. We also appreciated how perfect it was that the competition that year would bring people from four states directly to Baylor.

When it was finally time for the event, we all sang our hearts out, knowing this was the last time we would likely be referred to as students of John McFadden. As the various stages of the competition progressed, more and more singers were eliminated. On the night of the finals, with two thousand people gathered in the main concert hall, I had the chance to play for Natica as she sang in the senior women's division. Moments later, I returned to the stage to sing for the senior men's finals. Serendipitously, Natica and I both won first place in our categories. Later, we confided to each other that we hoped we had sent Mr. McFadden's Soul on his way, feeling proud of what this moment affirmed about his career as a teacher.

Although nothing could diminish all that I gained from Mr. McFadden in those few years at Baylor, as I looked back on this time, I also needed to admit that I recognized the continuance of a painful pattern. At some point in my final year of college, I had found a recording of me singing when I was eighteen. I felt that the depth of the rich sound—unusual for someone so young—was no longer the same. It seemed that being encouraged into the specific palette of colors that was so brilliant in Mr. McFadden's lighter voice had not been the best approach for my instrument.

Listening to that recording, I cried. Looking back in review, I realized that my guidance from Mr. McFadden hadn't set me up as well as I would have liked vocally. It triggered feelings similar to those I felt looking back at a mother and father who hadn't known how to provide the guidance that I truly needed early on. This was a complicated issue to face. It was a feeling that another authority figure who had been responsible for guiding me toward the higher levels of my potential hadn't been able to do that as fully as I needed.

Because I cared so much for this wonderful man, I wasn't sure what to do with those charged feelings. I felt a little guilty about the whole thing, to be quite honest. Fortunately, I received some comfort and affirmation some years later, when one of Mr. McFadden's teaching colleagues admitted that he had confided to her that he hadn't been sure what to do with my voice. Hearing that helped me to let go. I appreciated that he had showed up and invested in me fully. And I loved that.

Despite how I might have felt about the shifts that had taken place with my present technique, doors continued to open for my next steps. Toward the end of my senior year, I was faced with figuring out what I would do after graduating. Without knowing how to evaluate options, I decided to follow the path that a couple of other singers from Baylor had taken the year before. The University of Cincinnati College-Conservatory of Music (CCM), one of the two best graduate schools in the country, had renowned programs in opera and musical theater. So I chose this as the one place I would apply, to pursue my master's degree. Fortunately, my acceptance came once again with the offer of a full scholarship. This was great since my family was not in a position to help with these financial needs. I also secretly felt that this was an encouraging confirmation that I had chosen well, and it still supported me on this new path.

I was ready to move on. Actually, not quite. For me to feel done with my time in Texas, I still needed to look at what remained my biggest, unresolved challenge. It was one I had continued to ignore during my years at Baylor. For almost two years after I had arrived, I avoided getting involved in any romantic relationships.

Except for the few dates I took to various fraternity events, I focused most of my energy on deepening friendships. Only in my junior year did I decide to land more fully. That was when I started dating our fraternity's sweetheart, a wonderful girl named Cindy. Still stuck in confusion, I only let things progress to a certain point, particularly with our sexual exploration. Of course, this hadn't been fair to Cindy. Although

I genuinely liked her and hated the thought that my confusion might be creating an impact on her, I simply wasn't ready to go further.

Only as I reached my senior year did I decide that the only hope I had of finding peace with this disconcerting issue would come if I made a full commitment to a relationship. After spending some time getting to know Deborah, a beautiful, talented girl from the music school, that's exactly what I did. No holds barred. Because we got along well and had many things in common, our time together was great. We even enjoyed a full sexual relationship that I believe was special to us both. Those particular investments helped me realize that the inner conflicts I carried about wanting a core relationship with another man were not primarily about sex. I genuinely enjoyed the physical part of my relationship with Deborah.

That revelation made it clear that my desire came from an even deeper part of myself. Looking back as an older adult, I felt this need for male connection came directly from my Soul. Though I didn't understand it at the time, there was no denying that my need was authentic and unshakable, and so I gradually had to honor that truth.

Meanwhile, Deborah and I had been embraced as a couple the whole time we had dated, even at the small church where I led the choir and worked with the youth group. On the outside, everything seemed perfect. My time with Deborah helped me get really clear, and I decided that graduation was the most natural time to end our relationship. I was heading to Cincinnati, and Deborah still had two more years to go at Baylor.

At first, I made some lame excuse about not wanting to be in a long-distance relationship, which did not feel good to either one of us. It simply wasn't the deepest truth, and we had both developed genuine feelings of love and connection in our time together.

Since I felt sure that I would never put another woman in this position again, I had to return to what mattered: authenticity and honoring the people I cared about. That's when I faced the most difficult decision of my young life—finally revealing my scary secret.

Knowing that I didn't want to give Deborah any reasons to doubt her value, I focused on honoring her in order to summon the courage I needed to finally open up. Besides, I knew that if I moved on without taking responsibility, I wouldn't be able to live with myself.

Though facing Deborah felt torturous, I met her in my car, where I forced myself to say the first words. The conversation went something like this. "I know that my decision to end our relationship has been confusing and hurtful. The truth is that I love you...enough to be more honest than I have ever been. What I have to share is quite painful for me. No matter what I've done to find a new truth in myself during our time together, I need to finally admit out loud that I am a gay man."

Although she seemed surprised at what I had just shared, the love we had built held true. We both cried and held each other for a long time. Remembering those moments, I once again felt the comfort of knowing I had made love the priority, not fear. Some years later, Deborah told me our relationship had been the most honest and respectful of any she had experienced.

Though I didn't have the benefit of those perspectives in the first moments sitting in my car, I did find some initial relief that I could no longer hide from my truth. Scared and unsure, I also understood that I was finally freeing myself to become fully authentic again. I just wasn't sure how it would all unfold. Regardless, I was happy to make choices I could be proud of, no matter what anyone else might think or be able to understand. I knew it was much wiser than pretending and continuing to hide this part of myself in fear.

What I didn't know was that those choices formed the seed of what would become the most essential guiding principle of my life.

What I did know was that once I had honored Deborah, I could move forward—even if I had no idea what I would do to resolve the issue of having a primary relationship. Even so, I knew that in some way, I was starting to grow up. With that in place, I moved on to grad school, still hiding within my need to achieve.

12

DRINKS
AND DEBUTS

T HE REALITY OF BEING IN GRAD SCHOOL WAS A DIS-
tinctly new experience for me. Just as I had expected, there was
an entirely new level of pressure and competition to negotiate,
accompanied by the need to deal with the heightened egos that people
in competitive arenas often develop to deal with the pressures. That was
the challenge. At the same time, being around such talented people, I
had the chance to witness the gifts others had cultivated, and I became
more inspired than ever to better myself.

Looking back at this stage of my life, I was more practiced at recognizing the challenges and gifts. Now it was clear that those events had
served me when I was moving through them, and they were giving me a
second chance to learn.

Those of us who had won big scholarships and were cast in roles within the first few weeks of our arrival became the more obvious focal points for the pent-up feelings we were all negotiating. Sometimes people's pressures turned into resentment. I often felt that some people were just waiting to see if those of us who'd been singled out would live up to the hype, or whether it should have been them performing some coveted role.

My voice teacher at CCM was Andrew White, a gentleman in his seventies who was unquestionably one of the most famous baritone teachers in the world at that time. His "once-in-a-lifetime" student had been Sherrill Milnes, an imposing man who had become the world's most famous operatic baritone of the time.

Another consideration about school in Cincinnati was learning to function in colder northern weather for the first time. Driving and getting around in ice and snow were particularly tricky. Sadly, I learned how true this was one evening as I returned to my car from the grocery store and encountered black ice for the first time. I fell fast and hard. With bags in both hands, I had no way to catch myself or ease the impact of the fall. Once I was down, I remember lying on the sidewalk feeling stunned and alone.

This took place in my first few weeks in Cincinnati, at a time when I had no obvious friends to call for help. Having never learned to feel comfortable reaching out for help was also an issue. For those reasons, I chose to hop on one leg up the stairs to my apartment. In truth, I hoped that everything would magically feel better in the morning.

Looking back at the situation, I was reminded of another Gabriel teaching regarding how we all manifest conditions in our physical bodies, which reflect what's going on for us emotionally. *Your body acts as an outer physical barometer of the flow or resistance of emotions you are negotiating. When you resist in fear or shame, that energy becomes charged before it becomes buried deep in the subconscious. When you manifest a physical challenge in your body, it is often your body giving you clues about those specific issues and the feeling energy that is out of balance.*

By the time I looked at this moment in review, I'd already learned that each part of the body typically represents a specific aspect of our lives. It just so happens that the left ankle represents one's ability to move out of what's familiar, ready and willing to stand on one's own feet. My broken left ankle—which is what my injury turned out to be—reflected that I was fighting many of those exact feelings and fears. I was afraid of leaving what had been a time of great success and security, and I was now facing a much bigger fear of the unknown. My success in this new place hadn't been established yet, and I was feeling quite exposed with my recent admission to Deborah. While trying to work my way through all those charged feelings, I had little idea how to stand solidly on my own feet.

Alone and scared, I had gone to hide out in my bedroom—a choice that I had developed in adolescence. I didn't even consider going to a hospital until the next morning, at which point my ankle had become quite swollen. It was telling that I didn't even reach out for help at that point. I got myself to the hospital without telling a single person what was happening.

This revelation really touched me as I continued to review. I was also grateful that I had learned so much about nurturing both my inner child and my inner adolescent as I had moved through so many stages and lessons. In addition to working through some of the feelings that had been suppressed, I was now getting better at offering those parts of me the clear guidance that I had needed early on.

Back to the events as they were transpiring, many people were surprised when I showed up to school on crutches and in a cast. Thankfully, a few of them invited me to go out with them to a bar that weekend.

What they didn't know was that I had such a charged history with my mother's drinking, I had never even tried alcohol. However, now that I felt truly vulnerable and wanted to be connected more than alone, this felt like a good opportunity to try it out.

When it came time to order, I was clueless. One of the people in our group said, "I know. What about a Long Island iced tea?" Naively, I confirmed that I loved iced tea. And so it was decided. My first sips proved quite tasty, and I began to gulp the drink down rather quickly. My friends kept watching me and waiting for some reaction. They knew this drink was famous for being quite potent, and it consisted of all the clear versions of liquor. When no obvious response emerged, and I simply enjoyed the evening, I thought, *Wow. I guess drinking is no big deal for me.*

A few weeks later, I decided to go out again, this time with just one friend. The only difference I could pinpoint on this trip was that I was no longer on any medications. About halfway through the Long Island iced tea I ordered, my head fell forward on the bar. I passed out cold. Though I could laugh about it the next day with my friends, it was now evident that my body had a very low tolerance for alcohol.

What got me through the rest of an emotional first year of negotiating pressures and missing Crockett, Natica, and other friends from Baylor was knowing I had an amazing summer to look forward to. What made it so clear was that I'd already spent the summer before my first year of grad school performing at the Brevard Music Center in North Carolina's Blue Ridge Mountains.

Now that I was having to deal with heightened egos and other exposing feelings, I was anxious to return to a place where I had first met grounded, gifted adults—successful professionals in the music world who had already learned to keep their egos in check. Without that light at the end of the tunnel, I'm not sure I would have even wanted to continue forward on a performance path. That is how challenging my first year in Cincinnati had been for me emotionally.

Just like returning to an oasis after enduring a long journey through the desert, I was grateful that my adult friends who were once again at Brevard could relate to the things I confessed about that first year in grad school. Many of them offered comfort and helpful advice about existing in a competitive environment. I soaked in every moment of their love and support.

In addition to performing exhilarating roles and concerts, I used my time there to laugh and play, doing fun things like riding the younger kids around on my shoulders at mealtimes. I desperately needed those opportunities to reconnect with innocence and joy.

When I returned for my second year at CCM, I began to fear that I was in a continuation of my wounded pattern—being in the charge of an authority figure who didn't know how to guide me into the next levels of my specific potential. Andrew White, my venerable voice teacher, was an amazing man. And although he felt like a nurturing grandfather to me, his approach to singing turned out to be a giant pendulum swing, moving from one vocal extreme that didn't work well to another that was equally problematic.

Because he encouraged me toward a huge open throat, I ended up putting great pressure on my vocal cords. What I really needed was someone to guide me into an easy flow of my most natural, authentic sound. As I reviewed the situation, I wondered if those outer circumstances were mirroring my internal swings, which for so long had led me away from expressing my most authentic Self.

Not wanting to repeat pressures similar to those of my first year at CCM, I was ready to try some new approaches. One of the more fulfilling choices I made came out of identifying the areas of study that interested me most, rather than simply going through the program that had typically been followed. I began reaching out to teachers in other majors, asking if I could take dance classes with the musical theater students and acting classes with the acting majors. Most of those teachers responded to my enthusiasm for learning and happily opened their doors—once again, unprecedented firsts for most of them.

The only challenge I faced was being limited to a maximum of twenty hours of credit per semester. When I knew I wanted more, I started asking teachers if I could unofficially audit their classes. I promised each one I would fully commit and participate. I just wouldn't expect credit or an official grade. Once I had followed through successfully for one semester, my instructors were even more willing to continue.

Little did I know that following those instincts was helping me to build new confidence for proactively seeking out opportunities to invest in whatever genuinely interested me going forward. That was a huge gift that I recognized, looking back. Applying this new approach made the rest of my time at CCM much more fulfilling. I also met a more diverse group of friends in this broader exploration, which was simply great for me.

I recognized that my diverse training was paying off when I was cast as Marcello for an international tour of Puccini's *La bohème*—another unusual opportunity that presented itself to all of us at the conservatory. I was thrilled to be cast as this would be my first experience doing an opera that would allow me to combine gorgeous music with a moving story, where I could express my acting chops in a more meaningful way. Perhaps most thrilling was the chance to tour parts of Europe and to sing a whole role in a foreign language!

The adventure of being in other countries was stunning. I loved performing and being introduced to new cultures in a gorgeous part of the world. When I read my first reviews, I remember thinking I had certainly come a long way from Pinetops, North Carolina. One of the German newspapers asserted, "The baritone, Ron Baker, became a shining centerpiece in this performance of La bohème"—all written in German, of course. Even though I had to work around some frustrating confusions in my vocal technique, my willingness to convey honest, raw emotion helped me make those important first impressions.

After completing the master's program at CCM, I chose to continue my studies there to get the equivalent of a performer's doctorate—only offered at a handful of conservatories in the States. The summers before and after I began that program, I spent my time doing apprenticeships in Central City, Colorado. The structure of that particular program provided opportunities for a handful of young apprentices to train as well as perform. It was there that I got to sing Marcello in a second production of *La bohème*, this time with a stunning group of young singers who all went on to build important careers. Having time to develop friendships with a handful of established professional singers who were also there performing was once again invaluable.

John Moriarty was the awesome man who put this program together. He was a motivated, intelligent guide whom I grew to admire and care for. Fortunately, I thrived in that environment, enough to be invited back for a second summer. That is when I met a charismatic young woman who would become my best friend from the opera world. The stunning mezzo-soprano, Denyce Graves, felt like a sibling to me from the moment we met. It was fun reviewing the time we had shared, enhanced by knowing she would eventually go on to become a much sought-after performer and one of the few official cultural ambassadors for the United States. I also knew that our careers would parallel each other in meaningful ways.

During this important time of developing as a young artist, I continued to long for an authentic, deep connection with a primary partner. After meeting and performing with people from all around the globe, I was now well aware that there were millions of men and women in the world who had the same feelings and needs that I did. Of course, I also met many people who had some arduous challenges in their journeys with being gay.

Even as I looked back at this time in my review, I realized there were still many unanswered questions about the subject of Souls and sexuality. I made note of how much I looked forward to asking Gabriel about those very things. When I was in my early twenties, however, it was helpful just knowing that I wasn't alone in these feelings, which was part of my deep struggle for so many years.

What was also clear was that I needed to start putting my toe in the dating pool if I was ever going to create solid solutions for myself. I began by going out on a couple of casual dates in Cincinnati, aware that I was too vulnerable and inexperienced for anything serious. Truth be told, I did everything I could to keep my first dates a secret. However, I also noted that when I had told some of my colleagues at school about this part of my life, my sexuality was no longer a big deal to them. Who I was dating was not that interesting to other people and had no direct impact on our connections. Now I could get on with being just another person who was trying to create something meaningful in my life.

Once I realized that it was impossible to please everyone, I started taking even more initiative to commit to the things that mattered most to me. This made my time in this final stage of grad school a beautiful stretch into more meaningful experiences. With each of the stretches I was creating, I felt safer and more confident to continue with that opening to Life.

As one example, I got an invitation from a friend to attend an evening with an intuitive clairvoyant. Though I wasn't sure what an intuitive clairvoyant was, I loved the idea of experiencing someone with unusual gifts. The moment I heard about the opportunity, I got one of my clear green lights with energy surging up my spine.

A few nights later, I joined about ten others in a small room. The clairvoyant began by telling us that he could not only see the energy that surrounds all living things—mostly people and plants—but that he would also often receive intuitive messages. He then proceeded to move from one person to the next, offering messages to each one. Most received clues and hints about challenges they were negotiating. At some point, he mentioned that we all have guardian angels and guides who are there to help us, though most people aren't aware of that guidance in a conscious way.

When it was my turn, the message began with a confirmation that I was on a distinct spiritual path and that I needed to trust the way things were unfolding in my life. "What I am seeing now is quite unusual. You have a master teacher who has shown up. He wants you to know that you will have many opportunities to open and grow in your life, and if you allow it, the two of you will eventually become quite connected— almost like one." That was the end of the message, and although I had no logical idea what this might mean, I was excited by the possibilities of greater spiritual learning and connection.

This experience made me think even more fully about the next logical steps that were waiting to unfold for me. As I approached my final semester in Cincinnati, I needed to begin creating a more solid bridge into the professional world. Though the more obvious opportunities were limited, what made most sense to me was going after one of the extended apprenticeships offered by a handful of the biggest opera houses. To set myself up better than I had in previous transitions, I decided to schedule auditions for all four of the big apprenticeships in the US, which I knew would attract young singers from around the world.

Once the dates for those auditions were in my calendar, I bought plane tickets for the first two events. My first stop was New York City, where I would be singing for a place with the San Francisco Opera. Out of hundreds of candidates, there would only be twenty singers chosen. I arrived at the audition both nervous and excited. A few weeks later, I was informed that I had indeed been chosen. I felt thrilled to have a clear option on the table. I then had three auditions to go.

The apprenticeship for the Houston Grand Opera only offered space for two artists. For that day of auditions, a rather large contingency of singers from CCM flew to New York City. This second audition process was more comprehensive than the last one had been. Secretly, I felt particularly grateful for the depth I could bring, having learned so much about language and style in my training with Mr. McFadden. After I'd sung for the panel, I went out to the lobby to wait with the others.

At the end of a very long day, when the door finally opened, the messenger was direct and to the point. "Thank you all for coming. We would like to speak with Mr. Baker. The rest of you may go." While of course I was pleased to have made a good impression, familiar pangs of guilt surged through me. I had already been accepted into one program. Why had I chosen to come to this audition? Old worries about how my choices would impact others immediately surfaced. As strange as it may seem, I felt embarrassed as I stood there in the lobby with my colleagues.

Without any real guidance on how to work through the confusion, I only knew that the way to avoid further awkwardness was to cancel the other two auditions. Then, still conflicted over the results of being invited to two apprenticeships, I made my final decision by saying yes to the opportunity that had come first.

This all happened just a few months before I completed my studies in Cincinnati. Naturally, that's when I ended up meeting a handsome guy and starting my first relationship with a man, whom we will call Justin. Justin was from a very small town in Kentucky where he'd been shuffled from one foster home to the next. He was sweet, and I deeply enjoyed our first months getting to know each other before I was scheduled to leave for San Francisco. Knowing that the date was coming fast, we spent as much time together as possible. As my departure approached and we grew more attached, we began to consider how Justin might go with me to the West Coast. After I agreed to buy him a plane ticket, he assured me he would look for work as soon as we got settled in the new apartment. I promised myself that having Justin around wouldn't take my focus away from the opportunity that lay before me: apprenticing with an international opera house.

In San Francisco, on the first day of meeting the group of twenty apprentices, we were asked to sing for the main staff in the huge historic theater. That is where my pattern of fear about not deserving too much success seemed to play itself out.

When I'd first been accepted into the program, I was asked to prepare for the title role in an opera called *Gianni Schicchi* as well as a second leading role in an opera called *Don Pasquale*. After singing for the bigwigs, I was informed that the role of Gianni Schicchi was no longer mine. They were offering it to someone else who wasn't even in the program, and they provided no explanation.

Once I reached this point in my review, I asked Gabriel about the situation. He suggested that part of the reason this had taken place was indeed a reflection of the limited beliefs about what I deserved that were still solidly fixed in my subconscious. In an effort to not be resented or perhaps deprive someone else of an opportunity, that fearful part of me had created a form of sabotage. I also saw, looking back, that the decision may have been equally influenced by this highly educated staff recognizing the flaws in my technique.

Since most of the singing in that role was very character-like, I will never know for sure. However, I was certainly aware that the technical gaps were there. Though I wish the staff had been more direct in their feedback, which would have been the more nurturing way to guide a young singer, if this limitation was indeed the issue, they did end up delivering a clear message at the end of the summer.

Prior to twelve of us going out on a tour of *Don Pasquale*, the whole group gave a concert in the big opera house, which was a huge highlight for all of us. At the end of that concert, the staff handed out a few grants for certain individuals to continue their studies. I was not one of those. Fortunately, one staff member I admired took the time to tell me that I had not been awarded a prize simply because my grant proposal had included continued study with Mr. White. It was interesting that I hadn't actually intended to continue those studies. I just didn't have a new teacher lined up when I had to put in the specific ways I would use the money from a grant. The result was that they held back support to assert that they didn't support me continuing down that particular path.

One perk of doing that final concert was that it motivated my dad to get on a plane—which he hated—and fly all the way to California. Even though I was touched that he made the effort to attend this final concert—the first time he'd attended a performance of mine since high school—I interpreted the gesture as confirmation that I could only get his attention when I had achieved something truly impressive.

At the same time, the grandness of the moment didn't affect his ability to plant seeds of doubt for me to contend with. While we were all standing in the lobby after the concert, my dad felt compelled to comment to the person standing next to him, "I noticed that practically everybody on the stage was taller than Ronnie."

I had grown up constantly evaluating whether I measured up as a person, so his comment stung. My height was already something I worried about. This was mostly based on my mother having told me long ago that doctors had made an early prediction about the height I would reach as an adult. Based on my initial measurements and weight, six foot one was the magic projection—which just happened to be my father's height. When I stopped growing at five foot ten, I remember feeling panicked that I was not measuring up to yet another expectation of me as a man.

After our summer in San Francisco, Justin flew back to Cincinnati, and I went out on the extended tour of *Don Pasquale*. He and I talked every day, and I continued doing what I could to support him financially. To help with the bills, he worked at the front desk of a hotel several nights a week. I knew that he had long dreamt of going to college, so even though I had only been out of school for three months myself, I used the small amount I had saved to pay for his first classes. I thought it would be a meaningful focus for him while I was gone.

Things were looking positive from my end of the relationship, so I took a big step and invited him to come to North Carolina for Christmas. I knew this would not only give us time together, but it would also give us a chance to celebrate his birthday, which would take place just a few days before Christmas. I was both touched and surprised when my mom—who had never met Justin—brought out a birthday cake for him on our first night there. Justin was shocked and speechless. Only later did he tell me that this was the first time anyone had thrown him a birthday party. He also had presents waiting for him under the tree on Christmas morning. I was moved by the generosity my family showed, especially because I had never brought anyone I was dating home before.

After the Christmas break, Justin returned to Cincinnati, and I flew out for a few more months of touring. At the tour's conclusion, I returned to Ohio to prepare for our next big move—this time to New York City. Grateful to have a familiar place to regroup and plan, I moved back into the apartment that I had kept as a home base for us.

One of my top priorities during those months back at home was to start working on my technique. Rather than trusting yet another authority figure, whose efforts might end up not serving my particular needs, I decided to return to what had always been most reliable for me: teaching myself. I did ask for hints and feedback from some wonderful coaches in Cincinnati and New York City during those months, but I felt it was time to take charge of my career, figuring out the best ways to reclaim my own most natural voice.

I remember how relieved I felt when my mother heard me sing not long after. "Congratulations," she teased lovingly. "You've now taught yourself to sing like you did when you were eighteen." While that wasn't the whole truth, I definitely understood the compliment she was offering. With that extra affirmation, I admitted it was now time to look for an agent in the big city.

Just as I felt things were really coming together for this next step, my world was thrown into a major upset. After returning from a quick audition trip to New York, it occurred to me to listen to the messages on our answering machine. I wanted to make sure Justin hadn't missed passing on some important information about the auditions I was starting to schedule.

Answering machines in the late eighties simply kept a record of one message after another on a cassette tape. These eventually had to be erased to make room for more. Hitting the rewind button, I prepared to review what was there. After a couple of mundane messages, I heard Justin's voice. It immediately struck me as strange that he was the one calling the apartment. Then I heard another voice—an unfamiliar man's voice—confirming to Justin that he had picked up their laundry. I don't remember anything that was said after that. My heart had stopped.

It seemed Justin had been living a double life. Someone was practically living with him in the apartment that I was paying for and doing intimate things like sharing chores with him. Hearing this conversation about their joint laundry felt like being punched in the gut.

After regaining my senses, I rewound the tape, picked up the phone, and dialed Justin at work. When he answered, I placed the handset on top of the answering machine and hit "play." After a few sentences of their conversation had been revealed, I hung up and waited. Ten minutes later, he came bounding through the door, out of breath. After offering some easily challenged cover story, he admitted that he had been seeing someone. He tried to downplay it, of course. Unsure what else we might do, I asked him to gather some of his things so I could take him back to the hotel where he worked. I needed time to think.

When I got back to the apartment and reality set in, I realized this was exactly what my family had gone through with my father, years earlier. Yet again, I had manifested a situation that held strong feelings I had only recently begun to process. In my devastation, I now understood just a little of what my mother must have felt. By the time I had grappled with my churning emotions for a few hours, I realized I didn't want to lose Justin. I decided that if he was willing to work through things with me and seemed genuinely sorry to have betrayed our relationship in this way, I was willing to forgive him.

With a great sense of urgency, I jumped in the car and drove back to the hotel once again. It was about nine o'clock when I arrived, which meant that his shift was done. His coworker at the front desk recognized me and gave me Justin's room number. I practically ran to the room and knocked hard, barely holding back tears. After a pause, Justin cracked open the door and poked his head around to see who it was. The room lights were off, and he was shirtless. Rather than looking happy to see me, he looked awkward and surprised. As it turned out, he was already in the room with the other guy. Gut punch number two.

There was no other option at this point but to turn and leave. The fact that I was in shock became even more apparent once I reached the parking lot behind my apartment. Though I didn't know how, I had somehow driven all the way home with the emergency brake on in my car. The next week, I moved out of that apartment.

As always, I redirected my wounded feelings into a more intense focus on performing. This time, I was grateful to be preparing to leave Cincinnati for good. For this next step, I returned to my earlier pattern, setting up just one audition for one agent. Driven by the desire to make a choice that would set me up for the best opportunities, and to impress any of the people whose opinions truly mattered to me, I auditioned for one of the top agents in the world. Ken was part of the prestigious Columbia Artists Management, Inc.—commonly referred to in the business as CAMI. What I hoped was good news, but was ultimately not-so-good news, is that Ken took me on.

For the whole year that followed, it was clear that being the only newbie on a roster of impressive, world-famous singers had not been a wise choice. Because my agent was always busy taking care of the immediate needs of some of the most revered singers in the world, he didn't have time to offer the kind of guidance that I needed to build a new career. Therefore, once my contract ended at the close of that year, I bit the bullet and made an important change.

One of the highlights of my time at the new agency was getting cast in my first handful of roles at the New York City Opera, all of which took place in the infamous summer of 1990, when I first met Robert. Once that major contract was in place, I moved full-time to New York City. Looking back, it was undeniable that my wounded patterns and pressure had reached an unprecedented peak by the time I made that important debut. Therefore, meeting Robert and Gabriel couldn't have come at a more opportune time. I was primed and ready for some healthy guidance and a new direction.

ADULT

13

COURAGE AND CONFESSION

B Y THE TIME ROBERT AND I HAD FINISHED WORKING
our way through our individual life reviews, making sure
to spend time nurturing many of the wounded feelings that
emerged along the way, we had spent a full three years going truly deep
into this new approach with Gabriel. Even though I was learning to
become the nurturing authority in my own life, it was also important
that we were both learning to give and receive support with one another.

I remember how comforted we both felt sharing many of the important revelations that we each made along the way. For instance, when it
was unmistakable to me that I was the one most responsible for holding
many of my own limitations in place, based on making decisions out
of fear or shame, directly owning this fact with Robert made it even
more real. That process became such an important part of practicing

accountability, and it brought all the inner discoveries fully to the outer world I was learning to trust. Once I could see how my wounded patterns, challenges, and gifts had formed the primary focus or curriculum of my life, talking those things over with Robert helped to solidify my understanding.

I remember discussing with him how reassuring it was to consider that our Souls set up our core challenges in order to serve us. It encouraged each of us to learn from our choices, and we gradually learned how to resolve each myth that we had carried. For me, one of the most immediate myths involved perceiving that I was not lovable, simply because the primary adults in my young life didn't know how to nurture me with consistent communication and acknowledgment of my individuality.

What a relief to see through the eyes of my adult Self that this was not a personal commentary on my worth. Their limitations had nothing to do with my perceived lack of value. No matter who had been born into their family, they wouldn't have known how to champion or nurture them. I loved getting to share this revelation with Robert when it was finally becoming clear. I could also consistently reiterate that deeper truth for my inner child.

The impact of feeling alone and without guidance had been debilitating for so long. And now I had started to understand that hiding parts of myself that I hadn't learned to love or accept only guaranteed I would continue to feel alone. In other words, I had been the one separating myself from other adults who might have been capable of offering real support as I got older. Equally as exciting, I recognized that I held the power to be the primary nurturer for each facet of my authentic Self. By the time my review was complete, I realized that the more authentic I was willing to be, the more meaningful my connections with others were already becoming.

One of the other patterns that became obvious to me was how trapped I had felt, caught between the desperation to achieve and the fear that having too much success would deprive others. With that approach, there was no way I would have found peace. No matter which side of the equation I looked to, I was sure to have remained unhappy. Just as powerful was discovering the adult truth that when I sought another's validation, I would often have to invalidate what I authentically felt or wanted. How futile it now seemed to seek someone else's approval if it meant simultaneously negating myself.

Prior to doing my life review, I had no idea how committed I had been to so many of the perceptions I had formed as a child. There were so many limitations that I had embraced as "the truth," while it was only my wounded child's perception of things. For years, I believed that being a unique individual was a threat that would cause others to reject or dislike me, merely because I wasn't just like them in some way. Perhaps the most defeating was my belief that others' opinions about me were the most important. I had always spent so much time focused *outside* myself, and I neglected to consider how I felt about myself.

Now that I had spent so much quality time learning to look from the compassionate eyes of an adult during my three years of reviewing, I was starting to trust the profound truth that how we feel about ourselves colors every part of our lives. Until we understand this, we tend to spend a great deal of time looking for others to affirm our childhood myths—no matter how limited or false those perceptions might be.

Seeing my childhood through more informed eyes helped me to consider that my parents had truly been trapped as wounded children on the inside. They were stuck in their own versions of early wounded fears and projections. Now that I was exploring Life as a series of Soul challenges and gifts that are perfect for each individual, a great weight was being lifted from my shoulders.

In my review, I was also grateful to identify tons of qualities that I honestly loved and appreciated about myself—like willingness, sensitivity, courage, curiosity, tenacity, and determination. In addition, I could see how genuine and innocent I had always been and how much I loved other people. That remained true throughout, no matter what challenges had been on my plate at any given time. I adored my relentless desire for healthy connections, and I genuinely wanted everyone around me to find a healthy, fulfilling path.

I also valued my ability to sense my own Soul truth from the time I was a child. I recognized there had always been deeper answers that would allow Life to seem fair and supportive of our individual journeys. I had been willing to honor that inner hunch by continually searching until I found some truly comforting answers.

In taking plenty of time to learn how to trust my new eyes, I began to finally understand one of the verses I had memorized at Ambassador Camp. "You shall know the truth, and the truth shall set you free." I now believed the verse needed a few more words: "There are more complete adult truths and even Soul truths that have the power to set your wounded child free." (A more complete version from Ron Baker. Ha.)

Fortunately, from these new, more informed perspectives, I could see that challenges and a lack of nurturing didn't need to be anyone's fault. Even if we must honor and release the way those limitations impacted us, we don't have to get stuck in the stage of working through our blame, shame, and judgment.

Once any new, expanded truth became clear, from this point forward, I now had the capacity to be more enthusiastic. I was willing to look for chances to practice the new approaches, truths, and nurturing tools that needed to become more integrated into my life.

For instance, it was amazing for me to see how responsible I had always felt for the suffering of others—all the way back to my feelings of guilt for hurting my mother in childbirth. Then, when I asked for horseback riding lessons, and our dog had been killed, I had blamed myself, rather than understanding that tragic things sometimes happen. There was no need for blame or shame. It had merely been a heartbreaking convergence of events. The deeper truth is that we are all learning together in each experience. We serve each other to have various experiences on a Soul level so we can gradually learn to move beyond what we would have originally defined as good or bad.

I felt excited about seeing my successes and achievements as important parts of my learning and evolution as an individual. Each one had allowed me to build more confidence in my developing Self. And that had been necessary for me to prepare for building a career on world stages. Only by investing in my gifts had those opportunities become possible, and only then was I in a position to touch and inspire others with my gifts.

The abundance that came from doing this deeper life review was stunning. I was grateful to finally see that it was only because I had so often felt deprived and alone on my journey that I had been so afraid of depriving or hurting others—even though it was never my intention. I hated the experience of deprivation so much that I hadn't been able to see how that challenge had been a big part of what motivated me to seek out and identify what I needed. The challenge was not to be avoided. It was there to serve and guide me toward the bigger answers I was seeking.

Perhaps most important from my review was seeing that it is nurturing and compassion that make all the difference in our healing journeys and in the development of Self-value. In addition, it is whether we receive nurturing or not when we are young that sets up many of our core lessons—the Soul curriculum. And whether we receive it early or not, it is never too late to learn how to nurture ourselves later in life. No matter when we have those experiences, it is nurturing that forms the foundation for trusting our value as sacred individuals on unique Soul journeys.

After a few years of this education about the Whole Self, I started to truly understand that I get to choose who I most want to be. By practicing the qualities that are important to me, I am most capable of becoming that person. For me, this was exciting.

Once these seeds of wisdom were firmly in place, I paid closer attention to which of my choices set me up well and which ones did not. To transform and replace any choices I decided to relinquish, I knew I would need lots of quality time with my inner child and adolescent.

Of course, having a wiser understanding of a particular subject didn't guarantee shifts of behavior or positive outcomes. As a matter of fact, I had been told many times that each of the new perspectives I started to champion would require a healthy learning curve, complete with plenty of mistakes along the way.

For instance, just running into friends and acquaintances on the streets of New York provided a constant stream of opportunities to practice letting go of my addiction to validation. The fear of not being seen in a positive light was still scary to me in those first few years of interrupting my protection racket—so much so that I often felt I had to share something impressive about my life before I could relax. Even when I made a clear decision to let my addiction go, I would often hear things coming out of my mouth before I had a chance to make a conscious decision. "Oh yes, I've just gotten a call back for that," I might casually mention, or "Oh sure, it was great to talk with (big name-drop) earlier this week."

Perhaps most difficult was finding compassion for myself within the patterns of needing validation and allowing myself to make mistakes. It was all too easy to judge myself for even *needing* a learning curve, when the behaviors themselves were not pleasant to admit. I also found that my wound was quite clever, doing things like wanting validation for my new, healthier approaches. "Now I am doing the *right* thing. Surely *this* will make me lovable." I clearly needed lots of practice.

Fortunately, I was also beginning to trust being more authentic in relationships by sharing myself in order to connect, nurture, encourage, or simply enjoy healthy friendships. It helped when I learned to really take others in, showing genuine interest and taking time to get to know their beautiful, confusing, wonderful journeys as well.

That is the process that gradually developed into a sense of safety, a willingness to share my vulnerabilities and failures without feeling threatened. Though this took a great deal of time to trust, I knew this was the level of freedom and intimacy that I longed for. And that is exactly what I began to choose and practice. Happily, some beautiful people showed up in a big way. Healthy, new experiences were key for building confidence in each set of healthier choices.

The more I took stock of the foundational discoveries I had made in my review, the more I realized how wise Gabriel's way of teaching had been. Rather than laying all the answers out, he had provided just enough clues to encourage me toward the healthier truths that I most needed to discover. This was true for both Robert and me. Having revelations that came out of our own explorations and experiences then created a far more powerful impression than simply being handed the answers we were seeking—though I must admit that it took me a long time to stop asking for immediate answers.

In our weekly get-togethers, Robert and I got into the habit of sharing our main discoveries out loud. Somehow that made it all seem more real and gradually safer. Bringing what we had both been holding inside out into the open was a crucial part of healing our fear and our shame. Naturally, we both loved having a safe place to share vulnerable things. Having another's eyes of acceptance and compassion was priceless.

A real standout for me at one of the meals we shared together took place when Robert agreed that much of my wounding had come from a combination of invalidating experiences with my father and the confusing time in middle school when my mother had been drinking. Then he noted how interesting it was that right when I had finished this bigger review, my father happened to be scheduled to come to New York City to see me perform. Once I thought about it, I had to admit that the timing couldn't be ignored—particularly since it was so rare to get him on a plane to visit.

When Robert suggested that I ask my father to fill me in on some of the gaps I held from that time of peak challenges in middle school, a passionate surge of anger and resentment poured out. "How the hell would he know? He wasn't even there!" Having an outburst like that was unusual for me. However, it revealed that there was still lots of wounded anger that needed to come out. Once I understood the immediacy and the opportunity that lay before me, I leaped up from my seat in the restaurant to find a pay phone. Fortunately, there was one hanging close by.

When my father answered, I jumped straight in. "Dad. I'm calling to ask about your trip to New York. Do you think that when you're here, you and I could find time to sit down and talk—just the two of us? I've been realizing how many things I don't know about you, and I'd love a chance to hear more."

Based on the short silence that followed, my father was taken by surprise. Once he eventually spoke, he agreed to what I had requested. Both relieved and nervous about what I'd just set in motion, I returned to the table. This was a huge moment for me. If the conversation I had suggested to him took place, it would literally be the first time in our lives that the two of us had any quality time alone. That prospect stirred up a flood of emotions that I knew I needed to process.

In the days that preceded my father's arrival, I spent time thinking about our relationship, not only reviewing what had already been, but also looking forward and contemplating the kind of relationship I wanted us to have. I must admit that daring to wish for something more was scary. It meant I was risking more disappointment. What drove me forward most was realizing that I could either spend the rest of my life resenting and fearing this man, or I could own the fact that I was no longer a child. As an adult, I was now half responsible for the success or failure of our relationship.

I made sure to spend time releasing some of the anger that I had been holding into a pillow. I was hoping that would leave me less charged when we finally sat down. Once I emptied out the old energy, I imagined filling in that inner space with the energy of compassion for us both. I knew that equaled sitting still and immersing myself in the actual experience of compassion. I also focused on acknowledging myself, proud of having made the courageous choice to call him and set the opportunity in motion. Just focusing on new possibilities felt better than continuing to hide.

When I spoke to Gabriel about my new choices, he confirmed: *We are so happy you are taking such bold forward steps. This is the beginning of a new, healthier track. Focusing on the experiences that you are choosing to create in your life, rather than trying to move away from the ones you most want to avoid, will empower you to shape and color your life with more fulfilling experiences going forward. Trust the process.*

Much to my surprise, my father ended up taking some initiative for our time together. On the day he flew into New York, he told me that he had asked his wife, Wilma, to spend time exploring the area for much of that afternoon. I could hardly believe that he was clearing space for the two of us. He then suggested we meet at his hotel room. That option made me happy as I preferred that we spend time in a quiet, private space, rather than having to deal with the energy of a noisy restaurant.

Once we were there, my dad sat on one end of a bed, and I sat in a chair close by. Since I was the one who had asked for the meeting, I took responsibility for beginning the conversation.

"Thanks for doing this, Dad. When I realized how little I know about your life, I felt sad. So if you don't mind sharing, I would love to know what life was like for you growing up and how you felt about some of the important events that have taken place since we became a family."

Again surprising me, the man who had been silent for the majority of my life began to share without hesitation. He started by describing what it was like growing up on a tobacco farm in a house crowded with eight older siblings. All of their lives revolved around the farm, and getting the crops in had been such a priority for their survival that he'd ended up missing tons of school. As a matter of fact, there were two years when he had missed so many days, he was required to repeat those grades.

This was shocking to me. I had long been aware that my father was a very intelligent man. It would never have occurred to me that the pressures of farming might have affected his early life in such a distinct way. Just hearing this one piece of his history made me realize that I'd never seen my father as an actual person, complete with specific challenges. I had only seen him in the role of my father. Fortunately for us both, having just completed my review, I was able to listen with a real sense of compassion.

He then told me that repeating two grades meant he was bigger and stronger than most of the other kids by the time he reached high school. He confided that this was one of the reasons he was able to stand out as an athlete. I then considered that, much like me, his achievements were what had given him the confidence to take his own powerful steps out into the world. This was particularly obvious when he told me he had not only been the first but the only person in his family to pursue college, and that he'd only been able to consider that choice because he had been offered athletic scholarships. Even more impressive to me was the fact that once he'd completed his first degree, he found a way to continue on to complete his master's in business.

In a way, I felt like I was hearing about the life of a stranger. At the same time, I was thrilled that each new piece of information made this distant warrior seem more human. Particularly hearing about the obstacles he had faced, I felt proud and surprisingly protective of him. It was clear that venturing out into completely unknown territory had required big courage from him, a farm kid in the fifties. And I was happy to begin seeing glimpses of similarities we shared. Those provided new hope that we might be able to connect more fully than I had imagined.

The more my dad shared, the more I relished each clue that helped me understand the man who had always been a mystery. Naturally, I asked some questions, which contributed to our talk lasting almost three full hours. At some point, he admitted that it had never occurred to him that anyone would be interested in hearing all these things about him. This was literally the first time anyone had ever asked about his life in such a direct way. That made me sad.

It was also amazing to me that he was so willing to reveal such personal, vulnerable things about himself, particularly because it indicated that he likely had doubts about his own value—never trusting that anyone was interested in truly knowing him. Though I wouldn't have wished for him to have Self-doubts, I had to admit that knowing he had a similar struggle took away some of the shame I had always felt about my own.

The man I had grown up with had always seemed strong and in control. Therefore, it was surprising to find out that he had waited for someone else to take the lead before opening up in this way. By the time he was done, our experience had surpassed anything I had hoped might happen, and I was genuinely touched by the whole experience.

Later that night, I spent time reveling in each thing my father had shared with me. I also paid close attention to how I had always looked at him through the lens of my emotional wounds—of my child Self. I had imagined that all the limitations which had been present growing up were a personal commentary on my limited value. Fortunately, our first adult conversation came at a time when I was ready to understand that all children personalize their early experiences. So I wasn't too hard on myself.

I then let in the final shock that had come from my dad at the close of our conversation. This man who had never shown a single sign of interest in getting to know me as a child actually said, "I may have been a terrible father. I just don't know." At first, I couldn't imagine that he could be so out of touch that he didn't realize he'd hardly been a father at all. I guessed that must have been one of the effects of losing his own father so early. He simply had no real reference points.

Once I had time to digest his last admission, I felt humbled and moved, which was a far cry from angry and resentful. With those few words, he had been willing to trust me, and he had revealed an innocent part of himself. His vulnerability made me particularly glad that I'd spent time getting out some anger prior to our talk. Otherwise, I might have gone into this all-important conversation choosing to blame him and act out. Instead, I had been able to hold a safe space for something truly meaningful.

More than anyone, Robert knew how much this intimate conversation with my father meant to me. We both acknowledged that the nurturing approach we had been learning was likely the reason these astonishing breakthroughs were becoming possible. Excited with what had taken place, we both wanted time to include Gabriel in the celebration.

Dear one, how wonderful it is to see the impact of your new choices and how they opened you and your father into some truly meaningful experiences. How wonderful that you were able to create a loving space for your father to share. Love is what allowed this beautiful new beginning. It is also important to remind you that outer changes become much more possible when inner shifts have been established that can support them. Be clear that what you just experienced was a combination of inner and outer choices. And that is the best combination for creating reliable, healing transformations.

Inspired, I spent a great deal of time in the weeks that followed meditating again on specific moments from my childhood, looking for other choices and perspectives that were no longer serving me as an adult. I made sure to hold a safe space for my inner child, just as I had done with my dad, so that he would begin to express more of the feelings that I'd buried over the years—a natural choice for a nurturing authority to make.

It was also helpful that I had spent so much time during my review thinking about some of the specific words of encouragement I wished my parents had known to say to me. That is what prepared me to offer some of those same messages to my inner child during this next round of meditations.

Several weeks into that deepening process, something new started to nag at me. My father had made such courageous steps in sharing so honestly and vulnerably about himself during his trip. Now it was beginning to dawn on me that I hadn't yet matched him. Until I did, I realized I would still be hiding in fear, and I would ultimately sabotage half of the healing potential that we had begun to explore.

It didn't take me long to identify the choices I needed to make. Once I did, I imagined that I would feel empowered rather than afraid. It was now time to be vulnerable with my father. Facing this new challenge brought up some definite fear. I was more nervous about this step than I had been when I'd asked my father to share.

Speaking with Gabriel prior to taking any next steps was helpful.

In order to consider making this new choice, it is helpful to remember that you have already begun to claim a place of real authority in your own life. Without that foundation, you might go into this next conversation looking for your dad to finally take the position of nurturing authority that you needed as a child. You would be wiser to go into this conversation as the one responsible for holding a safe emotional space for your vulnerability. By creating a space to claim your own feelings out loud, you will be the one who determines that your feelings matter—no matter what your father's response might be.

You are now ready to begin sharing yourself with your father, just for the purpose of sharing your personal truths and feelings. You are the only one who can decide that those experiences are valid. That is a stage of ownership that every young person needs to be encouraged to claim as they grow older. This is the way any one of you learns to stand on your own feet, acknowledging the feelings, opinions, perspectives, and priorities that you value at any given stage—no matter what anyone else thinks, feels, or projects.

If you approach this next conversation with your father as an opportunity to practice being the Source—fully prepared to acknowledge your own value—you will create a space that releases some old fear and shame. These choices will feel more empowering, no matter how your dad chooses to respond or to react. Once again, it is how you feel about yourself that you carry around every day. In addition, if you free the other person from needing to validate you, you will free them to have their own authentic process, which also allows them time to work through whatever feelings they discover in the interaction. This is what would be most loving for you both.

Once I had time to live with Gabriel's suggestions, the adult part of me started to see the wisdom in the suggestions, and only then did I feel calmer about taking this next step. Just before making the call to my father, I took a moment to connect with my inner child. I knew what a big step this was going to be for him, and so I assured him how proud I was of him for taking this powerful step with me. No matter how much time Dad might need to process his feelings about what we were going to share, we were doing this to free ourselves as the top priority. And I acknowledged that it is okay that we sometimes feel scared when making courageous choices.

When my dad answered the phone, I thanked him again for taking the time to talk with me on his recent trip, assuring him how much it had meant to me. I also let him know that I was interested in us continuing to get to know each other. When he seemed open to the idea, I asked him if this was a good time to talk some more. He replied, "Sure," without hesitation.

"I guess I'll start by letting you know that I've been happier with my life in recent years." Though he didn't say anything specific in response, I could feel that he was open and curious to hear what came next. I was then painfully aware that what I most needed to share, I had spent more than a decade hiding—particularly from my dad.

In the brief moment before I continued, I was acutely aware that tons of other young men and women had been rejected after sharing this part of their lives, simply because their individual needs brought up fear and stretched well-protected comfort zones. On the verge of claiming my truth in front of such an important figure, I wasn't sure I was ready to face that possibility. However, I brought the focus back to myself and the fact that I was so ready to let go of being ruled by my own fear. I was determined to clear this hurdle for myself. That much I was in charge of.

I eased myself into the conversation in a rather careful way.

"What you already know is that I've had some awesome opportunities to perform. However, I've also been happy dating a couple of wonderful people over the last few years." Gulp. I could feel a distinct shift in my father's energy.

I had already decided that I didn't want to use any uncomfortable words, like "being gay" as I let my father get to know this intimate part of my life. Therefore, I chose to give hints from a specific experience that he and I had shared a year before. "Actually, you met one of them. We all went to dinner together when I came to North Carolina for my high school reunion. Let's see, where did we go...?" Here, I created an open-ended question, knowing that my dad's response would reveal whether he now understood what I was telling him.

"Country Squire?" he asked after a brief pause.

Relief flooded through me. "Oh, yeah," I affirmed. "That's right." I then continued to share more details about Bryan and some of the fun things we had done together. Right away, I felt relieved to be introducing this important part of my life to my father by making it about two real people. I also remembered how much my father had liked Bryan. And I must admit that I felt particularly comforted by the fact that Bryan had been a linebacker at Michigan State, and he happened to be wearing a Big 10 Championship ring the night he had met my father.

After I finished sharing, my father surprised me yet again. "I'm glad that you've been happy and that you have love in your life."

After we got off the phone, I cried really hard. I then spent some time thinking about how much I wished that the world didn't even need terms like "gay" or "straight" to indicate the specific genders of two people who are having a meaningful relationship. To me, those terms automatically created unnecessary separations. And I had just demonstrated that focusing on the humanity of two people created ease for us both. The fact that everybody goes through the same scope of challenges and gifts, learning how to open to the vulnerabilities of relationships, gave my father and me a clear way to relate to one another's experiences.

Rather quickly, I shifted my focus to being proud of my choice to match my father's courage. The moment also brought me back to how grateful I had been just a year before, when I had shared this important part of my life with my mother and sisters—or to be more accurate, how they had taken the initiative with me.

Soon after my journey to North Carolina, Bryan had ended our relationship—choosing to take all that he had learned in our time together back to a long-term relationship that didn't feel complete for him. At the time, I felt really sad. It just so happened that my mother phoned that very next morning. After hearing me speak only a few words, she had asked me what was wrong. Suddenly I was aware of the separation that my silence about this part of my life had always created in our relationship. "I don't want you to ask a lot of questions, but I could really use your support right now."

"I don't have to ask a lot of questions," she responded gently. "Intimate love relationships can be really difficult." Since she knew that I had just been to North Carolina with Bryan, it was clear that she had understood the closeness of our connection. Once she had made her support so clear to me, tears that I had been holding down for such a long time flooded out of me—finally free.

While I cried, my mom continued. "How can I be there to truly support you unless I tell you that I know you well? I am so proud of the person you have become. You are an amazing man. I also know that when any of us ends an important relationship, it hurts. I love you, sugar."

In the years since my mother had become sober, the four of us in the core family had grown much closer. Therefore, it shouldn't have been surprising when both of my sisters ended up calling on that same day without having first spoken to my mother. Somehow, this was the right time for each one of them to find a unique way of closing the gaps I had put in place, and I gladly received their support.

Now that my dad was also informed and included, I felt a complete freedom that I had longed for since my teens—to be able to live my life in a fully honest, authentic way. I no longer needed to watch everything that came out of my mouth. Once the truth about my personal life had been shared and received, I began to wonder whether the shame I had always felt about myself hadn't been about being gay at all. Perhaps that had only been the most obvious justification I had come up with for hiding anything I feared others wouldn't acknowledge or accept. Perhaps if I hadn't felt confused about my sexuality, I would have come up with other reasons for staying hidden and in shame. After all, my father had made the same choice for most of his life, fearing that no one was interested in really knowing him.

Now that I understood this as a possibility, I began to pay attention to my conversations with others. It seemed that so many of them insinuated at various points that they also carried doubts about their value and lovability. As this became clearer in my mind, I felt such a deep desire to do whatever I could to help others move out of those wounded myths and fears and into the same clarity that I was now beginning to find. At this point, I just wasn't sure how.

14

GRADUAL PERCENTAGES

WHILE I CONTINUED PERFORMING FOR HALF OF the year at Lincoln Center and the other half in various places around the world—which was highlighted with some world premieres in New York and doing other Puccini roles in warm places like California—I continued investing in my time with Gabriel and the community of seekers who had become wonderful friends.

One of the gifts of going to new locations practically every month was that it gave me lots of opportunities to try out new choices. The bigger challenge, having always had sky-high expectations of myself, was not being too hard on myself when I discovered more specific issues that were out of balance.

Fortunately, Gabriel understood my struggle and showed up with constant kindness in the moments I was able to have phone sessions from somewhere on the road. *It is important to understand that the process of lasting transformation is a gradual one for every person. People think they want immediate, profound shifts; however, that desire most often comes from wanting to escape the pain that they've been carrying. We remind you that healthy change takes place in small percentages—giving you time to make discoveries and then build a sense of trust in the new possibilities that you are working toward.*

The level of transformation that you have now reached has been a process of literally re-parenting your own inner child. In order to do that well, you must first identify deeper truths about each subject, and then get clear about some of the choices that will set you up more effectively than what you have known. This is what has prepared you to release the choices that you have decided no longer serve you thus far. And of course, it is always helpful to approach your learning curves with nurturing compassion.

We also suggest that by taking time to become intimate with each step of the transformation process that is required to shift from wounded child to empowered adult, you will become prepared to guide others through their own version of that same journey. Teaching is a choice that has always been configured into your Soul plan as a likely possibility. However, as always, that is a choice that is fully in your hands.

Hearing that we all shift by percentages was helpful. I had so often felt the need to be at the end result of any goal "by yesterday." I knew that slowing down enough to become more intimate and acknowledge each step of my transformation would definitely help me to feel genuinely proud of myself, rather than how I felt when I had worked to prove my worth to others. The more I began to slow down, calming the habitual impatience of my inner child, the clearer I became about setting myself up well. It was simple. Certain choices naturally inspired peace, and others left me in frustration or yearning most of the time.

Once I began to simplify each of the steps I was identifying, I gradually whittled it down to one simple practice: asking myself, as often as I could remember, "What choices could I make in this moment that would leave me feeling great about myself?" Asking and answering this one question is what helped me create some of my greatest breakthroughs. As a matter of fact, this simple question gradually became my one guiding principle. And while I was happy to be coming up with wiser approaches, I definitely accepted that I still had tons to learn.

Sometimes the challenges that Life offered, as the Soul's attempt to bring wounded feelings to the surface, were quite intense, particularly when I faced more than one challenge at a time. One of those perfect storms began when I was on stage performing the world premiere of a new opera at Lincoln Center. The first sign of trouble came as I was getting into my costume backstage. That is when I noticed that my right ear felt a bit clogged.

It didn't take long into the first act for things to become much worse. Within minutes, both of my ears became so clogged that I could hardly hear a thing. The sensation was very much like one that I'd had as a child—putting a finger in each ear and then talking, the sound of my voice would resonate inside my own head. Only now that it was happening in such an intense setting, I realized that almost nothing from the outside could get in.

Singing over a full orchestra, without a microphone, and filling a space big enough for three thousand seats is a tricky thing, even under the best of conditions. Healthy hearing is crucial to do that successfully. Once my ears became blocked, I began to panic. I knew this modern opera had all kinds of high notes for me to hit over the next couple of hours. It was hard to simply concentrate, much less be effective as an actor. I could barely hear the orchestra—particularly once I began singing. I felt so vulnerable, without any real solutions, that tears began to stream down my cheeks. The only thing that played in my favor was that I have what is known as relative perfect pitch. For me, this meant that I was able to remember what a particular line of music felt like in the muscle memory of my throat once I had sung it a number of times. I'll just say that I had to count on all my gifts to get through that opening act.

As soon as the curtain came down for intermission, I ran downstairs to the conductor's dressing room. Christopher Keene, who happened to be the main director of the company at the time, was also the maestro conducting this world premiere. As soon as he opened his door, I blurted out, "Am I singing on pitch?" He looked a bit shocked that I would ask such a thing. "I know that's a strange question, but something is going on with my ears, and I can't hear a thing, not even the orchestra."

He was immediately reassuring and helpful. "Do you think you can get through this next act, Ron? I assure you that you are singing on pitch. For now, if you need help in this second half, just look at me and I will indicate the best I can if an adjustment is needed or affirm that all is well." As vulnerable as I felt, it was also wonderful knowing that I wouldn't be going through the second act quite as alone.

Fortunately, for the rest of the performance, Maestro Keene gave me quick nods of affirmation anytime I happened to catch his glance from the pit. The day after what had been a harrowing performance for me, I got myself to an ear/nose/throat specialist. After examination, we discovered that the nasal passages that go from my nose to my ears were unusually narrow. Apparently, I had developed a mild infection and the swelling that resulted had literally blocked those passages enough to shut down my capacity to hear. The doctor also discovered that the infection had resulted in fluid becoming trapped in my inner ear.

"This is the bigger challenge because this will foster bacteria to grow. If untreated, that phenomenon could destroy the tender mechanisms of your inner ears. In short, you could lose your hearing altogether. To avoid this, we need to get you into the hospital for surgery as soon as possible."

At the same time I was presented with that challenge, I happened to be dating an exuberant, sweet man from Brazil named Aldo. He was a very generous guy who worked an incredible number of hours to help his family back home. He was also a big fan of opera, and so he loved being involved in my crazy life. The week before I went into the hospital, he discovered that he, too, had some unexpected issues to work out. Not knowing how to add one more thing to his already full plate, he decided that the best way for him to relieve some pressure was to let go of our relationship. Feeling that he had no space or energy to consider anyone else's needs, he simply moved into self-preservation.

No matter the reason, breakups don't feel good; however, on top of going into the hospital for career-threatening surgery, it just sucked. At the same time, I was aware of how far my family lived from New York. None of us had lots of money, so traveling by plane was not something that any of us did very often. Still unable to give up playing the strong guy who never admitted that he had actual needs—perhaps still influenced by early experiences like having spoken up about wanting horseback riding lessons—I downplayed the seriousness of the situation and ended up going through the whole experience almost completely alone. Fortunately, Robert and a couple of other friends were there to check in on me.

Still. So many challenges at once made each of them seem worse than they would have been otherwise. Throughout the ordeal, I felt alone, abandoned, rejected, insecure, unsure about the future, and therefore, unsafe and resentful. With so much to juggle, I collapsed into a pit of wounded feelings. Who knows? Perhaps I needed an experience this intense to realize how out of balance I was where receiving and acknowledging my own needs were concerned.

There was one moment when it all erupted and got the better of me. When I'd first begun to regain consciousness in the recovery room after surgery, my doctor said, "We have drilled through several inches of bone, creating a wider passage, and to support that new structure, your head is literally packed with yards of gauze. Just make sure that if the edge of that packing begins to show up in your throat, you don't start swallowing it. If you do..." at which point his voice trailed off and I slipped out of consciousness again.

Sure enough, the first time I woke up in my new hospital room, which I discovered I was sharing with an unknown roommate, an end piece of that gauze was hanging in the back of my throat. Much like when food is lodged there, every instinct in my body told me to swallow what was there. At the same time, I remembered the first part of my instruction. I just couldn't remember why this was such a threat. Therefore, I panicked and hit the button to call for help.

When the attending physician arrived and I told him what was happening, he lashed out. "I cannot believe that you called me in here for this. I have serious problems to deal with, and this is just silly." His callousness pushed me over the edge. Not recognizing myself, I grabbed him by the tie and pulled him closer—within inches of my face. "I have never had surgery in my life or even been in the hospital as an adult. I'm feeling vulnerable and afraid. I thought you were supposed to be here to help. And I need help. Please!" It was all I could do not to choke on the packing in my throat as I finally expressed some of my pent-up feelings.

Once the surgeon clipped the offending gauze and left, the stranger who was my roommate jumped in to champion me. "If you hadn't said something, I was going to come over there and do it for you. That guy was an ass." How cool to be championed by a complete stranger.

Though I knew I hadn't expressed myself in the best of ways, that moment made a real impression on me. It seems that all the feelings I had ignored by not letting others know that I needed help had come up in that moment. Though I did need support from the doctor, I was half responsible for the issue. Being stoic had proved nothing except that I was unwise. It was yet another choice I had been making that didn't set me up well.

The whole situation made me grateful to have spent time building up trust with Gabriel, to whom I eventually vented about this convergence of challenges. "I feel like I can't trust anyone! No one really cares about me. I had to go through most of this alone. I now realize I've been doing that my whole life, and I'm sick of it! When I think back, I can see that I've been angry at tons of people—like all the authority figures who have done such shitty jobs at being leaders, guides, and nurturers!"

Though I knew this was not the whole truth, but rather the perspective of the wounded child for the most part, it was still crucial to get those sentiments out. Otherwise, I would have continued carrying that energy around in my body. Gabriel assured me this was a necessary part of everyone's healing process, and so I took him up on the opportunity to continue expressing some of my long-suppressed anger—and sometimes rage—in future sessions. There were a couple of meetings when I yelled so hard about what I was negotiating that I ended up losing my voice for a day or two. That was not a decision I took lightly, being a professional singer.

What I eventually discovered was that I had grown so accustomed to avoiding any less-than-acceptable parts of myself that I had never understood how much those wounded feelings were building up inside me. I had so often tried to diminish anything that would reveal weakness because I didn't want to seem like less of a man. At some point, I even came up with a spiritual justification for avoiding my anger: "My Soul set up this challenge. It must be serving some important purpose. Therefore, I shouldn't get so upset about this." Ha! The truth was, I didn't want to be a burden or want people to get upset with me. I was afraid that if I upset them, they would leave.

Once again, I needed to face the fear directly, as an adult, and I had reached a point when I simply couldn't hold the feelings down any longer. I was pissed and deeply sad about so many things. I had moments that felt threatening or diminishing, moments that I had felt forgotten or misguided, and I knew it didn't serve me to continue suppressing and building pressure. So I didn't.

I slowly began to process regular release sessions, honoring different moments from my history and finally championing the child with a safe place to express and release it all. It helped that Gabriel affirmed and encouraged my new choices. *As long as you get the feelings out in a responsible way, such as in private sessions, being sure not to act them out at anyone, you will most often feel relieved and calmer. If you don't release them, quite often they will seep out, and you will find yourself acting out before you can take charge of the moment as the adult. This is why it was helpful that you emptied some charged feelings prior to asking for a conversation with your father not too long ago. For now, know that this new approach will require a gradual learning curve, and you will likely fail any number of times along the way. Shift by percentages. Do your best to remember that you are safe and you are loved when it all seems overwhelming.*

I did my best to use those tools for admitting, expressing, and releasing feelings with sound, often yelling into a pillow to honor whatever was coming up from the inside. Over time, I released the pressure cooker in a more complete way than I had before. Most often, I felt safer, and the process of working through conflicted situations became easier.

The last challenge that emerged as a part of this most recent cluster took place two weeks after I left the hospital, when I stopped by to see my agents. Almost immediately upon entering, both agents looked up. From the awkward pause that followed, I could tell that they were trying to work out why I had just shown up. One of them eventually said, "Weren't you just in Detroit performing?"

A bit stunned that yet another set of authority figures who were supposed to be core supporters had no idea what was going on with me—and this had become a pattern with these two—I was momentarily speechless. However, it was also clear that this was an important moment of choice. Do I continue in the same old ways, or do I speak up and take care of my deeper needs?

Without hesitation, I made a decision. "I'm afraid it is time for us to part ways," I said in a voice that was calmer than I felt. When they asked me why, I reminded them that I'd just had a major surgery that could have ended my career. They both looked embarrassed but said nothing. I also knew that they had hardly ever come to see me perform over the years, even though I was offered many roles at Lincoln Center, which was only six blocks from their office.

The first response was "Why are you leaving?"

I merely said, "Do you really want me to lay it all out?"

Then the other one said, "Where are you going? Who will represent you?"

"I don't know yet," I replied honestly.

"Well, that's just not good business to leave one agent before you find a new one."

Perhaps they were trying to convince me to stay. I didn't know.

Though I didn't say it out loud, I wanted them to know that I was leaving them because of their disappointing behaviors, not because I had found a better deal. It was simply that I was finally ready to interrupt unsupportive relationships in my life, particularly with people who were supposed to have my back. I hoped my gesture would give a clear message to the Universe and to my inner child that this was no longer okay with me.

Fortunately, it seemed that the Universe responded, affirming that outer shifts are easier once the inner shifts have been made. This time, I was sitting in my apartment on a random afternoon watching television when the phone rang.

"Hello. Is this Ron?"

"Yes," I replied, not recognizing the voice on the other end of the line.

"This is Marilyn Horne."

I could hardly believe it! Marilyn Horne was an icon in the opera world, and she was calling me. The only person more famous in that world was Pavarotti.

Ms. Horne shared that a friend of hers had just told her all about me. "I was wondering if you'd be willing to come and sing for me next week."

After I almost dropped the phone, we agreed to the following Friday. "I'll get Carnegie Hall," she said. "Just show up at three o'clock, and know that I'll only have about ten minutes. I look forward to hearing you. Bye now."

Thrilled, I showed up to the stage door of Carnegie Hall well before my time to sing. I didn't want to take any chances that I would be late, which often happens in New York City because of traffic or subways.

Knowing that Ms. Horne was a Rossini specialist, I chose to sing one of my favorite Rossini arias from *Guillaume Tell*. After I sang, she said nothing, but asked for a second aria and then a third, which I knew was taking us well beyond ten minutes. She then called me from the stage to come down into the auditorium and chat.

She had many nice things to say, and then she questioned me about the progression of my career. This eventually included her musing aloud, "Why are you not singing Billy Bigelow in the Broadway production of *Carousel*? I went earlier this week and think you would have been the perfect choice."

Little did she know that I had been one of the final two or three candidates up for the role.

"Who's your agent?" was her next question. When I told her that I had recently left my agent, she asked where I was planning to go. I explained that I had just done an audition for Jeff Vanderveen at CAMI, and I explained that I wasn't sure what would happen there, since they were going through a process of downsizing. She took in all of the information and then thanked me for coming.

The very next day, I got a call from Jeff's office. "We've decided to take you on as a client. We just ask that you keep this to yourself for a few weeks."

I thanked the woman who had phoned, and as I was preparing to end the call, she surprised me with, "By the way, did you know that Marilyn Horne called here on your behalf?"

Smiling, I got off the phone, deeply grateful for such a clear sign of support and a new place to land, both of which I considered beautiful affirmations that I had shifted something powerful in my recent decision to interrupt a very practiced pattern. In that moment I felt both humbled and encouraged.

By this time in my empowerment process, I was not surprised that our lives are inevitably structured with the next challenges to work through. I knew at this point that the process of facing challenges allows us to claim more levels of our personal potential. Only a few days after getting the offer from CAMI, I sat down to meditate with my inner child. When I started the conversation with "I love you," the child promptly retorted. "That is crap! You only love me when things are going well or after you've achieved something impressive." Ouch. It seemed I wasn't the only one ready to be more honest.

After taking a moment to absorb what I'd just heard, I was glad that my inner child felt safe enough to call me out—something I had occasionally wanted to do with others when I was younger. It seemed it was now time to receive a little of the medicine I had begun to dish out. After more conversation, I realized that what he was trying to tell me was that I hadn't been very good at honoring and holding a safe space for some of the more vulnerable, less developed parts of me that I had perceived as weak or unlovable.

That moment felt like the inner child was trying to re-parent me. It was a reminder that I needed to hold an even greater space for what seemed like an endless litany of wounds and confusions. Once I made the choice to face this one, I imagined that Life would soon present me with opportunities for practicing the new, healthier choices that were necessary—basically, chances to "put my money where my mouth is" in real time. Of course, I was not disappointed. Chances to practice soon revealed themselves.

I was hired as one of four singers from New York who would lead a holiday extravaganza with a major orchestra in a city that shall remain unnamed. For that production, they hired dancers, a puppet troupe, and a large chorus. Everything about the rehearsal process went well, all the way through the final dress rehearsal. That final evening included an invited audience, which was an important chance to deal with nerves and get honest feedback about the show. Fortunately, that final run-through went well, and we all left the theater happy and gratified.

Our first official performance was scheduled for the following day, so the four of us from New York expected to have a needed day of rest. What happened instead was that each of us received an early morning call from the director's office. Much to our surprise, we needed to come in for an unexpected meeting. They did give us hints that they would make some surprising cuts to the show. They suggested that the show had run long, which we all knew was not the case. Nevertheless, we all jumped in a car and went to the theater together, each of us clearly frustrated.

When we arrived, we were surprised that so many people had been invited. The head of the symphony, the musical director, the production director, and some of the office staff made us a group of about fifteen people who sat around a long boardroom table. Two of the directors began by offering the same story we had all just heard on our respective calls.

"We want to make sure everyone understands the need for a shorter version of the show. As you have been told, we will be eliminating all of the major songs from *A Christmas Carol*. This is what we feel works best."

What was so surprising was that the songs from that segment of the show had been some of the test audience's obvious favorites, clearly predicated by their enthusiastic applause. This boiled down to several songs being done by the four leads from New York, and one sung by the sweet six-year-old boy they had hired to play Tiny Tim. It's hard to explain the strong feelings that came up for me, now that we were hearing the story in person.

I knew that none of us from New York felt we were being honored with the truth, which we had discussed in the car on the way to the meeting. The fact that we were on point was later confirmed secretly by someone on the staff. Our best guess was that the resident composer must have been upset by the enthusiastic response that series of songs had received, while the response to his pieces had only been lukewarm. While it was easy to understand his disappointment, it still didn't seem acceptable to allow that to impact so many other people.

The longer I sat there listening to the story, the more I began to feel this was somehow a destiny moment for me. It became deeply clear that I was being faced with a bold set of choices to speak up and claim a new depth of myself—definitely a new sensation for me. My old default would have been to please the authority figures in the room by trying to protect how I was perceived. However, at this moment, something more important was brewing inside me. Finally, expressing that inner truth felt more important.

When the director finished speaking, he looked around the table at all of us. When he came to me, he said, "It seems clear that you have something you need to say, Ron."

I gathered myself and prepared to share with as much honesty and heart as I could manage.

"I'm sure there must be important reasons that you're making these choices. And while I fully honor that you must choose whatever you think is best for the show, I want to focus for a minute on the sweet little boy who is playing Tiny Tim. Just last week you cut half of his song. After you delivered the news, we all watched his mother back him up against a wall, only to shame him by saying, 'If you'd been good enough, they wouldn't have cut your song.' It was heartbreaking to witness."

At this point, I started to get more emotional. "Now, the morning of the show, you are telling us that you're cutting more songs. As an adult, I feel confused and disappointed. You happen to be cutting my favorite moment from the show. While I may be able to handle that choice, he is only six years old. And I can't let this moment pass without speaking up. With all due respect, he is just as important as you are, as the head of this symphony and you, as the director of the show. To me, he's like the child inside each one of us. So I simply ask that you consider what he will likely have to endure if you cut the rest of his song."

As I shared those last few sentences, a wonderful level of what I will describe as heart passion bubbled up in me, causing a few tears to escape down my cheeks.

When I had finished sharing, there was obvious tension in the room. To be honest, I was hoping that some of the other three singers might join in to back up what I had shared. After all, they had all been so vocal in the car ride over. Then I remembered how new this choice was for me. This was the first time I had made a decision to stand so fully in a truth like this, and I needed to have more compassion for them in that moment as well—though that one took me a few days to reach.

Eventually, the director of the orchestra spoke again. "You've given us a lot to think about, Ron. Thank you all for coming. Have a good show tonight."

At that point, most of us stood and moved out into the hall, and it was clear to me that none of the other singers felt comfortable to stand with me right away. However, the one who did come over was our musical arranger, a man whose formidable gifts had been obvious from the time he was a teenager. Even when he was in high school, he had done musical arrangements for celebrities like Liza Minelli. As the story went, the egos and pressures of being in the music industry had eventually gotten to him. He was now choosing to only do one gig per year.

Once he was standing next to me, he said, "I just want you to know that until the moment that just took place in that room, I didn't understand why I chose this as my one job for this year. However, what I just witnessed was the most Christ-like thing I've ever seen. I want to thank you for your courage and your compassion." Then he joked, "Based on who you've shown yourself to be, I predict you will either have a very long...or a very short career."

We both laughed.

Later that day, we all got another call, letting us know that they had chosen to cut all of the songs from *A Christmas Carol*—except for Tiny Tim's ballad. I was so pleased. In every performance, when we reached his moment to shine, I beamed with pride for him. As he sang with such an innocent heart, I was reminded that sometimes it is indeed possible for compassionate truth to affect others' lives.

I was also thrilled that my inner child was now bursting at the seams, proud that I had shifted my commitment to move beyond protecting myself from being seen in a negative light. He now felt more convinced that I was someone he could count on. While there were still people on the staff who felt more distant in the weeks that followed, I remained steadfast that this had truly been a destiny moment for me.

Even better, that is not where the story ends. When we completed the final performance of that holiday extravaganza, we were all invited to a cast party, which included close friends and family. While everyone was unwinding over food and drink, I was presented with another important opportunity. This time it involved a moment with the six-year-old's mother.

"I just wanted you to know how much we all enjoyed working with your son. I would also like to tell you a story, one that I hope you will pass on to him at some point when he needs a real boost in his life," I said.

"After our final dress rehearsal, the staff realized that the show was too long, and they needed to make some cuts," I told her. "Because we are the leads, they were originally focused on taking out songs performed by other people. However, when they brought up cutting your son's song, we all jumped in and said, 'No. Don't do it. He's wonderful. Cut our songs instead.'"

Her eyes widened with shock and then began to well up with tears. After a moment of taking in what I had shared, she thanked me. I smiled and simply moved on to say more goodbyes. When I left the concert hall that night, I felt as if I had moved through a powerful initiation. I now knew what it felt like to risk moving through fear to stand in the courage of my personal truth.

Somehow, I knew this meant that fear would no longer hold the same sway over me that it had previously. By deciding to move toward things that truly mattered to me, I had taken back my personal power in unexpected, meaningful ways. And I definitely felt good about my choices. There it was again: my one guiding principle. I was indeed shifting by percentages—only this time, the percentages were a little bigger than usual—and I was also choosing to become the kind of man I most wanted to be.

15

OUT OF THE FRYING PAN, INTO THE FIRE

WHEN I GOT BACK TO NEW YORK AFTER THE CON-cert, I discovered another sensitive arena that needed some of my newfound honesty. My primary relationship. For a little over a year, I had been dating a warm, creative, and success-ful man I will call Sam. While I valued many things about Sam as an individual, there were some core issues that were constantly limiting our connection. The main frustration was that Sam wasn't open about his sexuality with most of his close friends or family. This meant he couldn't be open about my place in his life.

From the very beginning of our relationship, he had asked me to sup-port those limits. For a while, I was willing, as I believe it's important that we accept people where they are, and then grow with them moving forward. The only problem was that over the course of a year, there were no signs Sam was making any forward moves. Even after a year of living together, he still asked that I not answer the phone in our apartment. Since we didn't have cell phones in the early nineties, this meant I was cut off from people being able to reach out to me directly. Instead, my friends had to call, leave a message, and then wait to see if I picked up or called them back right away. In short, it was a major pain, and some of them questioned why I was willing to do such a thing.

There was the issue of spending time with his friends, with me introduced as his buddy. Even though I fully understood his fear of exposure and rejection, I hoped that as we became closer, he would make some shifts. However, his refusal to progress meant that I was back in hiding. I had done that for so long that over time, it became really frustrating for me.

Sam was also uncomfortable with some of my spiritual explorations; talking to an Archangel went well beyond any explorations he had considered. When he suggested that channeling might even be a conflict with his religion, I was stunned. Though I appreciated his honesty, I knew these were all areas we would need to resolve if we were going to stay together.

I responded to this last conflict by simply asking if he thought that being gay was bad and wrong.

"No. Of course not," he replied.

I asked him why he was so sure.

He merely said, "Because my experiences are loving and good. Just take our connection, for example."

"I am glad you see that because I want to make that same point to you about my explorations of spirituality," I said. "You are worried about what people in your religion might think, while those same people might tell you that your relationship with me is wrong and bad. I just ask that you evaluate what I'm choosing based on what you are experiencing with me as well. I have assured you that my experiences have been loving and good, and you can answer for yourself whether you see anything about my choices that seems unloving in any way."

While he agreed that my choices had all seemed healthy and loving, he continued to question and negate that part of me on a number of occasions.

Eventually, while I was away doing another show, I took time to evaluate the constancy of these issues. I realized that as long as my partner chose to negate my choices and to keep our relationship hidden, we would always have frustrating walls between us. I didn't need him to embrace my choices as his own, but I did need him to trust and support me to be my best self.

When I added these impasses to his lack of forward moves, I decided it was time to end the relationship. Although we cared for each other a great deal, it was too important for me to stand in my own deepest truth. Only then could I set myself up well. Because I had spent so many years wanting this kind of close connection, this was a difficult decision. However, at this point in my life, being true to myself was more important than my fear of being alone.

Even though a breakup would require that I work through a myriad of feelings, I was much happier than I had ever been—on a clear trajectory of improving my own life. I even used the roles I was portraying on stage to release old energies. Free to express the feelings of villains and heroes, young soldiers, and even middle-aged grumps made me an even better actor.

I also learned a great deal about being true to my deepest feelings from my acting teacher, Diaan Ainslee. A particularly intuitive woman who encourages her students to identify and express whatever they are feeling "moment to moment," Diaan's class gave me consistent opportunities to explore and release whatever was coming up in my life. From anger and rage to deep levels of raw vulnerability, I was learning to feel much safer emotionally being seen in Diaan's class.

The other place I was offered a safe emotional space was in my weekly therapy sessions with Lula, a gifted bioenergetics therapist. I will always be grateful for having these two powerful women in my life. They were both well-informed, courageous authority figures who taught me a long list of healthy approaches.

At this point in my process, I felt deeply supported on a Soul level, reinforced by numerous chances to practice all that I was learning.

While performing a Strauss opera at the Kennedy Center in Washington, DC, I was offered a powerful chance to stretch through some fears. *Ariadne auf Naxos* happens to be a play within a play. In the first act, we meet a group of actors backstage at a theater, all preparing to perform an opera. The second act then reveals those same actors performing the actual opera, providing the audience with a more personal connection to the players.

For this production, I was cast as the Harlequin, the lead baritone in the second act. One of our performances happened to be scheduled on the night that DC faced a big snowstorm. Living in a rented apartment close by, I could make my way to the theater rather easily. As I was just finishing up getting my makeup and wig applied for the evening, Ed Purrington, the head of the company, rushed in.

"Ron, I'm afraid we have a problem. John Shirley Quirk"—who was singing the baritone lead in the first act—"is stuck in this ice storm, and he won't be able to get here in time for the performance. The audience is already being seated and there's no time for us to bring in someone who knows the role. You're the only other baritone in the show. Therefore, you're our only hope." Then he shocked me by saying, "Would you be willing to go on stage with a musical score in your hands and sight-sing your way through the role?"

I don't know if I can adequately convey all the things his request would require. The opera was being performed in German, and just reading those foreign words aloud for the first time was a big ask. There would be no time to translate and understand the words, much less make sure that I had the correct pronunciations. I would also be sight-reading musical lines that were not melodic and often required huge leaps, making it harder to be vocally accurate. It's a process singers would spend weeks preparing, so the shifts the muscles needed to make would align with healthy vocal technique. And if that wasn't enough, all of those things would be negotiated in front of a large, educated audience. This was the Kennedy Center, after all!

Then it occurred to me that I would be in strange costumes and a wig. I had no idea about the blocking—which are the movements that a character has to go through in the various scenes he shares with other actors. This meant I wouldn't even know where I needed to stand or to whom I would need to speak when I delivered each line. And though that was enough to make any sane person faint, there was more to consider. For this performance, there would be a guest conductor who was brought in to make his important debut on that particular evening. None of us had ever laid eyes on him!

Oh, my God. What is happening? If I said no, they would have to refund thousands of expensive tickets. We only had one more performance two days later, after which the entire cast would be leaving DC. There were simply no dates to add a make-up performance if this show didn't happen.

No time to think. Mr. Purrington is standing there, waiting for an immediate decision. I heard one voice shouting in my head, *Are you friggin' kidding me? I'd have to be insane to consider this!* And yet, I had that same feeling that this was another destiny moment. Apparently, that voice was loud and encouraging because I definitely heard the words "Sure, let's do it" as they passed from my lips.

Minutes later, they made an announcement over the intercom informing the audience that there would be a fifteen-minute delay to allow for a last-minute change in the cast. All the while, I was quickly getting out of my harlequin makeup and being put into a new wig and costume. Taking advantage of every moment, I began frantically reading my way through the first phrases of German. I figured that if I could become somewhat familiar with the words, prior to going to my dressing room, I would then speak those first phrases out loud. I would at least give myself some initial familiarity before trying to add music out on the stage in front of thousands of strangers.

In theory, this was a smart approach. However, what I found when I opened the first page was a reminder that I would be making the first entrance all by myself, immediately uttering a tongue-twisting phrase that had to be repeated three times really fast: "Mein Herr Haushofmeister. Mein Herr Haushofmeister. Mein Herr Haushofmeister!"

Once I was in the safe haven of my dressing room, I knew I would only have a couple of minutes by myself to practice speaking those crazy-long German words before they called me to the stage. By now the pressure was really building inside me. As it turned out, I had become so ungrounded that I couldn't even speak the first phrase accurately, and I was all by myself at this point. Stumbling and struggling over the words put me in a bit of a frenzy. It all happened so quickly that I actually burst into laughter at the very moment that the new conductor walked into my dressing room to introduce himself.

When he heard me failing so horribly and then seeming rather hysterical, he didn't say a word. He simply turned around and stormed out. I then heard him yelling in the hallway, "We cannot do this! It is not possible!" While that did very little to boost my confidence, the show still needed to go on.

All I could manage, once I found myself standing behind the Kennedy Center's velvet curtain, was a quick reminder that this would be a once-in-a-lifetime chance to face some deep-seated fears—very similar to some theater nightmares I had experienced over the years—where I would find myself out on an unfamiliar stage, completely naked, without knowing any of my lines. This wasn't far off.

It was hard to stop the panicked chatter in my head. I had spent so much time trying to look good in front of others. I was now facing the possibility of public failure in the real brick-and-mortar world—at the *Kennedy Center*, no less. For a moment, I became the eight-year-old me who had stood at the door of a basketball gym for tryouts without ever having held a basketball.

And yet, in some small space, there was a solid, quiet voice reminding me that I was as prepared as any other human could likely be for this challenge. That is when I heard the stage manager making a more complete announcement on the intercom about what the audience was about to witness.

Instead of what she conveyed in her professional, polished tones, I thought she should have said, "You won't believe it. Some crazy guy in our cast has just confirmed that he is indeed insane. He's about to come out onstage, practically blindfolded, and attempt to sight-read some crazy-ass music, reading words that have more letters than his wackadoodle mind can wrap his head around, all the while trying to stay conscious. Enjoy the show!"

With most of the cast crowded in the wings to watch the spectacle, I gripped the musical score I had barely begun to glance over and knew that the applause I was hearing meant that the equally hysterical conductor was now in place. Right away, the music began, and I was literally pushed out onto the stage like an episode of *I Love Lucy* come to life—once again all by myself as I faced those three difficult phrases. Just getting through those first lines felt like a little miracle, one that should certainly be written about in some book of too-strange-to-be-believed anecdotes. I now had only about a hundred more pages to go.

Constantly looking down at the score meant that I didn't have a second to look out at the audience, or even at my fellow actors, if I'm honest. I would sing a few phrases and then become aware of one person after another whispering, "Go over there now." Shuffling from one position to the next, I tried to wrap my brain around the stream of words and music without losing my place in the score. Whenever I made a mistake, there was no time to do anything but continue on. When some of the high notes came out surprisingly well, there was no time to celebrate. Just move forever onward.

At some point in the process, I noticed that time began to slow. Only then did I discover my body going into a survival mode that I had never experienced or realized was possible. Apparently, when fear becomes extreme enough, everything is perceived in slow motion, creating the illusion of having time to process what is happening. For the rest of the act, as I continued committing my butt off, page after endless page, I was living in that slow-motion world.

When we finally reached the end of the act, the applause coming from the audience and from the cast standing backstage was a brief, welcome relief. Without a moment to take it in, I was rushed back into makeup to get ready for my role in the second act. However, even within those familiar structures, my body was still in too much shock to remember much of what happened as the Harlequin—not even the gymnastics that I had to pull out of my past for that particular role.

When it was all said and done, I was numb from the adrenaline that still coursed through my body. The one thing I remember before finally falling into a deep sleep for the night was thinking that I would almost certainly never face anything that scared me in this same way again.

Two days later, when we were scheduled for a final performance, John Shirley-Quirk was back to perform his role in the first act. I was relieved to only be singing the role I had rehearsed. Fortunately, we had other wonderful distractions to look forward to in this performance. For this final run of *Ariadne*, two Supreme Court justices would join us on stage: Ruth Bader Ginsberg—someone I admired beyond words— and her dear friend, Antonin Scalia.

CNN was also in the theater to film this rare occasion. At the end of the show, we all had our pictures taken together for *People* magazine, and then there was a beautiful surprise waiting for me. Mr. Purrington came forward and handed me a "Courage Award." When I opened the small blue velvet box, I found two metal exercise balls that were intended for strengthening someone's hands. Inside the case were the engraved words he read aloud: "Ron's Extra Set." We all had a good laugh. And I was grateful that this challenging destiny moment was behind me.

After spending so much time identifying choices that no longer served me—choices I needed to replace or let go of—I decided it was high time that I also focused on celebrating my breakthroughs. After all, claiming

Self is not all about looking for weaknesses and gaps. Nurturing and championing our gifts and breakthroughs is vital for balancing and remaining motivated. Fortunately, I found many things to celebrate with my inner child. He and I had gotten so much better at nurturing feelings, facing fears, and treating ourselves well. I had even gotten better at asking for support from others; one of the most fulfilling places I had begun to practice this was with the amazing women in my family.

What helped was considering that when I asked someone for support, it meant that I trusted them and valued what they had to offer. That, of course, only mirrored how much I loved it when someone trusted and valued me. Basically, I was learning that these exchanges of true support encourage both people with the crucial message we all seek: "You matter."

The more I grew into my more authentic Self, there was one more truth I needed to face. Though I knew this truth might involve letting go of my biggest source of validation, I needed to admit that I wasn't feeling fulfilled in my career in the world of opera. My first guess as to why this might be led me to the fact that I'd never proactively chosen this specific path. It was more like it had chosen me, and I had merely walked through the opening doors.

Now that I was capable of a more informed evaluation, there were many aspects of life as an opera singer that I didn't like. I wanted to sing with a broader spectrum of sounds and colors than opera would often allow. I also didn't enjoy going from one show to the next so quickly. As was always the case, I wanted time to invest in deeper connections than those short stints ever allowed.

Don't get me wrong. I was still deeply grateful for the opportunities I had been offered. I simply felt compelled to evaluate what I needed and wanted for the next stage of my life. No matter what I chose, I knew it would need to support the possibility of having core relationships as a real priority. I also wanted freedom to spend more time with my family. By this time, we had added three wonderful nieces and a nephew to our ranks, all of whom were precious to me.

Once each of those priorities was clear, I began to prepare for change. I had been studying with Gabriel for seven years, and I felt a growing urgency to pass on the life-changing body of inspiring information that we had received to more people. How I would do that was still unclear. Nevertheless, it was a growing desire that I could no longer ignore.

No matter where I traveled in the world, I had started paying close attention to how much other people seemed to be longing for more complete answers and more fulfilling approaches. I had already enjoyed many opportunities to share about the key things I had been learning and working on in my own life. And I loved how people seemed so touched, hearing that we are all sacred individuals on unique Soul journeys.

I longed to reach more people with nurturing tools and the inspiring details of a Soul journey. And I imagined that to open more doors, I must become more widely known in the world. I wasn't sure if that meant attempting to do more musical theater, aiming for Broadway shows, or going to LA to start making inroads into the film and television industry. The only thing that was clear to me was that I needed to make some distinct shifts.

16

HELPING
AND HEALING

HILE MOST OF MY PERFORMANCES WERE BOOKED well in advance, one opportunity that came along out of the blue ended up being a great reminder that my travels were not just about building a career and making money. They also provided chances to impact people's lives.

Though it was unusual in the early nineties for Americans to travel to Russia, I was invited to perform in the first American opera ever produced at the world-famous Bolshoi Theater. *The Balcony* is an opera based on a play by Jean Genet. And although it wasn't one of my favorite shows by any stretch, being able to spend time in a country considered both mysterious and inaccessible to most Americans at the time was remarkable.

The cast and crew for our show all stayed in the one hotel that was reserved for foreigners. No Russian citizens were allowed inside, though we grew accustomed to seeing the young Russian soldiers guarding each entrance. Having always been an adventurer, I didn't limit my movements to going back and forth from the hotel to the theater, as many people in our company did. Instead, I ventured out as often as possible to explore the historic city of Moscow.

Whether I was visiting famous sites or riding the subway—which was filled with rich wood and beautiful chandeliers that had originally hung in one of the tsar's palaces—I talked with anyone I could find who spoke some English. Many of my new friendships began at the neighborhood gym, which was just a couple of blocks from the hotel. The guys I met there seemed just as excited to connect with an American as I was getting to know them. They appreciated how much I wanted to learn some of their native Russian.

Being someone who loves languages, this was actually the first time I had traveled to a country without already having a capacity to communicate in basic conversational phrases. Over time, I found out that some of my new friends were involved in what was conveyed to me as "the underground," though they were careful to protect me from that part of their lives. While I was grateful they didn't tell me until the end of my stay, I had to admit that it added a distinct level of intrigue to my journey.

One of the most interesting discoveries we revealed to one another was a rather pervasive message we had all received when we were young. Growing up during the Cold War, we'd all been told that people from the other country wanted to dominate or kill the people from our country. When I assured them that I had never personally known anyone who felt that way, they affirmed the same thing was true about the everyday people from their beautiful homeland. Grateful to be stewards of deeper truths at a time when it was rare to be allowed a visit to our respective nations, we moved past those myths quickly, allowing our own experiences to teach us more about what was possible.

Like the citizens of so many other countries I had visited, all of the Russians I met simply wanted the freedom to create meaningful lives. Desiring to do my part to be a positive influence and encouragement, I found simple ways to honor them. One thing that occurred to me was inviting handfuls of them to come to the Bolshoi for a performance. It seemed that many of them hadn't been able to consider such a choice before. When I showed up with tickets, they were really happy and appreciative.

At the hotel, through the repetition of all my comings and goings, some of the guards also became familiar. One day when I was returning from the gym, one of them approached me. With very little English at his command, he asked if I would consider participating in an arm-wrestling match with one of his comrades. I loved the idea of getting to make a more personal connection, so we agreed we would do it later that evening.

After I ate in a basement-level restaurant of the hotel, I headed back up to the lobby to find the guy who had approached me. For the first time since we had arrived, I found the outer lobby jammed with people. I was pondering what might be going on to have drawn such a crowd when it hit me. Oh, my God. Apparently, more people were curious about Americans than I had guessed, and now all of these people had come to see this American visitor arm wrestle with one of their own.

Rather quickly, the guy who had set things up found me and guided me over to a small table. That's when I noticed a much larger man with a serious face and lots of muscles emerging from the crowd. Once we took our seats, my opponent simply stared at me and waited. I wondered if he might be trying to intimidate me or if it was simply that we didn't have the option of language. For a moment, I even felt like we were doing a scene from a *Rocky* movie.

The officiator soon came forward, got us into position, and then placed his hands on top of our joined fists. Having done gymnastics for so many years, I knew that I had unusual strength in my hands, arms, and wrists—accounting for why I had never lost an arm-wrestling match up to this point. I felt rather calm about the whole event. When the officiator signaled, we were off. Right away, we engaged with tremendous force, likely both surprised that neither of our fists budged.

That same pressure went on for quite some time, and the Russian soldier's direct stare never wavered. At some point, he took a big breath and made what I would call a roar, most likely trying to create a sudden surge of strength. When my hand still didn't move, I saw the light in his eyes begin to dim, and almost immediately, our fists began to make small moves in my favor.

Thank goodness some higher part of me woke up fast. *What are you doing?!* it screamed. *This means nothing to you. He is surrounded by friends, and this is much more important to him.* I realized there was a more powerful opportunity taking place—the chance to value another person. I was thrilled that the choice seemed so natural and obvious to me.

Rather than allowing any continued movement of our fists, I began to relax the pressure that I'd been exerting, which my opponent noticed immediately. I could see it in his eyes. While I was fully prepared to allow our hands to move in his favor, he responded by releasing some pressure as well. Back and forth this progressed, until neither of us was pushing much at all. I thought it was cool that we were the only ones who were likely aware of what was taking place.

I'm not sure what inspired the officiator to come forward, but this is when he approached. With a single word in Russian, which I assumed meant "Tie!" we were done. Rather abruptly, the soldier stood up, nodded at me formally, and quickly walked off through the crowd. I thanked the guy who had invited me and went back to my room, assuming that was the end of the story.

Late the next morning, when I was making my way through the lobby to head out for rehearsal, I was pleased to find the muscular soldier from the night before standing by the entrance. Much to my surprise, his quick approach showed that he had been waiting for me. This was the first time we had stood next to one another, and it was even more obvious that he towered over me. He was at least six feet two inches tall.

Once he extended his hand to shake and it was clear that I was glad to see him, he broke into a beautiful smile for the first time. Only when we released our clasped hands could I feel that he had used the opportunity to pass something on to me. As he walked away, I found his gift was a Russian sportsman's medal—a lasting reminder that there is no greater prize than valuing another person. Even in our brief interaction in a hotel lobby, without words, we had made a lasting impression on one another's lives, transcending our different languages and traditions to briefly touch hearts. Priceless.

Experiences such as this one began to awaken a deep desire in me to touch more lives in whatever ways I could. To gain some clarity, I spoke with Gabriel about this at our next meeting.

If what you are saying is true for you, and we believe that it is, the most powerful way for you to become prepared for impacting others' lives, in addition to sharing this nurturing education about Self, is to learn much more about the flow of energy that moves through your body. You discovered years ago that you have a heightened sensitivity to energy. You now trust being able to sense where it is blocked in others' bodies. Now consider that creating more flow of energy is required for awakening into more of the Whole Self. What you need to understand is that it is ultimately the specific flow of energy that determines how conscious, aware, and evolved any of you can become.

This was all quite fascinating to me.

Gabriel continued: Just as you have three facets of the core Self—child, adult, and Soul—you have three energies that want to move through your body. All three are necessary to not only clear the wounds of the inner child but also to activate the greater potentials of the adult and Soul Self. For now, we will just talk about the first of those three energies, which is a force that is most familiar to people around the world.

From the time you are all born, there is an energy that begins to move up the spine called "kundalini." This is the sexual, creative force that is responsible for waking you up to your first layers of the emerging Self. You all have seven primary energy centers, each of which focuses on different facets of the Whole Self. Now we tell you that it is kundalini energy that activates the first levels of potential in each of those centers. Kundalini is the energy that inspires you to want to connect with one another and to Life around you, starting with your caregivers.

When you are young, kundalini only flows in small amounts, giving you time to learn how to navigate the foundation of your physical, emotional, and mental potentials. Then, after years of learning to connect to the child self, your kundalini goes through its first major surge. That acceleration of kundalini is what causes you to awaken into puberty. In what you call adolescence, kundalini creates tremendous shifts and changes, awakening more of your physical, emotional, mental, and sexual capacities.

Gabriel then reminded me about what happens when we don't receive the various levels of nurturing that we need in our first years. Instead of opening to receive and claim those first layers of our authentic individuality, we end up accumulating experiences colored by fear, shame, and judgment. When that happens, we don't open and learn to trust our emerging individuality or those around us. Instead, we learn to grip, resist, and block the flow of kundalini. Those blockages end up creating friction and impairing the flow of that energy through our bodies. Eventually, those blocks become the source of pains that we manifest in the body.

Soon after I began to invest in this deeper understanding of energy, I was scheduled to go to Hawai'i, where I would be singing in another production of *La bohème*. To give myself as much time as possible in that tropical paradise, I scheduled my flights with a couple of extra weeks for exploring. Little did I know that this choice would allow me to meet a shaman and then an indigenous healer known as a kahuna.

Though our time together was brief, both of them offered powerful clues for working with energy. When the kahuna acknowledged that he could sense a powerful capacity for healing within me, I was encouraged to take some proactive steps for investing in those untapped gifts.

When I returned to New York, I began to scan for places that I might study more about the healing arts. After a brief stint learning about the healing property of plants with an herbalist that I was really enjoying, I was hired to play the role of Javert for the Broadway company's tour of *Les Misérables*. Even though I would now be traveling from place to place, I was unwilling to let this new exploration die away. Not too many weeks into the tour, I heard about a gifted healer named Belinda Hymas, who lived in one of the cities we would soon be visiting. Without hesitation, I reached out and scheduled a session that would include another dear friend of mine from the cast as well.

When we met, Belinda told us that she had first discovered her healing gift when she was a child trying to help a wounded baby bird. Unfortunately, when her gift made her parents nervous, she ended up shutting it down. Only years later did she decide to pursue an official study. That is when she became certified through the Usui Reiki School. After Belinda was done with her certifications, in a much shorter time than was typically required, she began to sense there were more potentials than those activated in the three initiations of traditional Reiki. Exploring her intuitions further, she was being guided into the activations of twelve power centers that we all hold inside us.

What I learned from Belinda in our first meeting resonated so fully that I started flying her in to work with me in other tour cities. Once things started to unfold in affirming ways, I knew I had to complete all twelve levels.

It came as no surprise that soon after I received my first initiation, Life naturally handed me some ways to apply what I was learning. During one of our performances of *Les Misérables*, the actor playing Marius fell off a piece of the set and hurt his ankle. The few people who knew that I was studying Reiki called me over to help. Of course, I was happy to do what I could, but since this was one of the first opportunities I had to practice what I had been learning on someone who was in real pain, I didn't have any strong expectations.

Rather than trying to explain Reiki in a complete way, I will just say that a practitioner uses their hands and intention to increase a flow of energy in various parts of someone's body. It is much like turning up the flow of water that moves through a hose. By accelerating that flow, especially when combined with nurturing massage to help the person relax the muscles in a particular area, it is possible to encourage the release of blockages and pain in the body. Flow creates health.

At this moment with my friend, I found I was able to encourage that flow in his ankle. Almost immediately, his pain dissipated, and he was able to complete the performance. At the same time, the part of me that had always played the caretaker—wanting to take others' pain away from them—inadvertently ended up taking on the energy that the other actor had released. The result of my first healing session was that I ended up with mild ankle pain over the next couple of days.

I asked Gabriel for an explanation. *You need to honor whatever another person has manifested as a perfect part of their unfolding Soul plan rather than seeing it as something to take away,* he explained. *You need to trust that each person needs each of those experiences as each manifestation is attempting to provide important clues about what they are going through on the inside—revealing where they are in flow or in fear. When someone discovers an area of fear, which blocks the flow of energy in their bodies, then they have the opportunity to respond and resolve that fear. In other words, pain is there to serve, attempting to show someone where they need to focus and nurture themselves.*

After hearing the new instruction, to simply hold a compassionate space rather than approaching someone with sympathy, I started having healthier experiences. One of the most meaningful involved one of my nieces. When Lawson, the first of my three nieces, was quite young, she had lots of earaches. To resolve the problem, doctors inserted artificial tubes that would allow her ears to drain. A common procedure. After working well for several years, she began complaining about ear pain again. When her parents took her to the doctor, they discovered that one of the tubes had become attached to her eardrum. Therefore, when the eardrum began to grow with age, a small hole had formed, which was dangerous. Lawson was scheduled for surgery the following Monday.

As fate would have it, I was scheduled to be in North Carolina for a visit that very weekend. Naturally, I didn't want to make Lawson feel uncomfortable in any way. She was only four years old. And so I decided to take cues from her about how much energy work to offer. Thankfully, she gave me very clear signals. Though she didn't typically sit still for long, that weekend, she kept wanting to hang out in my lap.

Under normal circumstances, I would place my hands directly on someone's body to create a more nurturing experience. In this case, I decided to keep my hands a few inches away from Lawson's head to avoid confusing her. I trusted that if it didn't feel right for her, she would simply move away. Instead, within seconds of starting the flow of energy, Lawson laid her head down into my hand with complete trust.

We sat together for about ten minutes before she jumped up and moved on to some other activity that had gotten her attention. I knew that once we set the new flow of energy into motion, healing would likely continue—if that is what served her particular journey.

When her parents took her to the hospital for surgery a couple of days later, the pre-op examination revealed that the tube had not only separated from the eardrum, but the small hole was no longer there either. The surgeon was unsure what to make of it.

"We don't know what has happened, but surgery is no longer needed. You can take her home."

Lawson was actually a little disappointed at the way everything worked out. She'd really wanted to wear a mask in the hospital, like the one she'd seen me wear in a video of *Phantom*—from a performance I had done with Kristin Chenoweth as my Christine.

Over time, I began to work on more and more people, sometimes using massage and Reiki to relieve a migraine or a backache, and I eventually worked on issues that were much more serious or immediate. I found that the more I opened and offered people clues about what was likely going on for them emotionally and energetically, they became more invested in the sessions with me, which meant they also made distinct, powerful shifts.

When I was able to discuss some of the healing moments with Gabriel that had begun to transpire, including the process of having activated the twelve power centers with Belinda, he had some interesting things to share.

Moving through these activations has been important for both you and the channel [Robert], continuing to deepen your readiness for a direct connection to your Souls. The opportunity for awakening all three facets of Self was configured into your Soul plans as distinct possibilities for this lifetime. We are pleased that in addition to becoming the adult authorities in your own lives, you are now ready to begin negotiating the energies of the Soul.

You are aware that some of the people have key roles in your lifetime, and they are referred to as Soul mates. You may not know, but it is possible for people to have any number of Soul mates in a single lifetime. Soul mates are not always meant to be romantic connections. Instead, the term refers to the people who have chosen to play pivotal roles in your core lessons. Some come in as protagonists and others as antagonists. Some, a combination of both.

There are also other levels of connection shared by Souls. The one that is most relevant for the two of you we will call Twin Flames. All Souls have one Twin Flame—one particular Soul who is assigned as a primary support in your extended journeys. The typical setup of Twin Flames is for one of the partners to remain on the spiritual plane, while the other is experiencing their journey in the physical. As those Soul journeys continue, the two take turns and reverse places.

On some occasions, Twin Flames choose to incarnate together. When this happens, it is typically because they have chosen to work together to impact

and support large groups of people. We tell you this now because we want
you to be sure that you and Robert are Twin Flames who have come in with
the potential of touching large numbers of people.

Robert and I had always been aware of our natural connection, but we were both surprised and inspired by hearing about this next level of connection. The reason Gabriel wanted us to have this information was to help us realize the impact that our Souls coming together had already been creating, as we prepared to open to this third level of the Whole Self: child, adult, and now, Soul.

As I began to hear that we were preparing for a next stage, I wondered how closely related my restlessness to make a shift in my career was to this deeper awakening. In case I was not already clear, going to Monte Carlo for a world premiere of *The Picture of Dorian Gray* was about to provide more clues. Surrounded by truly gifted, creative people in one of the world's most glamorous cities, I still felt like I was betraying my deepest truth to move on. The more I ignored those feelings, the more disconnected and alone I felt.

By this point in my journey, I had performed more than sixty roles all over the world and had sung for opera luminaries like Pavarotti and Marilyn Horne, as well as surprise chances, like singing for Jerry Garcia of The Grateful Dead. Though I couldn't shake the idea that my time in opera was coming to a close, I still hoped I might find a new way to continue having exciting, meaningful experiences like these.

Fortunately, I was well practiced at following my intuition by this time, whether I fully understood what my inner green lights were leading me toward or not. Therefore, when I returned to New York, I decided to make a first shift: letting go of the opera agents at CAMI. At the very least, I knew this would allow me to focus more fully on performing theater roles, which I had begun to enjoy much more fully than most of my operatic ones. Performing the title role in *Phantom*, for instance, was a lifetime highlight for me. I loved the immediacy of communication that was possible in theater, as well as the ability to use the softer, more intimate colors of my voice, which was made possible when singing with microphones.

Having always had the luxury of being scheduled for shows two to three years into the future, I now found myself making a leap into a big "unknown." By the end of the summer of 1996, the only thing on my calendar for the next three months was a workshop that Robert and I had planned to teach in Upstate New York. After that, I had a tentative plan of heading to Los Angeles to audition for what is known as "pilot season."

Though it was a vulnerable time with so many unanswered questions, the intimate experience of being with people for the upstate workshop was great. Little did Robert and I know that our next synchronicity would come out of that time in the Catskills. I refer to meeting Deborah Rebolledo, whom neither of us had met prior. And yet, she was about to become a major player in our lives.

At the end of our three days together, Deborah approached us to say, "I have gathered a group of wonderful people from Brazil for a journey to Egypt and Israel this January. I've been searching for the spiritual focus of that journey, and I am now clear that the guidance you are able to bring through Gabriel would be perfect."

While the opportunity to travel to Egypt sounded fascinating, I knew it would conflict with my trip to LA. Since I had just canceled all future income, not going west would block my ability to audition for more jobs. This was a moment when I definitely needed some guidance. Naturally, I turned to Gabriel.

Dear one, we believe we have been speaking to you for seven years now. In all that time, have you ever heard us suggest what someone should do?

"No, Gabriel, I have not."

Well...this is going to be the first time. You were speaking to a friend this last week who suggested that the journey to Egypt sounded like the "trip of a lifetime." We are affirming that not only was your friend correct, but it is also more than that. We are suggesting that going on this journey to Egypt is the chance of all your lifetimes.

I was stunned and thrilled by Gabriel's words. What he didn't share was how important that journey would be for catapulting Robert and me into the Soul level of our journeys, opening us into greater levels of Life experience that we could never have foreseen.

IV

SOUL

17

UNPRECEDENTED SHIFTS

ROBERT AND I COMMITTED TO GOING ON A THREE-week journey to Egypt and Israel that promised to be unlike anything we had experienced before. Once we made our decision, we invited people from our core New York City community to join the individuals who were already scheduled from Brazil, bringing the total number of travelers to forty-eight. None of us had any idea what to expect.

A couple of months before the start of our travel, we noticed some surprising synchronicities. One of the most powerful involved hearing on CNN that a rare configuration of planets would form a perfect six-pointed star in the heavens on January 23, 1997. If this astrological event was important enough for a major news network to report, we wanted to find out more—particularly because it would happen while we were in Egypt. When we investigated further, we discovered that a worldwide meditation had been planned to coordinate with this rare configuration in the heavens.

As if all of that wasn't enough, Deborah phoned a couple of days later to inform Robert and me that some of the details for our itinerary had shifted. Once we sat down to put the new pieces into the journey calendar, we realized that January 23—the day of the alignment—was the very day we were now scheduled to have private time in the Great Pyramid in Giza. Upon closer inspection, what we found was hard to believe. Based on the new shifts in our schedule, that rare planetary alignment would now take place smack dab in the middle of the three hours we would be the only people in the Great Pyramid, one of the Seven Wonders of the Ancient World.

Robert and I had experienced many interesting synchronicities in our years with Gabriel, but this discovery took the word *synchronicity* to an entirely new level. We knew that Gabriel's approach to teaching typically involved waiting for us to make some initial discoveries from our lives before introducing a new topic. We would then bring what we were exploring for Gabriel to provide a more complete context. In this case, the response to the alignment of events was almost overwhelming to consider.

We are so glad you've been paying attention and that you're getting excited about this convergence of events. We knew it would be more mean-ingful for you if we waited for you to make some initial discoveries, which you have done beautifully. What we now have to tell you will help you under-stand why we have called this the 'opportunity of all your lifetimes.'

January 23, 1997 will be a profound moment for your entire planet—marking a time of new beginnings and awakenings, unlike anything your world has known. Since 1990, we have told you many times that your planet has entered a time of unprecedented accelerations, all intended to prepare and support a literal shift of evolution into Soul consciousness on your planet. What we mean is that this acceleration of energy will gradually equal a new awakening, shifting you individually and collectively toward the next level of your potential. Since that is too much for most people to consider logically, we will use the map of the Whole Self you have formulated to make it a little clearer. (See Diagram 1)

Up to this point in your path of evolution, the vast majority of people have been stuck in a survival level of consciousness, ruled in many ways by the accumulated experiences of the wounded child. In recent decades, more individuals are starting to seek out other more empowered choices, just beginning to claim more of the adult Self.

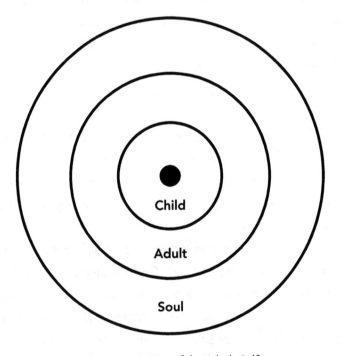

Diagram 1: A Map of the Whole Self

The acceleration is the very reason we have begun to introduce you to more about your Soul journeys. On January 23, there will be a tremendous download of energy taking place, which will create an unprecedented boost of energetic support for you to all begin a gradual awakening. Even though this will take place as shifting percentages, things will change much faster than anything you have previously known.

Over the next fifteen years, there will continue to be a series of these energetic events, like the one you have just heard about on what you call CNN. We have prepared you for this time of shifting by offering you a foundational understanding of the flow of energy that presently moves through your bodies, as well as the need to clear any blockages of fear, shame, and judgment that you have accumulated by your nurturing tools.

The energetic initiations or downloads that will begin with this event on January 23, 1997 will challenge you all to open to a much greater flow through your bodies. This shift will be very similar to what happened to all of you when you reached puberty. Keep in mind that the shift into adolescence impacted every facet of your young lives, and we assure you that this shift will be no different.

All of this made sense to us logically. We had already begun to see powerful shifts from the healing work we had both done with our inner children. Having faced many fears and released many layers of wounded feelings, we had already experienced our bodies starting to feel lighter. We were now anxious to hear more.

We now want you to just begin considering the bigger context of the alignment that will take place on January 23. This planetary initiation will involve an energy download that will be focused directly on The Great Pyramid of Egypt, the very place where you will all be standing. That download will set into motion the first of seven Soul initiations, which is why we refer to this first activation as the Birth initiation. This birth, which is an introduction of a new level of energy, will begin to impact every facet of your lives, starting with your physical bodies. You need to know this will be a powerful introduction of Soul consciousness.

We have also told you over the years that "Soul consciousness" is synonymous for "Christ consciousness." When we, Gabriel, came two thousand years ago to announce the birth of the Christ, we referred to the birth of a world teacher who was coming to introduce the integrated potentials of Soul consciousness. In other words, Jesus was referred to as a "Christed being" because he was a "Soul-integrated being." There have been others on your planet who have also opened to that level of the Whole Self, such as the one, Buddha. We have spoken to you about being sacred individuals on unique Soul journeys for many reasons. Part of that was to prepare you for this time.

One of the primary goals inherent in this powerful boost of energy is to encourage you to move beyond your systems of separation and duality, trying to define who is right versus who is wrong. For now, just consider that Jesus was a man and a world teacher who came to demonstrate that so much more is possible when you become Soul-connected. No matter what stages of learning you have presently reached, you all share this path of the Soul. It is a path that embraces the sacredness of all humans.

Unlike the first time we came to announce the birth of the Christ/Soul in a man, we have come at this time to communicate through any number of channels around the world that this series of energetic initiations will once again create a birth of Soul or Christed consciousness. The difference is that we are not here to herald the arrival of a world teacher. Instead, we are proclaiming an awakening of Christ/Soul consciousness in the hearts of all people. We hope you won't let the terminology typically associated with one particular religion or another get in the way.

This teacher, who was born into a Jewish family, came two thousand years ago to demonstrate a movement through seven initiations—archetypal steps *that are required for awakening and embodying your Souls. That awakening will, of course, require that each individual chooses to become proactive, willing to prepare and open to a deeper understanding of the Whole Self. This shift will not magically happen 'to you,' like some sort of rescue from your fear, shame, and judgment.*

This is the reason we've been teaching you how to prepare, how to nurture, and how to clear your bodies over these last years. This is also the reason that we have suggested that you pay close attention to each step, including the symptoms that you experience as these energies begin to move, as well as quantifying the specific tools that you discover are effective. The world will reach a point when many more will come seeking these powerful options and solutions in their lives.

Since we would be putting ourselves directly in the download of these unprecedented, accelerated energies during our journey to Egypt, we were grateful to be as informed as we could be. Even though I wasn't sure what was possible, at this moment, I was even more grateful for the opportunity of the profound education and guidance that we continued to receive.

We would like to continue working with you for years to come, providing more layers of understanding about the unprecedented shifts that you will all be facing as you begin to integrate these planetary activations. Though the bigger masses won't likely be aware of these events for years to come, many of the outer changes and discoveries that will become obvious in the world will be set into motion by this very series of energetic downloads.

This was interesting to consider, and I, of course, found myself wondering what the specific shifts—which I imagined would include accelerated breakthroughs and challenges—might include.

Your journey to Egypt and Israel, we say to you once again, will be coordinated with the first of seven initiations: the Birth of this new potential. The temples that you will be visiting along the Nile River are an exact reflection of the seven energy centers or chakras that you each have in your bodies. Those centers are located at various points along your spines. The temples of Egypt were all built to train initiates who were interested in moving through foundational levels of initiation. That training started at the temple of the first chakra, now known as Abu Simbel, and ended at the Great Pyramid, the highest of initiation temples. On your journey, you will visit each center as you sail up the Nile River.

Without having spent years building up trust in Gabriel and the guidance he had already provided, we would never have been prepared to understand such profound claims in such a short time before the journey. Even so, we were still stunned at the magnitude of what we had just heard. For weeks afterward, Robert and I could barely wrap our heads around what it all might mean and what we might experience.

It now made complete sense why Gabriel had recently begun to shift the focus of our sessions to present a more complete understanding of the Soul, as well as hinting that we would eventually want to expand our teaching of all the things that we had been learning to reach more people. After all, the results we had experienced working with others so far had already been inspiring. For now, however, making this information clear to all forty-eight travelers who would be with us for the journey was our most immediate task.

In order to set you up well, we return to your map of the Whole Self. We have already told you that your shift into adolescence takes place based on a surge of kundalini that awakens you into more of your potential—physical, emotional, mental, sexual, and spiritual. Having already experienced that awakening from childhood into adulthood, you are already clear that your entire reference point to Life shifted at that time.

What you now need to consider is that the activation of this Birth initiation will set into motion a second surge of kundalini, and you will begin to experience a new awakening that is even more powerful than puberty. This is a surge that is typically associated with midlife, and it will begin to take all of you on the journey into realms to which there is no logical reference point.

You will then begin to recognize even more benefits in the worlds of science, medicine, and technology. Those will open at a rate unlike anything you have witnessed, as it is, once again, a greater flow of energy that allows for the potentials of consciousness that have previously lain dormant to be realized.

As I contemplated what Gabriel had shared, I remembered all my childhood questions about Life and wanting to understand more about how it all works. I remembered how sure I had felt that there must be more complete answers, if only I knew where to look. Well, by this point, it was quite clear that Gabriel had been providing those "more complete answers" for years and was now promising a new connection to even more of what he called "the natural awakening of Divine Order" in our lives.

In order for the event on January 23 to have its greatest impact, we need your help in spreading the word. You will remember that we suggested you start sharing our messages with the world by building a website not too many months ago. (Having a personal website was not typical in the late nineties.) *We now ask that you use that website to inform as many people as you can about what is going on with this spiritual awakening. At this point, most people have only been made aware of the planetary alignment. We simply ask that you do your best to let as many people as you can know about this first Soul initiation.*

Just hearing about Soul initiations will begin to stir up greater depths of Self, whether people are conscious of those personal activations or not. It will likely be felt more like an excitement and a desire for "more." Let people know that they have a clear chance to play an important role in this unfolding. Simply by choosing to ground the energies that will be coming in on that important day, through meditation and setting clear intentions, each one will be serving a beautiful service for the whole. Over time, we will ask that you continue sharing many other layers of information we will be providing, revealing more of the specific ways this series of initiations will impact lives.

Over the course of many decades, your world will continue to go through unprecedented shifts and shakeups, asking you to transcend fear and separation, as you seek more complete solutions to your world's challenges, which will become more immediate and exaggerated. It will help tremendously to have as much of this new education available as possible.

People will be comforted by beginning to understand what they can expect and how to work with these shifting energies. You have all wanted to trust that your lives matter. This is a chance to play crucial, proactive roles that allow you to become part of something bigger than yourselves.

Even just beginning to consider the potential magnitude of the opportunity that this rare planetary configuration offered, I put all my efforts into getting the word out to as many people as possible. I remember being completely amazed when I sent out my first email and began to get responses from people all over the world. How great it felt to find out that people were excited by what we had to share.

One of the things that had been confirmed during my travels around the world had been the fact that people are much more alike than we are different. It felt good hearing perspectives about Life and the Soul that put us all on the same sacred page, learning together. And now, we all had so much to look forward to as the coming months promised new healing shifts.

We now want to help you understand more about the formation of the six-pointed star that will align in the heavens on January 23. The six-pointed star is an ancient symbol that represents the coming together of the Whole

Self—joining the lower Self (child) and the higher Self (Soul), all joined together in the heart center, which is the chakra of the conscious, empowered adult who will need to assimilate this awakening. (See Diagram 2.)

The six-pointed star is formed by two triangles. The three-sided object pointing upward represents the three chakras of the lower Self that must be healed to move up to the heart space. The triangle pointing downward represents the three chakras of the higher Self that must move down and become grounded into the body. When those two triangles come together in balance, there will be a more complete joining of the physical world with Spirit, which is what will activate the Soul energies to awaken in the heart center.

Diagram 2: The joining of physical and Spirit / the lower and higher Self

To set you up well for your time in the Great Pyramid, we will be providing you with seven ceremonies to do—one in each of the seven temples you will be visiting. This will allow you to prepare each of your chakras with loving intentions prior to the bigger download of energy on January 23. You can include that preparation information when you let others in the world know about what is going to transpire.

We knew we would begin our sailing journey up the Nile by spending time in the temple of Abu Simbel, which we had also been told represents the first chakra at the base of the spine. There, we would do our first of seven ceremonies, setting our individual intentions in place for the journey ahead. The first chakra is where the seeds of any new idea are planted, prior to making its way through all seven energy centers.

Our natural progression would follow that plan, gathering in each of the other six temples, and eventually reaching the final destination on January 23. The ceremonies Gabriel shared with us focused on deepening our commitments to giving and receiving in balance, identifying the things that no longer served us in our lives, and mostly centered on creating the new visions that we wanted to create in our lives moving forward.

Because of the importance of these initiations, we want you to be aware that you will be supported with some surprising manifestations—some on a grand scale. There will be many higher beings working with this unprecedented event who want to make sure you are left with no possible doubts about the power of this unfolding. Each experience will not only add to the emotional impact and opening that you will likely experience but will also give you clear stories to eventually share. Know that each choice is being made to help you inspire many more people around the world.

Before closing this particular session, Gabriel filled us in more fully about the power of the new energies that would pour in during our time in the Great Pyramid.

In many ways, Robert will act as a primary conduit for the downloading energies for your group. This is simply how his energy has been configured, very much like an antenna. You, on the other hand, will serve as a ground for that energy, much like a lightning rod. In order to become prepared for receiving these unusually high energies, we have been progressively preparing your bodies over these last years. However, we want you to be fully aware that

the energy you will be facing in the Pyramid will be many times more power-
ful than anything you have experienced before. In order to protect the people
who will be going with you, make it clear to everyone that no one other than
you is to touch Robert while you are in the Pyramid.

If that weren't enough, Gabriel then suggested that anyone unpre-
pared to handle those levels of energy could go into shock if they
touched Robert during those hours of direct connection. Once that was
clear, Gabriel prepared me for an additional role I was to play in that
sacred ancient structure.

We also want you to know that once you are in the King's Chamber, the
energy that will be moving through Robert will eventually be transferred to
you, at which point, we encourage you to allow the sounds that have been
awakening in your work over the last months to be resonated into the space.
There have been many reasons for you to develop your voice in this lifetime,
well beyond the most obvious opportunity for having a performing career.
One of those is for you to be able to use specific resonances to support ener-
getic shifts, both in individuals' bodies and in certain spaces.

So much of what Gabriel shared sounded like science fiction to us in
1997. As we were packing for the journey, Robert and I admitted that
we were afraid we wouldn't be able to live up to whatever was being
asked of us. However, as nervous as we were about our roles and respon-
sibilities, we also felt strangely like children who were on the verge of an
epic adventure—excited, eager to get started, and a little overwhelmed
with being responsible for forty-eight people who were learning to navigate a mysterious new level of energy.

18

MIRACLES OF BIRTH

ALL FORTY-EIGHT INDIVIDUALS BOARDED VARIOUS planes from many different starting points across North and South America, ready to come together for the first time in the ancient land of Egypt. By this time in the process, each of us knew that we had chosen to participate in an event that would mark powerful new possibilities, but we had no idea what to actually expect.

From the moment we landed, we found ourselves in a culture much older than any we had previously known or even fully imagined. Many of the local people were dressed in long robes called *galabeyas*, just like the one I had seen Jesus wearing in the chalk mural at my grandparents' home. I found the connection comforting, like a perfect bridge between ancient and modern times.

Right away, we received a warm welcome from our guide, Mohamed Shata, an Egyptologist who clearly loved his ancient homeland. Abu Shata, as we began to call him in the coming days—*Abu* meaning "father" in Arabic—was a gentle man whose eyes often exhibited a spark of childlike humor. Little did I know that Mohamed would become more like a father figure to me in the next two weeks than any male figure in my life had before. I would even say that getting to know him made me want to be a better man.

I mention this because I want to be clear that it was not only ancient temples, mammoth statues, and lush landscapes that inspired transformations in our group during the weeks we spent in Egypt. We also discovered powerful magic taking place in the authentic investments we all made in one another, and Abu Shata certainly set the tone for that.

The moment that initially cemented my connection with Mohamed took place at a shop filled with paintings—a gorgeous array of colors on the world's original paper: papyrus. While people from our group were strolling through the store, I found myself transfixed in front of one particular painting. The man, whom I imagined might have been a Pharaoh, was sitting with his right hand in a strong fist and his left hand opened on his other knee. A beautiful bird was nestled behind his head.

When Mohamed noticed my fascination with this image, he came and stood next to me. "Ron, the fact that you are pulled to this painting makes it clear to me that you are a very sensitive man," he said. "The statue on this papyrus represents many important things for me. His hands reflect the perfect balance of strength and gentleness. The energy of the falcon behind his head represents Horus—the same archetype for Egyptians that Jesus represents in the world—revealing that this leader is constantly guided by Spirit."

Mohamed had no idea that he had just described for me what I had been attempting to define throughout my life—what it means to be an inspired man and leader in the world. In a few brief words, he also enhanced the core intentions that I planned to set in motion in the temple ceremonies over the coming days. What a wonderful affirmation from a man I would come to admire greatly.

To close our conversation, Mohamed pulled out his business card, which featured a representation of that very statue. From that point forward, it was clear that he and I shared important core qualities. He then told me that the actual statue had been found buried in a small temple next to the Sphinx and was now housed in the Cairo Museum. To commemorate the moment and to remind myself of the beautiful qualities symbolized by the man joining with Horus, I bought a copy of the painting—which still hangs in my home.

When we entered the Cairo Museum the next day, we all became even more deeply immersed in ancient history. Mohamed took the time to introduce us to many of the primary archetypes of ancient Egypt, almost like he was telling us about close friends. Some in the group found that they were drawn to Hathor, the goddess with cow ears who represents the archetype of a nurturing mother. Others were struck by the energy of Sekhmet, the goddess who represents the fierceness of feminine strength.

At one point, when Mohamed started to fill us in about another statue, I felt an energetic pull that was quite unusual for me. I felt a literal force tugging at my chest, pulling me toward the entrance of another room just a few feet away. Trusting that Mohamed would take care of the group, I followed the impulse. As soon as I turned the corner, I understood. There, directly in front of me, was the imposing stone statue that had been discovered next to the Sphinx. The effect of the actual statue was even more powerful than the painted representation. Mohamed, of course, noticed right away what was taking place, and he soon shepherded the whole group into that space, bringing our shared appreciation to a satisfying completion.

Once the group finished exploring some of the many highlights that were housed in Cairo, we flew south to the place where we would start our journey up the Nile. This is when the real heart of the journey began for me. Robert expressed something similar when we had a moment to share in our cabin on the river ship we had so looked forward to boarding.

Each temple that we visited provided its own brand of power and unique experiences, starting with Abu Simbel. This first chakra site actually consists of two large temples, both built by Ramses II. The larger temple is where we put most of our focus, and it's where we did our first ceremony—stating out loud our individual intentions for the journey. While we were in that sacred structure, both Robert and I had unexpected experiences that stretched us well beyond familiar comfort zones.

Though our education about Soul journeys had been centered around the idea of having many lifetimes, I had only experienced occasional glimpses of intuitive familiarity in certain places that I had visited, whether those sensations had been pleasant or quite uncomfortable. That all reached a new level in this first initiation temple.

Just after we finished joining our individual energies into a group resonance, we were ready to enter the mammoth temple that stood before us. It boasted four sixty-five-foot-tall statues of Ramses II that seemed to be guarding the space. Prior, I had never seen anything that compared to the scale of those statues. After a brief tour, we gave everyone time to explore the temple grounds on their own. Gabriel had encouraged us to give people time to have individual experiences whenever possible as that would be a crucial part of their journeys.

I was surprised to feel so pulled to the smaller statues of Horus that also lined the front of the temple platform before going inside. From the moment I moved up those few stone steps, I started to feel a bit strange—sad somehow. Without logic, I felt compelled to wrap my right arm around the shoulders of the first statue. Doing so only heightened my emotion. Since I had already learned about the power of allowing feelings that want to move through my body, I connected to the sadness. As soon as I did, I experienced a full vision of myself as a young boy of about ten, standing in that very spot in some ancient lifetime. The experience was so complete that I trusted, beyond logic, that I had stood on those very steps before. In that lifetime, I had clung to the statue for comfort while I waited for my father's ship to return from battle. After a moment or two, the memory progressed to the point where I knew that my father had not survived and wouldn't return.

As what felt like unexpressed tears started to flow, I intuitively felt that these were feelings I hadn't felt safe to express in that lifetime. As I allowed the release, I was reminded of the parallel to this lifetime, when I had spent so much time yearning for my father to connect. At that point, my tears became sobs.

The next morning, Gabriel affirmed that we do indeed store mental and emotional imprints of all our lifetimes in the cells of our bodies. I was grateful that I had learned to feel safe enough with vulnerable feelings over the last seven years that I was ready to finally allow the release of that deep sorrow. Not surprisingly, I also needed to ask for some feedback for Robert and what he went through in that first temple.

While we were exploring the inside of the cavernous structure at Abu Simbel, some of the group joined us. I was glad to have them there as witnesses because Robert's experience was one that none of us will ever forget. After he brought through a beautiful channeled message in the main hall, we were all moving away from the heart of the temple, known as the "holy of holies." Just as we reached the next doorway, Robert's body was pulled by a powerful energy—one that seemed to be coming from inside that room. Unlike the pull I had felt at the museum, this energy was so powerful that Robert's body was literally lifted off the ground between two and three feet. With little time to process what was happening, I had the thought that if something wasn't done, Robert could end up being hoisted over the security partition blocking the entrance to the chamber.

I already knew this about myself: when something frightens me, I don't shut down or cower. Instead, I usually gain a surge of assertive energy, particularly when motivated to protect someone I care about. In this case, I grabbed hold of Robert's waist and pulled him out of the opposing energy. With him draped across my shoulder, I walked directly out of the space. As a matter of fact, I didn't put Robert down until we had moved back out into the sunlight. Once it began to dawn on him what had just taken place, he allowed his fear and began to cry. A number of us from the group hugged him until he was calm.

Two days later, we visited the second chakra temple of Isis, which is connected to the feminine receptive energies that we all contain in our emotional centers. We were told that this temple had at one time become immersed in water—which happens to be one of the main feminine elements on the Earth. Gabriel told us that the mother of Horus, Isis, carries the same energy as Mary, Jesus's mother. There in the main courtyard of that temple, we did a ceremony to align with the emotional center in our bodies. It was there that Mohamed approached me.

"Ron, I have had a vision. I see that one day you will write about our time together here in Egypt."

Each day, we returned to the ship and spent hours sailing up the Nile River, complete with a panorama of farming scenes lined with palm trees. This was much like watching a movie of ancient times. Some days, we gathered as a group to share our individual experiences, and on other days, we became part of celebrations and skits put on by the staff of the ship. The combination of joy, play, and deep contemplation, punctuated with occasional channeling from Gabriel, kept us all in a healthy balance.

At the Temple of Kom Ombo, representing the third chakra, located in the solar plexus of our bodies, we prepared to do another ceremony. This time we focused on healing the challenges of duality, or the opposition of two sides—like good and bad, light and dark. Reflecting that division, the physical Temple of Kom Ombo is divided into two distinct sides. According to the stories shared by Mohamed and enhanced by Gabriel, initiates working through the lessons and challenges of this temple had to face some of their deepest fears in this temple before passing on to their next levels of training.

For that initiation, there were underground chambers filled with water. When deemed ready, an initiate would dive into the waters, knowing they would be required to face some emotional fear—without any idea how that fear would manifest. The initiates were told that they would find their greatest freedom by looking deep within, and the test reflected their need to truly look deep. This was encouraged in the physical structure as well, which began with an opening into a series of chambers that were each separated by a wall.

After swimming underwater to find the opening to the second chamber, which was located at a point low on the dividing wall, they would naturally want to come to the surface for air. However, what they would find above them in the second chamber was a congregation of alliga-tors—representing their survival fears. If their preparation allowed them to face their fear with calm, they would realize a need to dive deeper still to find the second opening, which would bring them into the relief of the final chamber. This is what was required to pass the test.

Fortunately, Gabriel did not ask our group to participate in any such ceremonies. Ha! Doing so would have likely created mutiny. At the same time, we were all still facing various fears on the journey—even if that was a fear of getting in touch with wounded feelings or a fear of working out the conflicts that would come up between individuals along the way. Each of our fears required that we search for deeper levels of compassion and understanding in order to find resolutions.

***

The fourth temple along the Nile was one of my favorites. This Temple of Horus represents the heart chakra, the center of the conscious, empowered adult. Since the heart is also the integration point of the Soul/Christed energy we were there to initiate, our ceremony focused on choosing to demonstrate certain qualities of the heart. Being at that temple, which was the home of the Horus/Jesus archetype, I was reminded how moved I had been hearing stories of Jesus from Aunt Sara so many years before. Gabriel had also assured us that Jesus's own training included being in these very temples for his initiation journeys. All of it was so exciting, moving, and surreal when I took the time to let the opportunity touch me.

Though I had already learned to appreciate Robert deeply over the years, this journey elicited a new level of respect. Not only did he bring us a constant stream of channeled messages from different guides and teachers along the way, but he was also a constant reminder that powerful new energies were circulating in our bodies each time we entered a new space. Though the experiences affected each of us in unique ways, the impact on Robert's body was most obvious.

In two of the temples, that new flow of energy had become so intense that Robert actually passed out and collapsed to the ground. Of course, we all rallied around him. Particularly helpful was a dear friend named Tim, who was a powerful practitioner and a natural leader who'd been an integral part of our Soul family from the beginning. Even with all the help, Robert still had to summon the courage to continue exploring these spaces each day, and that courage never faltered.

Naturally, each of those episodes left me feeling vulnerable about what we might encounter in the Great Pyramid. Fortunately, I had chances to check in with Gabriel privately on several mornings before we joined the group.

In some of those meetings, Gabriel reminded us about encountering obvious signs of the power of the journey, now naming some of the specific manifestations that might take place. He suggested that we pay attention to animals and birds we encountered. Each one represented a certain archetype of energy, as many indigenous cultures in the world understand. One thing we had noticed was that we would almost undoubtedly find hawks circling above our heads when we were doing our ceremonies. These "messengers of Spirit," who also represented the energy of Horus, were a rather constant presence.

Gabriel also hinted that there would be manifestations in the energy of nature around us. This indeed proved true. The first two that stood out aligned with the two occasions we traveled away from the Nile and into the desert for day-long excursions. On the first of those trips, Mohamed pointed out that dark clouds were gathering as we prepared to do a ceremony. Just about the time we started giving voice to our individual intentions, the skies opened, and rain began to fall. When we asked Mohamed why he seemed so excited by this, he told us that it only rained there about once every ten years. We also noticed that the rain stopped once we were boarding the bus after the ceremony had ended.

Anyone in the group who had been less than impressed by that first manifestation was likely inspired to reevaluate when the exact same thing took place on our second journey into a different part of the desert the very next day. The rain started to fall even more heavily that day, and once again, only for the precise duration of our ceremony. Each of these outer signs helped us to gradually build trust and excitement that there was more going on than just speaking our intentions aloud in these rituals.

In the group meetings we held with Gabriel after that second occurrence, he affirmed that the rain was not only getting our attention, but it was also part of a symbolic purification for the group—all of whom he now referred to as young initiates.

Each purification is further preparing you for your time in the Great Pyramid. Each event is a sign of support and an affirmation that you are more connected to Life than any of you have likely guessed or experienced.

After two weeks and six ceremonies, January 23 finally arrived. As we got closer to the Great Pyramid, the ancient structure kept seeming more vast. Quite honestly, standing next to it, it seemed too big to even consider. Mohamed told us that there were enough stones in the 481-foot-high pyramid to build a four-lane highway from New York to California. I can only say that our cameras did nothing to capture its scope and size.

Gabriel explained to us that the Great Pyramid is configured in such a way that it naturally reflects the three levels of the Whole Self: the child or lower Self housed in the subconscious mind, the adult in the conscious mind, and the Soul/higher Self in the superconscious mind. Those three elements are represented within the structure as three chambers: the Pit (subconscious), the Queen's Chamber (conscious), and the King's Chamber (superconscious).

To complete our initiation, we would spend time in each of the three chambers, moving from the lowest to the highest, just as we had done moving up the Nile. To prepare ourselves for entering this remarkable temple, we spent a great deal of time connecting our energies as a group and remembering all the intentions we had already claimed in the previous days.

When it was finally time to enter, we moved through some raw tunnels that led us to the stairs that would take us down to the Pit. Robert and I were the first to move into the small tunnel of steps—tons and tons of steps—gradually leading us down into the Earth. The ceiling of that staircase was about four feet off the floor, and the only lighting came from occasional light bulbs connected through one small silver conduit pipe. Many people eventually shared that they experienced some unprecedented claustrophobia during that descent.

In order to even fit into that small descending passageway, I had to hang my backpack down by my side, while I put most of my focus on steadying Robert. Even though Gabriel had told us there would be many times more energy in this space than we had previously encountered, this was the first time I had ever seen Robert's body react like a jackhammer. I had to hold him by both shoulders to make sure his head didn't bang on the ceiling. Again grateful for his willingness, I protected him the best I could.

At the end of a very lengthy decline, we finally reached the raw cave-like room called the Pit. I was surprised that it was so rough-hewn, complete with big boulders resting in seemingly random places. When everyone in the group arrived, it seemed that every one of us was grateful to have a moment to settle. We then took time to join our group energy with the higher beings who were working with us for this profound Birth initiation. After honoring that connection, we followed up with a meditation and called in the inner child. For that time of contemplation, I encouraged everyone to think back on some of the core lessons that had been set up in their early lives and then to show up as their own compassionate authority figures, acknowledging their connection to the child part of the Whole Self.

I had a brief moment of appreciating how I, as a child, had sensed that I was being prepared for something meaningful in my life. Once I connected to that innocent child, we both affirmed that this journey of initiation was well beyond anything we had imagined might take place. I thanked him for his willingness to trust me on the journey and affirmed that I would continue to be there for him in any way that I could.

When we had all finished our meditations in the Pit, we made our way back up the long staircase. Going up was a bit easier, at least for me holding Robert. While his body was still quite active, it had calmed during the meditation. Once we reached the top of the staircase, we were directly in front of the entrance to the Queen's Chamber. Once inside that space, we connected to our individual heart spaces and spent time honoring the visions we had first stated at Abu Simbel. We also began to include wishing for the visions that served each individual around the world in this awakening of Soul plans.

The pinnacle of our initial journey was focused on the time we would spend in the King's Chamber, something we had anticipated with awe since our first conversations with Gabriel. And now, it was finally time to move into that hallowed space. To reach that pinnacle, we needed to ascend through the Grand Gallery—the only tall, open passageway in the Great Pyramid. This remarkable space was lined with two staircases, each running parallel along opposite walls, capped by a vaulted ceiling. Once we reached the top, Robert and I went into the King's Chamber alone, initially asking the higher beings' permission for the group to enter—giving us a clear way to honor the sacredness of the moment.

The King's Chamber was a deceptively simple room constructed of huge blocks of rose quartz. These massive squared-off stones fit together so perfectly well, thousands of years after construction, that a sheet of paper couldn't be squeezed between any of them, a building feat that couldn't likely be repeated in present times. This space, too, was lit by a couple of isolated bulbs running along a silver conduit pipe. The room contained only one item: a partially damaged stone structure called a *sarcophagus*.

Gabriel had assured us in our preparation talks that this object had never been used for the burial of a Pharaoh. Instead, one of the main purposes of the Great Pyramid being built was as a temple of initiation, so perfect in its proportions and directions that entire volumes have been written about it. The chamber where we now stood had been the sacred center of the temple used by initiates over the course of many centuries. We were even told that Jesus had experienced some of his final initiations of preparation in this sacred space.

Gabriel also told us that the *sarcophagus* was no longer located in its original position, something that would become significant in the ceremony we had been encouraged to perform on this unprecedented day of initiation. When the group joined us in the King's Chamber, they had been asked to enter in silence, focused on retrieving the specific ceremonial items they had brought with them—including three specific crystals and a rod of initiation.

As we continued to prepare and find our places, forming the two triangles of the six-pointed star appearing in the heavens, the grandness of this moment was in the forefront of everyone's mind. And even though we were standing in that location, there was no way to wrap our heads around the significance of what the world was about to experience.

Robert and I were instructed to stand in the center of the configuration, which represented the two energies having joined together in the heart space. We began by saying a short prayer of invocation to the higher beings and guides that work with our planet's evolution. Afterward, we began to activate the space with the group sounds and pitches that we had been told would work best. When this was complete, both triangles of people started slowly moving in opposite directions—one triangle flowing clockwise and the other counterclockwise.

After completing this first part of the activation, we spent a few moments in silence, reaching out to acknowledge and receive the energy of the millions of people who were now gathering in groups around the world in meditation. All together at the top of the hour in every time zone, we would soon be reciting the exact same words, focused on this very space as we all set the intention to receive and ground this remarkable download.

At this point in the ceremony, I knew it was time for the transfer of energy from Robert to myself, which would be my cue for making the specific sounds I was prepared to offer into the space. I feel certain that a full minute passed, but it felt even longer, and I felt nothing. I wasn't quite sure what to do—although I didn't want to miss the precise moment of planetary alignment—so I decided that I should just begin, trusting the sound and intentions to move with the sacredness that I felt. To serve the moment well, I let go of my confusion and focused all my energy on the inspiration of sound to move through me.

Fortunately, several people in the group, including Robert, were gifted clairvoyants, which simply means they can see energy as it is moving in a space. What each of those people described seeing was identical. As I allowed the sounds to move through me, a column of silver light began to take form at the ceiling, over the very place where Gabriel told us the *sarcophagus* had originally stood. Gradually, the column solidified and began to descend to the floor of the chamber.

At a certain point, the sounds moving through me abruptly stopped, without any conscious decision on my part. Once there was silence, we all held the space as initiates, standing as proxies for the millions of others who were doing this from their homes around the world. After a few moments, the clairvoyants in the group noted that the column of energy that had been well formed began to rise up and dissipate simultaneously. When the energy had nearly disappeared, everyone in the room heard the crescendo of a sudden high-pitched sound that emanated throughout the space. Awe and amazement filled the room.

Once we created closure to the worldwide meditation, reciting the words we had encouraged others to speak out loud, we all sat along the perimeter of the space, and I sang the song Gabriel had asked me to sing to complete this time of initiation, "Amazing Grace," which speaks of moving from blindness or being unconscious into a new vision. "Was blind, but now I see."

The initiation ceremony was complete. Still silent, we all began to gather our things. As people approached the *sarcophagus* to collect their crystals, the first to arrive discovered that the energy that had moved through the space was so intense that it had shifted many of the crystals from their original places to one end of the *sarcophagus*. Some of the crystals had even shattered. So many of the things we experienced on the journey continued to go well beyond anything that was familiar or logical.

Before leaving the Great Pyramid, Robert and I took time to thank all of the beings who had participated in this journey of initiation and would be continuing to guide the process of assimilation over the coming years. Back at our hotel, we gave the group the rest of the day to rest and contemplate the possible impacts that this Birth initiation would begin to have in our lives and in the world as a whole.

19

A NEW MISSION

N O REST FOR THE WEARY. WE WERE NOW TWO WEEKS
into this journey, preparing to continue on to Israel. I tried
to use every possible moment with Robert, and some of
those were focused on hearing from Gabriel.

Almost straight away, he addressed my concern.

*Dear one, we know that you are concerned about the transfer of energy in
the ceremony yesterday. We assure you that the transfer took place. You simply discovered that your body was able to ground those new levels of energy
with much more ease than you had imagined. We never suggested that your
body would respond in the same way Robert's had. Your energy configuration
is entirely different as it is serving a different set of purposes. Be at peace.*

With that reassurance, I was ready to continue to the next leg of our
journey, where we would be retracing the steps of Jesus's seven initiations. What a thrill it would be to visit the exact places where the seeds
of Soul possibilities had been played out two thousand years ago!

On our way to Israel, the group made an important stop at Mount Sinai to visit the sacred location where Moses had received the Ten Commandments. It was something I had seen depicted many times in the movie starring Charlton Heston. Adding to the impact of being in such a holy place was the fact that the top of Mount Sinai was a spectacular vantage point from which we could observe the night sky. Part of the reason we were there was to see more directly the objects that had come together in the heavens for the initiation.

Sure enough, the canopy was lit up in a brilliant display on that night, the likes of which I'd never seen before, more stars than I had ever perceived. Taking it all in, the song from my childhood came back to me: "It took a miracle to put the world in place. It took a miracle to hang the stars in space. But when he saved my Soul, cleansed and made me whole, it took a miracle of love and grace." How those words took on new meaning at this time, tying together the experience of my child, adult, and Soul, I couldn't possibly have imagined this moment or this opportunity as I sat in that tiny chapel in North Carolina all those years ago.

As we prepared to move to the locations where ancient stories had transpired, I could hardly take it all in. There were many highlights during that week. However, I will only focus on one for this telling. It took place at the Dead Sea—a historic body of water that is so saturated with salt, everything floats on its surface. It is also the lowest point on Earth—yet again, a great place to start the journey of seven initiations.

At this point, it should have come as no surprise, but as we approached the place we had chosen for this first ceremony, the weather began to shift in a very dramatic way. This time, clouds that were practically black filled the sky as far as our eyes could see. I imagined we were well protected, but I must admit this brought up some concern about putting our group into the water for a baptism ceremony. Robert, Deborah, and I agreed to watch for any lightning that might put us in harm's way.

Of course, we were still new to these grand manifestations, but we might have guessed this was merely the background for another sign of the power and magnitude of a planetary initiation. As we moved from the bus to take our places in the shallows of the sea, a huge hole opened in that dark sky. The glistening, distinct beams of light that came through the hole formed a dramatic pyramid, much like what we had seen depicted on a number of temple walls in Egypt. That first opening was followed by three smaller holes forming on both sides of the central hole. It didn't take us long to recognize that this was a remarkable replica of the seven energy centers—three chakras for the lower Self, three for the higher Self, and the pyramid of light emanating from the heart in the middle. It was a wonder to behold, perhaps the most amazing of all the physical phenomena we had witnessed on our journey.

Just as had been the case in Egypt, this configuration stayed open for over an hour, long enough for us to complete our baptism initiation. When we finished and were making our way back to the bus, true to each of the past experiences, each hole closed, and the sky was once again covered in clouds. As amazed as I was at this dramatic event, I was equally shocked by the realization that I was kind of getting used to seeing those remarkable manifestations.

After visiting many locations, each with their special energies, our final destination in Israel was the site where Jesus's body lay for three days after the Crucifixion. Gabriel suggested that those three days metaphorically represented the transformation of fear, shame, and judgment in the lower three energy centers—the very process we must all learn to move through before a resurrection of the Soul can take place in the heart.

For most of the three weeks of our travel, Robert and I had hardly managed any moments to ourselves when we were in the actual sites. That's what made it so unusual that the two of us ended up in the tomb space alone. Not even any other tourists. As soon as we went in, Robert showed signs that he was about to channel.

Whenever one of the guides who had been connecting to us on this journey began to assimilate with Robert's body, I would tune in, preparing to receive whatever energies and messages were about to come through. Once a guide came through more than once, I could typically recognize the energy of that being before they spoke.

What made this moment so powerful for me was that the energy coming through seemed new, but it also felt familiar. As a matter of fact, if my hunch was correct, this would be the first time Robert had opened to channel this particular connection. As soon as that thought crossed my mind, I became skeptical. "No way. I must be wrong." And yet, that familiar feeling never shifted.

Seconds later, the voice that came through identified itself in this way. *When I lay here in this space, I was preparing my body for a revelation of the resurrected Soul. This is why you are now here, preparing to not only resurrect your own Soul energies, but to continue bringing the message of Soul journeys into the world. You have much to look forward to as things unfold over the coming years. Many surprises lay ahead for you both, and I will be with you quite often in the process. To clarify the part that you have chosen to play, as an initiate, you represent an "everyman"—preparing to demonstrate, as one example of many in the world, some of what is possible for every man, woman, and child.*

As you have been told, the process you are opening to allow will only become possible as each individual chooses a similar path—to open and prepare their bodies for these unprecedented, new levels of energy to flow through their body. This is the path that will allow the resurrection of the Soul/Christed energies from deep within. We are grateful to have this moment with you, to thank you all for the service that you are all bringing as young initiates of the Soul.

I was literally moved to tears. Speechless. Once the message was complete and Robert was becoming grounded again, I felt elated, but so small. I did my best to share what had come through. We both admitted that we felt awkward, even suggesting to the others that such a thing had just taken place; at the same time, we wanted everyone to feel the acknowledgment that had been offered to each one of us. More than anything, we felt blessed beyond all words for the opportunities and experiences of the past three weeks.

Returning to New York felt like returning from some timeless vortex. Most things about our familiar world now felt strange and different. We felt ungrounded and highly sensitive to everything for any number of weeks. Just having a television on in the same room felt like an assault on our senses.

Gabriel explained, *It will now take months, if not years, for you and others around the world to assimilate what has been set in motion from just this one initiation. Be sure that you will now begin to experience many symptoms in your bodies as you face the challenge of allowing these new energies to work their way through more of the blockages that you still hold. Trust that we will continue to be with you as you continue forward.*

As a matter of fact, now that you have completed one initiation journey, we will tell you that we are hoping you will agree to lead a total of fifteen journeys between now and 2012. That is how long it will take for all of the layers of energy to be activated for the seven initiations.

As usual, each thing that Gabriel shared stirred up feelings of overwhelm in us. However, we were more grateful than ever to hear that he would continue to be with us through the whole process that would lead us to 2012. So far, Gabriel had been with us for seven years—interesting number. What a joy to think he would be with us for at least fifteen more. For now, we had more on our plates than we knew how to handle. We recognized that we needed time to be with everything that had been set in motion.

We started hearing from many of the people from the group, who were all experiencing new and unusual aches and pains, just as Gabriel had promised. Some felt dizzy or lightheaded. Many people's sleep patterns were interrupted. And others expressed not knowing who they were any longer, in some strange way.

I had some strange encounters with electronics. After I rode in my brother-in-law's car, for instance, all of his preprogrammed radio stations disappeared. Another time, I visited my sister and stayed in a room that had a television and a computer. Both became completely disrupted and had to be fixed after I spent the night there.

I considered each of these strange occurrences to be powerful indicators of the energetic shifts that were taking place in our bodies, a great reminder that there was a bridge to what had taken place in the ancient land of Egypt and our modern lives in New York. It is strange how the mind will try to edit out anything that stretches familiar comfort zones too much.

The same shake-ups and shifts you are beginning to experience will be happening, just a bit more gradually, for people all around the planet. Anything that is out of balance will begin to become more evident. This new surge of energy will interrupt many of your familiar systems and approaches. This will all become a natural part of making you aware of the blockages that most need to shift or be cleared for the higher good of all. These will be some of the more immediate impacts of this second surge of kundalini as your planet begins to move through the equivalent of planetary midlife.

What we had already heard about the stage called midlife is that this second surge of kundalini has the power to awaken us into our deepest potential: the Soul. However, up to this point in our planetary evolution, the masses of us have not been prepared to handle those levels of energetic movement in our bodies—filled with dense blockages of fear, shame, and judgment.

Therefore, the experience of this second surge of kundalini has typically equaled energy slamming into those blockages, creating an accelerated breakdown and decline. This has been the Divine Order that has prepared each person for the end of a lifetime—until this time of new energetic support for awakening Souls.

Though there have been handfuls of individuals who have chosen an accelerated path over the centuries, it is only now that mass consciousness is reaching the stage of midlife with the energetic support needed to awaken into Soul. You might say that the Earth herself has reached midlife as the planet integrates the first in a series of energetic surges. You will all need to respond. As the next years and decades progress, you will all need to move through many shifts and get used to many changes. Whether you like it or not, this is the stage of evolution you have reached. And one thing is for sure. You will either go through an accelerated breakdown or an accelerated awakening. The choice will be yours, both individually and collectively.

As we prepared to shift from one millennium to the next, Gabriel assured us that there were many initiates around the world who were beginning to wake up, choosing to become pioneers, like us, who would bring their gifts into the world in new ways. He assured us that new leaders would begin to emerge in every field. Though each individual's path might differ in obvious ways—much the same as our Soul curriculums are set up to reflect our unique needs and interests during childhood—we would all learn to bring our individual pieces of the puzzle to create more complete solutions for our evolving world. One of the most important things we would need to learn was how to work together, honoring both our shared humanity and our emerging individuality.

These were the most important messages that concluded our first initiation journey. At that point, our core group hoped that the fourteen other journeys Gabriel mentioned would be as powerful as the first. Since I am sharing this story after having already lived through each of those journeys, I can assert with great enthusiasm that every one of them has been uniquely wonderful, each with astounding synchronicities, miraculous affirmations, and meaningful shifts into deeper intimacy with one another. For me, that final piece—the capacity for true connection—has remained, as always, my highest priority and greatest joy.

Some of the sacred sites we visited for the next initiations included Peru, Tibet, India, Nepal, Bali, Burma, Mexico, and England. Over time, we began to notice how often the specific locations that were being activated for an upcoming initiation would experience a major shake-up before our journeys took place. Whether it was a typhoon, an enormous fire, a mass shooting, a bombing, or simply a disruption of people challenging the status quo, each of those shake-up events served to bring the world's attention to the very areas where the next downloads were about to take place.

Over the next fourteen years, we organized fourteen worldwide meditations. Because the internet was not inundated with endless options and distractions in the late nineties, when we started our outreach, it was easier to get people's attention. Gabriel told us that as the momentum built, the numbers of people who became connected to those yearly initiations grew to over sixteen million. We welcomed this information as further encouragement that there are tremendous numbers of people who are indeed waking up.

Each time we returned home from a journey, our lives would change in ways we could never predict. Suffice it to say that Robert and I got used to living in the depths of "unknown territory" and newness from 1997 onward.

Soon after the first journey, Gabriel suggested that we now needed to consider how we wanted to start helping more people to understand the shifts that were beginning to unfold. We also needed to figure out as many ways as possible, combining all of our training with various teachers, that people could best prepare their bodies for tremendous shifts.

After going through the miracles of the first journey, Robert and I were both certain nothing could be more important than dedicating our lives to honoring this remarkable opportunity. All the shake-ups occurring in the world around us only strengthened our certainty. When we'd left for Egypt, Robert was still invested in his career as the head of the makeup department at the New York City Opera, and I was thinking that I would shift from a life in opera to a career in film or television.

Once we returned, those priorities had clearly shifted. I now felt a much deeper responsibility to help others—a remarkable evolution of my early desire to help when I went to college. We now had seven years of education. We had both enhanced our training as healers and as bioenergetic practitioners. We began putting together what would become a unique approach to personal transformation, empowerment, and energetic preparation for the Soul.

Within a short time, the Universe moved things along for Robert. While he had been putting more time and energy into other arenas, the New York City Opera had been deciding it was time to go in a new direction as well. The result is that Robert was unexpectedly fired from his position. Though a bit disconcerting initially, once Robert adjusted to the idea, he moved rather quickly into working with clients and offering private Gabriel readings full time.

In addition to deepening my commitment to the clients I was already working with, doing massage/Reiki sessions to help move energy more effectively through their bodies, I spent a great deal of time studying bioenergetics and putting the tremendous body of information we'd been receiving into a logical sequence and form. Of course, we didn't have a distinct vision for how it would all unfold. We just knew there was now no turning back. What we were on the way to creating, starting in 1997, was a School of Self-Mastery.

20

SOUL CONSIDERATIONS

OVER THE YEARS, I'VE HAD THE CHANCE TO ASK hundreds of clients to look back over their lives and see if they could name five healthy relationships. With just that much information, none of them answered in the affirmative. What I was actually asking about were relationships built on authentic sharing and mutual trust, with clear tools that allow the couple to grow into consistently deeper, reliable connection and intimacy over time.

After spending so many years learning to develop a healthy intimate relationship with myself, I understood that not having the tools and education for nurturing Self is what most often blocks people from creating healthy connections and authentic intimacy. That was certainly true for me for most of my life.

This was ultimately the discovery I tried to encourage for each of my clients, and I have loved letting each of them know that this is what they could look forward to, by taking the time to learn how to nurture and value Self. And that has proved true and consistent over the years.

Another privilege of being in conscious relationships of all types, where two people learn to come together in mutual support, is that we can learn to become emotional allies, playing proactive roles in helping one another work through core challenges and wounded feelings in a safe space. I only knew this was possible because it is what I had begun to practice in my most immediate relationships. Robert and I purposefully used our friendship as an opportunity to work through some of our most difficult individual challenges.

Gabriel assured us that the potential of the Whole Self is so vast that there would never be an end to the "next level challenges" that we could choose to face. Challenges are a necessary part of creating forward momentum. It was nice to be reminded that our challenges are vehicles that encourage us to show up and examine anything that is out of balance or that we haven't yet explored. Each one is a chance to claim more of our personal capacity, while we also build more of the qualities that are important to us as individuals. Courage. Willingness. Compassion.

The biggest joint challenge that Robert and I had to face with each other began back in 1997, after seven years of being Soul brothers and dearest of friends. Just before we left for the first journey to Egypt, Robert surprised me by sharing that his feelings about our relationship were shifting. He was hoping that I felt the same way and that we could become life partners as well. This presented me with a major conundrum.

I loved Robert like a Soul brother and a rare presence in my life, more than I could say, but I never felt drawn to him romantically. At the same time, Gabriel had just told us that Robert and I were Twin

Flames, and I knew that Robert was the only person I had met at that point who could relate to all the spiritual depths that I experienced. We had been pioneers in one another's lives, facing many things together.

Looking back, in some ways, I wish I had stood in my deepest truth when he first asked the question. But I couldn't shake the idea that my limitations might only come from being caught in some deep fear I needed to face. Perhaps this was a challenge that would reveal an unusual depth of love that I couldn't otherwise reach. With that in mind, I reluctantly told Robert I was willing to at least explore and find out what was possible. I made sure to be clear that this meant I was agreeing not to date anyone else, and even agreeing to move in together once we returned from Egypt.

As always, hindsight is more informed than foresight. Looking back, I could see that this was the second time in my life I ended up going against my deepest truth—and the period of confused frustration that came out of it lasted for six challenge-filled years. Perhaps this was what it took for me to be willing to deal with some of my deepest wounded feelings. One thing was for sure. I used every opportunity in those six years to process and reeducate my inner Self. I hoped that Robert was doing the same. One way or another, the whole experience only deepened the gratitude we both felt, having a trusted companion to work through countless fears and confusions.

What I appreciated as much as anything was that no matter how challenging things became, both of us kept showing up and communicating about whatever we needed to face—sometimes loudly. What each part of that process taught us was a rare depth of honesty, even in the face of disappointing someone so dear. And even though my truth never changed, we ended up reaching levels of the Whole Self that neither of us would have likely accessed otherwise.

Robert ultimately needed to face his fear of rejection and being "not good enough," while I was facing my fear that love required me to become a martyr—wanting to please and avoid depriving someone else. Over the six years it took for me to gain real clarity, things eventually came to a head.

I knew I had reached a point of no return when my despair over being untrue to myself became so crushing that I started to wonder if I even wanted to go on living. How ironic to be offered the opportunity of all our lifetimes, while also negotiating suicidal thoughts. Apparently, this was the depth I needed to reach in order to access my deepest set of fears.

This pivotal moment asked me to face the core fear of disappointing or letting others down in a profound way. If I chose to honor my deepest truth, I knew I would risk disappointing Robert. If he chose to pack up and leave, based on my decisions, then everything we had built over the last decade might collapse. This also meant potentially disappointing the hierarchy of higher beings who had handed us this insane set of opportunities. I doubt I could find words that adequately convey the depth of pressure I felt in that choice.

What I held on to, trying to create an equal balance for my fear, was that everything Gabriel had taught us over the years was an encouragement to make love the most important consideration—which starts with Self. I had also been taught that the depth of any fear is always matched by the level of empowered Self that is waiting to be claimed on the other side of the fear. So far, that had always proved true.

On New Year's Day, 2003, I woke up knowing my present course had to change. I dug deep and decided to choose love for myself—no matter what that choice meant for anyone else. That is when I called my friend Donna to ask for help. Being a wonderful therapist who loved both Robert and me, she heard the seriousness in my voice and asked me to come over right away. She then helped me put together all the pieces I was negotiating so that I could make a clear plan.

While Robert was definitely disappointed and sad about the decision, he was not surprised. The moment was hard for us both in different ways. Fortunately, we assured one another that we would continue to show up the best we could. And that is how I freed myself to return once again to a fully authentic place that I hope I never question again. My choice allowed me to show love to Robert much more fully than I had been able to in those last six years, when I was afraid of sending him mixed messages.

After the next year of reassuring and stabilizing this new kind of trust of unwavering friendship with Robert, I was ready to open for the possibility of a next relationship. Though it may seem quick in the telling of this story, it was one full year later when I met Todd, a wonderful man with an unusually big heart.

It didn't take long for us both to recognize how blessed we were to have found each other. We also had to admit that we were grateful we hadn't met years earlier. We both somehow understood that neither of us would have been ready to allow such a deep connection if we had.

After what I had just learned with Robert, I was prepared and determined to live with a greater willingness to trust and share a connection with Todd. I decided that no matter what fears might come up, I would face them. And that is what we gradually learned to do together—with some natural learning curves all along the way. Whenever a challenge became apparent, we would sit down and talk it through sooner than later—most of the time. No matter what I needed to share, Todd was always there in support. And I did my best to do the same for him. In many ways, this was the first time that I truly felt such a complete sense of "home."

Now that I was finally happy and at peace in a healthy, mutually supportive relationship, I knew it was time to ask Gabriel for more clarity on the subject of sexuality and how it plays such an immediate role in our unfolding Soul journeys. Prior, I had been somewhat afraid to approach the subject—mostly because I knew that some religions had such strong impressions of right and wrong around this issue.

For instance, I knew there were confusing messages in the Old Testament that many people had used to support their opposition to same-sex love relationships. And yet, because resolving so much fear and shame had been required for me to experience this awesome level of authentic intimacy, I knew that whatever Gabriel had to share would be important.

Gabriel's first inclination was to assure me that my Soul had indeed chosen this challenge for very specific reasons in this lifetime—setting up an inescapable sense of shame about Self that I could not avoid exploring if I wanted to find real peace. He said this was part of being an "everyman"—because every person must face their fear and shame about the Self in order to learn how to love and create an inner connection to the deepest truth—that we are all sacred individuals on Soul journeys.

Choosing to have such a clear, confusing issue that would exacerbate your sense of confusion and shame—which is inherent in all Soul setups in some way—was crucial for your journey in this lifetime. Remember that it is often when you have a challenge that you are willing to look at any specific aspect of your life. This particular challenge set you up with deep questions about your value as a man and what it means to be an empowered individual.

For each person to gradually activate and land in the heart center is the main purpose or destination of every Soul journey. The heart is the primary place where you experience meaning and value. Helping you prepare for moving up into the consciousness of the heart is the reason we, Gabriel, have come at this time. In order for you to help other people, you have needed to understand the entire journey—from the reality of being stuck in fear, shame, and judgment, and then moving through the many steps of resolving those challenges in order to activate your sacred heart. This is the journey from wounded to wiser that you have taken.

I had waited for decades to hear these words. The best news was that the words affirmed the journey I was already taking. In other words, I had already begun to love and value myself as an individual and as a man in the world in meaningful ways, and that was something I knew I would continue to deepen for the rest of my life.

The specific challenge around sexuality and shame that you have carried has been one of the main motivators to search for more complete truths and answers that promote peace. People carry an endless array of shameful myths about themselves. And in the course of your extended Soul journeys, which takes place over many, many lifetimes, each one of you grows through learning about love in many variations.

From the beginning of our time together, we have told you that very few people have a real understanding of the Soul and the setup of Soul challenges in a lifetime. Without that awareness, you have not been ready to consider that your Souls do not even have a gender. Each one of you is a perfect balance of male and female energy—reflected in your mental/assertive and emotional/receptive energies. This balance is intended to teach you the natural flow of giving and receiving, which very few in your world truly understand or practice. The Soul Self can only be integrated consciously when you have learned what it means to actually love—which can only be achieved when you create a balance of male and female energy, giving and receiving in sacred acceptance of Self and of one another.

At various points on your extended Soul journeys, you all have lifetimes when you learn from incarnating as men and as women. You also have lifetimes when you learn from your male or female energies being distinctly out of balance. When that happens, one way to work through the challenge to come back to center is for you to focus most fully on exploring male energy or female energy in a lifetime. This is one way your Souls can teach you about the natural gifts and challenges of both.

In learning those lessons, you all play the roles of protagonists and antagonists with one another. This is the natural way that Souls learn together, exploring many sides of each issue. This is ultimately the process that teaches you how to love all that you are. It is a huge process, which is why you need so many lifetimes. You all have infinite potentials, and it is learning to love and value that allows you to awaken more of your potentials.

All of this was making great sense to me. Actually, this particular conversation seemed to encompass the totality of how Life operates to support our Soul journeys rather than only applying to my specific issue. I loved that. In some ways, the conversation was providing clarity that I'd been seeking since I was a child. The experience left me feeling grateful and humbled.

The deeper truth about sexual expression and intimacy is that there is no bad or wrong combination of individuals who are exploring love and connection in the eyes of God/Goddess/All That Is. Notice that we used a name for the Divine that purposefully demonstrates the inclusion of male and female energy. After all, everything is made up of a balance of those two energies— even the Divine. God consciousness embraces all that is, because every challenge, lesson and expression is sacred. As individual Souls, you are all facets or manifestations of God consciousness.

When you are children, you don't know that you hold the capacity of adult consciousness. When you are adults, at your present level of evolution, you don't know that you are also Souls with much deeper potential of consciousness. The same goes for not understanding that you are all part of the Divine Order of God consciousness.

Learning to love—in sacred acceptance—every facet of the Whole Self is your goal. Oftentimes, the most powerful lessons about love are explored in your primary relationships. As for who you choose to love, it is only possible to find real peace when you embrace the most authentic truths that are held inside you in a lifetime.

Again, we assure you that you hold all of those truths from the moment you are born. That is the perfection of Soul plans. We are also aware that almost no one likes their particular challenges. That is the nature of challenges. However, your Souls know what you each need to explore in the various stages of your growth and evolution, including an awareness of the specific Souls with whom you need to explore love most fully in a lifetime.

If you are a man and need to explore what it means to embrace your sacred male energy, you might very well choose to explore what it is to love another male physically, emotionally, mentally, sexually, and spiritually. If you are a woman and need to explore what it is to love and value the depth of your feminine gifts, you may choose to love another woman in the same ways.

Much of the confusion and fear that have been so prevalent on the planet have come from interpretations of the documents that have been embraced by each of your religions. Keep in mind that we are not here to make any of those documents or the interpretations that you might need to explore at any given stage of your individual and collective development right or wrong. Each of those messages and the interpretations that you choose to embrace as you explore can become important tools in your lives.

However, be aware that how you interpret those messages is colored by the level of Soul development you have reached in a lifetime. Keep in mind that every level is sacred and perfect for you at some point in your journey. In other words, on a Soul level, all things operate beyond good and bad. Everything is simply provided as an opportunity for learning and growth. You decide what serves your journey into love and what does not, in each stage of your growth.

Within that process, it is important to remember that you are all making the choices that you believe are the best at any given time. This was true when you were in third grade and when you were in college. If you think about it, we bet your specific choices and perspectives evolved from the time you were in third grade to the time you were in college. Each step along the way, you were basing your choices on the convictions that you held at any given time. Only through what you experienced were you able to evaluate what continued to serve you and what did not. As you grow wiser, you let go of limited choices that you recognize no longer serve you—anything that keeps you from the next depths of love that you are ultimately trying to reach.

Now consider that the documents which have defined your religions have been written down and passed on, quite often in oral traditions at first. They have then been translated by individuals who were doing their best as well. And yet, those messages could only be communicated based on how clear any of those individuals happened to be at the time they passed them on.

I loved hearing these perspectives. The fact that they held no judgment but allowed for the humanity and evolution of all people was comforting to me.

All things, including the documents that have been created throughout history, are naturally impacted by whatever unresolved agendas or desires to control each individual is carrying. For instance, Emperor Constantine tampered with messages in what you call "the Bible." As one example, all references to Soul journeys and the reincarnation of Souls were removed at that time. This was a choice he believed was for the good of the people. It helped to keep them in a healthy level of fear so that they could be kept in line with the behaviors that he thought were best. If people thought they only had one lifetime, they would feel more pressure to "follow the rules."

Messages about the flow of male and female energy have also been interpreted or misinterpreted by many individuals, all doing the best they knew how. The truths that were truly intended to be conveyed on this subject included the need for male and female energy to flow in balance. In some ways, you might say that is what forms a perfect marriage—of energy and connection, not of genders.

Now just consider how fully you—yes, you—understand the flow of male and female energy today. If it were up to you to document the impact of male and female energy for future generations in a book at this moment, how effective do you suppose you might be? We live in a time when there is much more shared information and developed consciousness than was typical two thousand years ago.

Just look back to what you perceived about any given subject twenty years ago, and then look to the perspectives that you have grown into today. If your earlier understanding had been written in stone—as a requirement of acceptance in society—would you now be in conflict with your own words or claims from an earlier version of your own growing Self? And would you wish that others whom you love had to be held accountable to or ruled by your twenty-years-ago understanding? Religions and governments have often suppressed growth and change, all in the name of forcing a rather frozen approach or principle.

Just consider how many individuals have been excommunicated or even executed for exploring any perspectives that challenged the norms of the day— such as Galileo suggesting that the Earth was not the center of the Universe or that the Earth rotated around the sun. Blasphemous, they all screamed!

Those particular perspectives may seem silly to you now that you have grown into a twenty-first century society. However, at a different time, you would all be considered heretics by your religions—all based on people doing their best to passionately protect whatever perspectives or approaches they decided were frozen rights and wrongs. That behavior has often equaled trying to feel safe within the rules of governments or religions. We now remind you that each stage of learning has eventually needed to realize the limitations it had embraced and explored, with the inevitable need to eventually evaluate more complete truths and perceptions in order to improve the quality of Life in that period.

This has also been true in the evolution of your personal relationships. You still live in a world that has much to learn about healthy relationships, and that is true of all combinations of people, no matter the genders. You have much to look forward to as you continue learning about love and healthy relationships—if you are willing to open to the Soul truths that are attempting to rise at this time.

If, on the other hand, you decide to use the few passages in the Bible that have been translated as limited, negative passed-down interpretations of those subjects—such as the passages from the book of Leviticus—then some of you will find that you must condemn some surprising things. You would have to stone, condemn, or reject those who eat shellfish, as well as those who have chosen to divorce.

What is important is that you each learn to evaluate your individual, most loving truths. Clinging to frozen absolutes doesn't allow you to consider each idea with compassion, allowing each individual to explore the things you each need, in order to grow and evolve. As one example, divorce is sometimes the most loving choice possible for the two Souls involved in a deep conflict— particularly if one person is not ready to move into the next stages of their potential. It is also true that divorce has often been used as an escape, prior to seeking help or trying to work out the conflicted lessons you are there to explore. When that is the case, most often the two individuals will eventually find that they manifest similar issues in their next relationships. This is because it is not possible to escape your core Soul lessons.

There are so many perspectives and truths that will become clearer as your planet opens to the practical perspectives of the Soul in the coming years and decades. However, we know that whenever wiser perspectives are introduced, those more expanded or inclusive approaches typically challenge familiar comfort zones, which is another name for the "accepted norms of the day." When that happens, there is often pushback, resistance, and acting out in fear. Sometimes the pushback is quite reactive, all in the name of defending something that an individual believes is the only truth possible. That approach has never worked, and it never will.

Gabriel's answer to my question continued to become more comprehensive and inspiring than I was expecting. Each piece of the puzzle was helping me understand even more fully how important it is that we look at each facet of our lives and choose the most compassionate perspectives that we can. This was a great confirmation of the work I had begun doing with clients all around the world. I was helping each one to find greater peace and understanding about what is possible in their lives.

In closing, let us repeat once more that male and female energy operating in balance is what allows any two individuals to achieve or create a "perfect marriage"—giving and receiving in equal value. Seemingly simple. And yet that message has been misunderstood for centuries.

We can only assure you that the passage that refers to two male energies coming together or laying together as an abomination was never intended to refer to two men having a loving sexual connection. The actual abomination is for the male/assertive energy of any person's will to become aggressive and then met with any other willful energy. The will is a driving force in your lives, and it is male in nature—in both men and women. The abomination is two willful energies choosing to control or to act out in fear and defense. Two people, two political parties, two nations, or two races. It is all the same lesson.

When you operate from the wounded assumption that two differing approaches or comfort zones must imply that one must be right and the other has to be wrong, you have a real problem. It is called duality, and it is a myth, not a truth, from the perspective of the Soul.

We merely encourage you to ask yourself whether the truths that you claim are more focused on love and value—honoring the journeys of all individuals and the planet herself—or whether you are embracing wounded limitations, based on the fear of anything that doesn't directly validate your present perspective.

Having spent so many years at this point learning to claim my most authentic evolving Self, I was deeply grateful for any new perspectives that allowed me to lead with even more love and less fear. I celebrated the fact that the answers Gabriel had just provided could be applied to every challenge of fear and shame that people might continue to face in their lives.

More and more, these have become the very tenets of love and value that have guided our School of Self-Mastery. We believe that is why we have attracted such a broad spectrum of individuals seeking to discover more complete answers and more fulfilling solutions—including teachers, healers, therapists, psychologists, and other types of leaders.

Before we knew it, 2012 was fast approaching, which signaled Robert and me to begin planning the last of our fifteen journeys—this time, to the heart chakra of the planet: Machu Picchu, Peru. I was sure it would be powerful. And yet, there was no way I could have guessed the depth of upheaval and change that was about to take place in our lives, yet again.

21

PROFOUND CHANGE

ECEMBER 21, 2012, BECAME A MUCH-TALKED-ABOUT date in the empowerment world. Various individuals introduced theories, describing what they thought a twenty-six-thousand-year cycle coming to a close would mean for us all. Some even assumed that the Mayan Calendar "ending" might mark the end of the world. That perspective never resonated for me, though we had the advantage of Gabriel assuring us that this would be a time of bigger cycle shifts than anything we had previously known in our planet's history. Again, another huge claim.

When I asked him to share more specific perspectives on this particular date, he suggested, *The upcoming shift will indeed be "the end of the world as you have known it." However, like all calendars, the Mayan system merely marks a natural ending, followed by a new cycle beginning, and change will become the name of the game. As we have told you many times, the changes that this series of initiations has already begun to set in motion will become nothing short of a complete evolutionary shift on your planet, with enough power to catapult those who prepare out of survival conscious-ness and into a profound, surprising awakening.*

We also need to point out that none of those shifts will be immediately evi-dent on December 21, 2012. Change will take place at an accelerated rate, but it will still take many years before people begin to understand the evolution-ary shift, even at the foundational level. It will likely take much longer before people have access to an understanding about what is happening on a higher level. They will first focus on the shifts and how their familiar comfort zones are being interrupted.

Because we had been told many times that these journeys had already begun to inspire a shift into planetary midlife, we trusted that people's lives and the systems that govern those lives would either choose collec-tively to participate in an accelerated awakening or they would experi-ence an accelerated breakdown. No matter what people chose over the coming years, we felt sure we would all be presented with an accelerated learning curve. That was for sure.

Even though I had been preparing for years for these initiations, I began to experience an illogical fear and resistance of going on our final jour-ney to Peru. What was particularly surprising was that I had always been the primary champion who drove these bigger explorations. This time, however, I couldn't get the idea of "death" out of my head.

I already knew that each new beginning required some letting go of what no longer served. This was different. I wondered if I might be preparing for a near-death experience, similar to the one Robert had gone through in 1987. I also wondered if some death process was required for the awakening that we were working toward. Lots of ideas about my gut reluctance swirled around in my head right up until the day we left for Peru.

Though each of the other initiations had been unique, what remained consistent in each was the growing depth of connection and support that the groups we attracted were able to experience—a wonderful sign that we were all showing up and growing up. For the final journey of this series, many of the ceremonies Gabriel gave us focused on proactively embracing the endings that needed to take place in our lives, while we continued to refine the visions that had evolved since 1997.

On one of our first days in Peru, while we were staying at a beautiful stucco hotel that had tons of local charm, we ran into a vendor who had become rather familiar to us on our last journey to Peru. When he and his sister called a couple of us by name, those of us who'd been on the previous trip were really touched. Who knows how many thousands of tourists they had encountered in that gap of time? Once they told us they had heard of our return, the gentleman felt compelled to bring me a beautiful amethyst crystal that he thought I would love.

Though I can often feel a distinct energy when I hold various crystals, I had never been truly enthusiastic about them. In this case, however, it seemed that the vendor knew something I didn't. When I picked this one up, the energy emanating from it caused my whole arm to move in a large, sweeping motion. I would have to be pretty dense not to have seen this as a beautiful synchronicity. I bought the amethyst and thanked him, feeling that this object could become a wonderful memento for me of all the journeys.

Nine of our ten days in Peru passed in meaningful ceremony and exploration, and then December 21, 2012, finally arrived. Our group entered the sacred site of Machu Picchu, excited to see what would happen. Naturally, we had organized our fourteenth worldwide meditation and trusted that millions of people would be gathering around the globe to join their beautiful energies with us again in just a couple of hours. In preparation for that coming together, we did a meditation to join the proxy group's energy, just as we had done so many times. For this round, however, Robert and I had arranged for a special surprise. We wanted the group to experience the energy of a local shaman, one who already had a deep connection to the site.

Having the shaman guide this opening meditation meant that I could relax from my position as leader, taking advantage of those few moments to have my own experience. The first symbols that appeared when I closed my eyes were the three animal archetypes typically depicted in Incan art—the serpent, the jaguar, and the condor. I loved knowing that these three animals archetypically represent the three levels of the Whole Self.

I then got a clear picture of a double tetrahedron, which is a 3-D representation of the six-pointed star that had begun our initiation journey in Egypt. The 3-D version is often referred to as a Merkabah, which is the form of the energy or light body that surrounds each one of us. In order to awaken into the consciousness of the Soul, that light body must be activated—a process that we had begun teaching in our School of Self-Mastery. When it appeared, I figured it was likely indicating an activation of my own energy field. However, what happened next was completely unusual: the two pyramids of the double tetrahedron split apart. One of the pyramids rose up, though it remained connected to the lower one through a spiraled rainbow.

As soon as the shaman guided us all to come out of meditation, I asked Robert if he knew how to interpret the split Merkabah in my vision. He said that he'd never heard of such a thing, and so we figured that only time would tell. With no time to linger, I returned to the opportunity of leading the group to prepare for the main event.

For this day of shifting cycles, Gabriel told us that the Earth would align at the very center of the Milky Way. The center of anything is typically the point of neutrality. In a point of neutrality, there is no duality, separation, or opposition—the very goal that we are all working toward in moving to the heart space, the center of our beings. What is cool about any point of stillness and balance is that this is where the greatest amount of energy can flow. In this case, we knew that a tremendous influx of energy was soon to be downloaded.

Once we gathered for this second part of our initiation, our group joined hands, took some deep, proactive breaths, and then brought our attention to connecting our energy with people from all around the planet who were focusing on Machu Picchu—the heart chakra of the planet. Afterward, we recited the same powerful words that millions of others were simultaneously reading aloud.

We planned to complete our journey in Peru by ascending to the highest point in the area—Huayna Picchu, the peak that overlooks Machu Picchu. Because the climb is quite steep, some people in the group needed more time than others to make their way to the top. Wanting to make sure everyone was safe, I chose to bring up the rear.

Halfway up the mountain, our little group stopped to rest for a moment. While we were sitting, my dear friend, Donna, asked if she could see the amethyst crystal I had been holding so often on the journey. Simple and elegant, this amethyst was adorned by a beautiful piece of silver that wrapped around its center.

When I handed it to Donna, she immediately said, "That is the brightest rainbow I've ever seen in a crystal."

Surprised by her comment, I took the crystal back for a moment. I'd become quite familiar with the amethyst over the course of two weeks, and yet, I had never noticed a rainbow. As soon as I looked this time, I saw that Donna was correct. Somehow in the last few hours, a bright rainbow had formed in the center of my crystal.

When the last of us eventually made our way to the top of Huayna Picchu, we all looked out at the amazing vistas, which included Machu Picchu below us. It was there that we did our full closing of the fifteen initiations, which naturally included a huge "thank you" to all the guides who had put up with us—oh, I mean worked with us and would continue to guide us over the coming years of integration.

As one final gesture, I closed my eyes and spontaneously sang a particularly meaningful phrase from *Phantom of the Opera*. With my heart as open as I could muster, it just felt right to sound this beautiful encouragement out into the world: "Let your Soul take you where you long to be!" I loved reverberating that final high note, which seemed to proclaim, "We are here. We have responded. We have witnessed the remarkable things that have taken place. We now stand as witnesses in the world."

Once all of our hugs were done, the group began the steep descent back down the mountain. About halfway, I had another surprise. As someone who loves hiking in nature, I would never have guessed that I would be the one who ended up falling. In an instant, as I stepped on a slippery rock in just the wrong way, my feet were no longer under me, and my body plunged downward. I ended up catching the entire weight of my body with my clenched right fist, which happened to be the one that held my beautiful crystal.

For a moment, I thought I might have broken all my fingers. Even so, my more immediate concern was the crystal. When I checked it and found that it was intact, I placed it in my pocket and then focused on nurturing my hand. Throbbing, but fine.

As was so often the case, the schedule on our journeys was tight. We didn't have time to dally, even if one of the two fearless leaders had gone down. We all returned to the task at hand and reached the bottom of the mountain where our luggage was already waiting. We now had only enough time to grab a snack and make a quick trip to the bathroom (ha!) before we were on our way to the airport.

In those few brief moments, I sat with Robert to have some tea. It was there that I once more retrieved the crystal from my pocket. Right away, I had the feeling that something was wrong. As it turned out, that thick piece of amethyst had been completely cleaved into two pieces when I fell. The silver fastening was now the only thing that held the two halves together. I was sad, tired, and a bit angry. The one object I had decided to give some meaning was now ruined. All I could do was allow myself to have a brief, exhausted cry.

However, this was nothing compared to the challenge I had to face once we returned to New York. One evening when Robert and I were hanging out at my apartment after the journey, we were reminiscing about some of the highlights we had enjoyed over the past fifteen years. It was then that Robert told me he was having a strong intuition that he was somehow complete with what his Soul had chosen to do in this lifetime and that he no longer felt a desire to be here.

I was stunned. I couldn't understand why he wouldn't want to stay and enjoy the next levels of Soul that we had relentlessly worked to prepare for. After all, we had been told that the hardest part of the journey by far was all the preparation and clearing. Graciously, Robert was willing to talk about it several times over the coming weeks, but his mind never shifted, and his feelings definitely persisted. Those conversations, of course, left me wondering if this was the death I had been sensing before our journey.

By this point, I honored the fact that Robert had every right to follow his deepest truth. That is the loving support I held on to. Only a few months later, Robert manifested lymphoma and found himself in the hospital. Over the course of a week, we had some very tender conversations. One of the most important things I had the chance to say to him was, "Robert, I probably know everything there is to know about you—even the things that you have tried hard to keep hidden. No matter what happens here, I want you to know and trust that there is no part of you that is unlovable. No matter what your journey has required, I see you, and I love you in every way that I know how."

He looked at me with the tender gaze I knew so well and replied, "It is only because of you, Ron Baker, that I know that love is actually possible."

After we, his staunch supporters, had gone home that evening, things accelerated. The doctor called in the middle of the night to tell me that Robert had experienced heart failure, though he had been revived. By the time we were able to be with him in the morning, he was again unconscious, lying in the ICU. When the doctor called Robert's medical proxies in for a conference—which meant that I was joined by our dear friend Brian and my sister JB—he explained that the only things keeping Robert's body alive were the medications they had begun to provide.

We all agreed that we needed to honor Robert's wishes. To prepare for letting him go, we gathered a few close friends from the core Soul family and created a simple ceremony that involved each person offering him some acknowledgment and a blessing for the next stage of his journey. When it was my turn, I reminded Robert of the near-death experience that had begun our journey together. "You must go back, for you have not yet learned how to love." I then thanked him for including me in completing that circle of learning about love over the course of our twenty-two years together. I also wished for him that he would now be free of all the fear and pain he had carried in this lifetime, and that he would do his best to remember the profound depths of love that we had shared.

Once the ceremony ended and the group had left the room, I sat down next to Robert's bed and took his hand. The moment I did, the vision from our final day in Machu Picchu returned to my mind's eye. The same two halves of the double tetrahedron split apart, and as the one rose to a higher place—still connected by a complete rainbow—I heard Gabriel speaking inside my head, *As Twin Flames, you have been two halves of a single whole. Robert brought through higher messages from Spirit that served you brilliantly, and you held a grounded space for all of him to land and feel safe. He is now moving more fully back into the higher realms, where he will be able to best support you, as you take your next steps. Trust that the two of you will continue to be joined by all seven levels of a complete rainbow—the Whole Self.*

The moment the message was complete, I felt Robert's energy leave his body, and the EKG machine monitoring his heart went flat. My precious Soul brother, Twin Flame, and rare companion had moved on.

22

LOOKING FORWARD

I FELT THAT I LOST TEN PEOPLE THE DAY ROBERT PASSED. He was invested in so many parts of my life, wearing a multitude of hats and playing countless roles. And now he was gone. With only three days to get his apartment packed before another month of rent was due, I gathered with some invaluable helpers to get it all done. It was one of those times when I was steeped in gratitude that I had spent so much time learning how to receive support. Even so, it was intense going through our twenty-two years of memories. Overwhelmed and raw, I packed a little and then took time to cry.

On the second day, as I moved through the room where so many of our client sessions had taken place, I was shocked out of silence by hearing Robert's voice in my head, calling my name. It was so clear that I froze. Because I was in such a vulnerable state, I jumped into my testing mode. At this point, I had spent decades being able to hear guides through a form of telepathy. But this was different.

After pausing for a moment, I made my way to the office where I had originally been headed. "Robert," I said aloud, "I think this is you I am hearing, but I have to be sure. I'm now in your office and need to find your checkbook. If this is you, I just need you to help me locate it."

Standing in front of one of the shelf units that housed thousands of hours of recorded Gabriel messages, I heard, "Just look up." Without moving, I tilted my head upward and there on the top shelf, I saw an inch of Robert's checkbook sticking out. The phenomenon of being able to hear him broke me open, and I collapsed, sobbing into his desk chair.

Once I could focus again, Robert started talking really fast. He affirmed that being able to connect like this made it seem like he had just stepped into the next room. He then assured me how loved I was by guides and other higher beings on the other side. Once he had shared a few other things and seemed complete, I sat motionless and in silence, trying to take in what had just happened.

In case what I've just shared is confusing, let me clarify. About a year after Robert had begun to channel Gabriel, I discovered that I, too, could meditate and hear guides inside my head. At first, I thought I must be making the whole thing up, much the same as Robert had felt when he began channeling Gabriel. When I focused on the messages, which were clear and helpful, rather than the mystery of what was making this possible—as Gabriel had advised we do way back on that first evening that he'd come through Robert—continuing to explore and listen seemed an obvious choice.

I also appreciated that in one of my private sessions with Robert channeling, Gabriel had affirmed that he'd be happy to come through me as well. As much as I appreciated the offer, I suggested that he talk with me privately any time that seemed helpful. I didn't want to make the fact that I could channel public and interrupt the roles Robert and I were both playing in our growing community. However, now that Robert had passed away, I was beyond grateful for the ability keep bringing through guidance, continuing those sacred conversations.

Much to my dismay, after connecting telepathically with Robert for a few weeks, he informed me, "I'm being told that we can't continue talking like this, at least for a while." I already knew that "a while" could mean many things to beings beyond the physical world.

"In order for you to take your next steps as a leader," Robert continued, "it's important that you stand even more fully on your own feet. For you to continue bringing all that we were taught out into the world, you will need to trust yourself more than ever.

"You have many things to look forward to as you continue growing into the next stages of your life, and as always, this will include some next-level challenges. Keep in mind that much of what you will be facing will be opportunities to build the strength you will need in order to fulfill the things that will be asked of you. Know that I will be with you as you continue to individuate. Even when you can't hear or sense me, I will be there." With that said, Robert went silent again.

True to what he shared, the process that I've been through in the nine years since he passed has been exactly as he suggested it would be. I've been faced with some distinct next-level challenges, much of which has been centered around going through my own death process—letting go of so much of my "familiar," in order to continue creating space for more Soul energy to be assimilated.

Some of that has also been facing the next levels of fear about being alone. After more than two decades of conversation, even the guides became a part of facing that fear, when they went silent for a period of time. At various points, they affirmed that they, too, want me to trust the power of the man I have become. Though that shift felt like an abandonment of close friends I had come to know over the course of more than two decades, I could see the wisdom in standing even more fully in a trust of Self.

Within all of the growth, I was also comforted by the affirmation that they have occasionally provided about me being well prepared to take my place in the next opportunities that have just begun to become clear, including sharing this story. And, of course, the most amazing affirmations have continued to be the consistent shifts that my clients have made. Getting to share in the intimate journey of a whole grid of people moving from survival and separation to a state of empowered connectedness—and for some, even moving into the initiations of Soul consciousness—has undoubtedly been the greatest privilege of my life.

Of course, I've had to continue my own work as well. Perhaps the most significant shift, in some ways, has been the resolution of the relationship that was set up with my father in childhood. After our initial conversation back in the summer of 1990, we didn't make too many purposeful strides toward a deepening connection. Then, at my dad's eightieth birthday party, in a room full of people who were particularly important to him, he made another of his awkward comments about me. After acknowledging everyone in the room with charming, touching anecdotes, it was his turn to say something about me. I couldn't believe it when he opened with, "Ronnie almost made it," referring to my performing career. What I think he was inferring was that because I had left my first career, it equaled some form of failure. What I did know was that the comment cut straight to the gut. However, the moment gave me a chance to see how much I had become the source of my own value and the true authority in my own life.

Still, I decided it would be helpful to reach out with a letter and share the only things in my heart that had remained unsaid. Rather than choosing to call him out or make him wrong, I used the opportunity to fill him in on the amazing role he had played in my life—even from a distance. What better way to convey the journey I'd been on than by using all I had learned to also acknowledge him—one of the key players who had motivated me in countless ways.

I told him that he'd always been more important to me than he would have ever had reason to know. I told him how stuck I had been for so many years, looking to him for approval—even if I had never said so. For much of my life, I had made pivotal choices based on what I thought might make him proud of me. Out of that desire, I had always cast him as my potential hero. However, I also needed to own that whenever he hadn't known how to fulfill the role of hero, I would often swing the pendulum and cast him as a failed villain.

I then apologized to him for any ways that acting out my wounding might have hurt him over the years. I closed by making sure he knew I was glad to now see him beyond his role as my father. I looked forward to embracing him as simply a man on his own sacred Soul journey.

Much to my surprise, my father reached out to me the day after receiving my letter and told me that he'd already read it many times. He then suggested that if we were both willing to work on it, we could surely make things better. Neither of us knew when he shared that heartfelt wish that we would soon have some unexpected opportunities to do just that.

Within two years, my father developed a major sore on his right foot that just wouldn't heal. Right before Thanksgiving of 2015, it was clear to my two sisters and me that he needed help. We decided that I would be the one to fly down first. Only once I was there would I be able to assess the situation. Thank goodness we listened to our intuition. When I saw how serious his wound had become, compounded by not getting the quality of healthcare that he needed—not even close—I took him to Wake Medical Center in Raleigh.

It turned out that he had such poor circulation in his right leg that there wasn't enough blood flow for his wound to have ever healed. It would have likely become infected, putting his life at risk. Once the doctors had done a thorough evaluation, my father was told that his right leg needed to be removed from about the midpoint of his thigh. This was the only place that had enough blood flow for the amputation wound to recover. My sisters flew in within days to help.

Having a leg removed would be a profound physical and emotional challenge for anyone to face. However, much to our surprise, the more vulnerable my father became, the more he opened to receive our support. Just days after the surgery, he surprised us all.

"Do you know what this leg is turning out to be? It is a second chance for families."

In the coming weeks, my sisters and I got to see many new sides of this man—from the scared child to the inspiration that he had become to many people around him. Doctors, nurses, visitors, and other patients were touched by his courage and willing spirit. He never lost his gifted sense of humor. The honest conversations that he allowed among the four of us also created a deeper connection than we'd ever experienced. And it was only the process of facing challenges—in this case, life-threatening ones—that allowed us to move into this more complete authenticity and love with him.

In a few private moments that I had with him, he offered an acknowledgment that I never would have imagined hearing from him.

"I want you to know that I've been impressed with you since you were six and sitting on a piano bench. I've also been moved over the years by the person that you are. I want you to know that I see and appreciate all that you do for each person in the family. None of that has been lost on me. And finally, I want to acknowledge that anyone who has the privilege of really knowing you is truly blessed."

I felt so fortunate to hear these words coming directly from this warrior athlete. I was acutely aware that many people never have such an opportunity. I was also aware that these healing experiences had ultimately been made possible because my sisters and I had all shown up for him with nurturing, compassion, forgiveness, and love. By having learned to love and nurture ourselves over the years—facing many of those lessons in our relationships with each other—we had become capable of loving our father in his moments of real need.

Once we got his apartment wheelchair-ready, he returned home, determined to be an inspiration for the other older people who lived at his retirement complex. Six months later, however, he came down with an infection. Surprisingly, it had nothing to do with his leg. This time it was a systemic infection called C. diff.

Again, my sisters and I took turns being with him in the hospital in North Carolina, and it was obvious to us that his health was steadily declining. There were a couple of close calls when I was with him where I thought we might lose him before my sisters had a chance to get back to us. When they did, and it was eventually time for me to return to New York, I had a strong feeling that this might be the last time I would see my father alive.

Kneeling beside him, I spoke a few words that I hoped would be comforting. Looking him straight in the eye, I offered, "Thanks for sharing the journey with me, Dad. I love you very much."

He smiled and nodded, and then said, "Thank you, son."

Within a day or so, he told my sisters that he was ready to let go. He then took the time to share some particularly healing messages with each sister, also including some things that he wanted them to pass on to the people who couldn't be there with him. His final message to me was, "I may have helped Ronnie get to Broadway, but he helped me reach the mountaintop."

At some point after he felt complete, he pulled both of their faces in right next to his in a tight squeeze, and then he allowed himself to weep in their loving embraces. I was so happy for all three of them to have shared such a moment together. Then, on Father's Day of 2016, my father left his body, having created more healing with each of his children than any of us would have ever guessed possible.

Sometime after he died, someone at a convention I attended asked me to elaborate on some of the most important things I had learned and discovered about myself over the years. The final question of his interview was, "What do you think of as your superpower?"

I answered without hesitation, "My willingness to love beyond fear."

Who knew that such a simple question would bring my journey into such clarity? Learning to love, nurture, and value is the most immediate purpose of the Soul. I now trust that as the primary truth I was so desperately seeking as a child.

In order to reach the conviction and celebration I now enjoy, I have needed each person whose life has touched mine. Whether awakening, inspiring, or simply frustrating me along the way, they have all played an important role by revealing facets of the Whole Self that I've clearly needed to explore.

Perhaps most comforting at this point is being able to claim from direct experience that our lives all operate in Divine Order—whether we are able to recognize the signs or not. At every stage, our journeys are shaped by unique challenges and gifts that attempt to encourage us toward our next perfect steps.

Only by embracing both have I been able to follow my earliest hunches that were was "something more" within the privilege of loving freely and courageously. I am now more committed than ever to bringing a practical and inspiring message of Soul journeys into the world.

FINAL WORDS OF ENCOURAGEMENT

Reviewing the abundance of highlights I've just shared from my journey, I feel inspired and amazed at how our lives are configured with more Divine Order and support than most of us have ever been taught to recognize or appreciate. I began this lifetime feeling alone, insecure, and disconnected much of the time. I spent decades longing for someone to offer consistent, nurturing support. I simply wanted to know that I mattered. And in the end, that is exactly what I discovered—even if the knowing ended up coming in a completely different way and from a completely different source than I ever imagined: from me learning to align with my own Soul.

How amazing to now look back at the journey through different eyes, having learned to view each stage and lesson as a beautiful part of my awakening Self, guided and colored by each of the core challenges my Soul configured for me along the way. Even with my early hunch that there just had to be deeper truths about Life and how it all works,

I had no idea how beautifully and meaningfully facing my own challenges would allow me to eventually guide thousands of others toward their sacred Self.

The most obvious example, which I feel sure is clear to you by now, involved having a father who offered no nurturing or acknowledgment of my young Self. I now realize that if I had received even a mediocre level of nurturing, I might have been willing to settle. If that had been the case, I might never have awakened such a deep commitment to search for solutions. This also means I might never have been able to identify the nine levels of nurturing that have not only transformed my daily experience but have also opened the door for me to support so many others.

Just as powerful as learning to make allies out of my challenges has been learning to recognize and invest in my most natural gifts—my authentic interests, qualities, priorities, preferences, and talents. Some of those gifts were present as initial inspirations, such as my initial curiosity and determination, as well as some early intuition that there were deeper truths waiting to be found. Other gifts only became possible as I showed up and invested in the first layers of my emerging Self. No matter when each one was discovered, I recognize that each gift has played an important role.

Oftentimes the two have worked together as well. For instance, my wounded motivations to impress and prove myself drove me forward in distinct ways and fueled me to invest in certain talents. That investment was also crucial in leading me to an important education about the world—where I got to know various peoples and cultures, and how we are all ultimately the same around the world.

Each sacred piece that I've chosen to develop and invest in has allowed me to deepen my capacity as the nurturing authority in my own life. Rather than remaining desperate for validation from others,

I have learned to trust that I'm the only one who can ultimately recognize that I matter, and this has always been a truth, in each stage of my growth and development—just as it is for you. I am also the only one who can decide what kind of man I choose to be, most powerfully shaped by making choices that leave me feeling proud of myself.

Gabriel assured me for years that "all things are there to serve us" before I was prepared to live into the truth of such an audacious claim. And each of the examples that I've just outlined affirms that this is true. Only by taking each step and facing each lesson have I been able to open to the fact that our experiences are what inform and teach us most fully, as we evaluate which choices set us up well and which ones do not.

I am grateful that I not only understand this as a concept, but I also experience this as my ever-deepening reality. Just as every child needs to be told things over and over when they are young, I have needed each of these core Life lessons reiterated to even consider that I am a sacred individual on a unique Soul journey.

In closing, I return to my initial motivation for sharing this story. My greatest hope is that some facet of my story will have inspired you to feel clearer about your life, encouraged you to see yourself through new eyes, and awakened a real determination within you to show up for yourself with compassion and courage, all enabling you to recognize that you matter. You deserve to grow into love and wholeness, as you become informed and guided by core challenges and learning curves.

Only your particular path can lead you, in your own perfect timing and pace, to the ultimate truth that you are the grand prize that you seek.

What a joy it is to know that no matter what challenges have arisen for the people who have explored this nurturing approach with me over the last twenty-five years, having a clear foundation of nurturing has allowed each one to build a more reliable sense of safety in the world than they had known before. Each one has been able to incrementally empower themselves, creating a life of authentic meaning, value, and purpose.

At the same time, we are always and forever works in progress.

To now be able to dance with the magic of Life in such conscious, meaningful ways is what keeps me showing up every day—even in these times of worldwide challenge and shaky systems. Just as our personal challenges are there to serve us, so too are our global challenges. I try to remember that each one is an important guidepost, attempting to get our collective attention, constantly encouraging us to respond and adjust into more fulfilling choices.

Any imbalances that we discover in the world around us naturally reflect the imbalances we need to nurture in our individual lives. And the more we learn how to nurture those challenges, the more we prepare to offer our particular strengths and clarity to those around us. This is the path that will allow us to heal a world that has become deeply out of balance in so many ways. The truth that we must begin to acknowledge is that these challenges are also part of the Divine Order of our lives, attempting to remind us that we all need one another more than we may have ever realized in our wounded separation.

In order to keep moving toward the collective healing that is so desperately needed, we now need more people to realize the power of becoming proactive nurturers. As we enter this time of planetary midlife, the world is literally crying out for help. It's becoming more and more aware of a need for deeper truths and more fulfilling approaches than what we have chosen to embrace thus far in our collective journey.

As a community of humans, we are now being faced with a distinct choice. Will we choose to face this planetary midlife in ways that are all-too-familiar (and less than fulfilling), or will we finally interrupt our wounded habits to seek more of the tremendous potentials that we all hold inside—potentials that are encouraging us all toward the heart?

Naturally, I would love the stories I have shared to begin a dialogue. If you need a clear place to land and explore how you can take the next perfect steps, I hope you will reach out through my website: *RonBaker.net*.

There, you will find a way to become connected with a community of people who are not only dedicated to creating personal transformation, but who are also ready to become more proactive in making a difference in the world around them. I call this group of inspiring individuals a Global Tribe for Transformation.

The more of us who learn to nurture, the more inspiring models the world will have who demonstrate that so much more is possible than the habitual choices of wounded children. The more empowered nurturers that we have, the easier it will be to realize that none of us is alone in the process of facing challenges and claiming Self. What we need is to understand that we are all wounded—with no need to judge and shame—so that we can finally create safe spaces to come together.

Today, there are so many agendas at play in the world that seek to keep all of us in fear—even fearing one another. If we allow ourselves to be pulled into that fear, we run the risk of creating more separation and mistrusting one another, rather than moving toward the heart that is calling.

It is crucial that we remember we are infinitely more powerful and capable of creating a world of meaning, value, and purpose when we learn how to come together as unique individuals who are learning unique lessons and working through unique challenges—yet, who all share the need to live in a world of mutual support.

Only when we come together can we learn to value the gifts that we each possess, encouraged to truly move toward solutions that serve the good of the whole. Only those choices will allow us to create a wave powerful enough to inspire the unprecedented enhancements that are so needed in our world.

My final words of encouragement are the same ones I shared at high school graduation many moons ago—that we all choose in whatever ways we can to love and be loved. That is still my greatest wish for us all.

ACKNOWLEDGMENTS

Writing this book has been quite a journey. I love learning and growing as a human. So many people have taught me, planted crucial seeds, and offered loving support. Priceless.

I will begin by thanking Kris Carr, the one who encouraged me to write this story as a way to introduce myself and my School of Self-Mastery to more of the world. I'm not sure I would have considered doing such a thing without her guidance. Thank you ever so much.

Next, I thank Angela Sperry, whose courageous honesty was responsible for bringing out much more depth than I imagined offering. Thank you for your consistent loving presence throughout this process. It means the world.

The process continued with the support of Noam, Andrew, and Brian taking the time to read the first drafts of a comprehensive journey through my life and lessons. Thank you for such a loving investment of time and encouragement.

There is no way to describe the intimate dance that takes place with a great editor once the initial story is on the page. The eloquence, gentle directness, and generous guidance that I have received from Nan Satter has made the journey of exploring words a real joy. And that is saying something tremendous. Believe me. I have learned so much from you, Nan, and I look forward to many more adventures moving forward.

Based on having heard some daunting stories over the years about publishing, I have been so pleased and surprised by the consistent support I have received from each member of the team at Scribe Media. Thanks to Erin, Miles, Skyler, Erin, Michael, Candace, Natalia, and Tara for offering your gifts to this project with such a generous spirit.

Finally, I thank my family—both my original family and my Soul family—with whom I have learned most of the lessons outlined in this memoir. Without you, I would be unsure what love actually asks of us and gives back to us when it is shared in mutual value. I thank you for putting up with my long list of learning curves over the years. Thank you for showing me what is possible when authenticity and generosity are on the table.

There is actually a long list of other players who have come into my life for the specific lessons, opportunities, and challenges that have shaped my life. Know that I am all the richer for it, even if that is just a poetic way of saying thanks, and I love you.